Men and Power

Men and Power

edited by Joseph A. Kuypers

Prometheus Books

59 John Glenn Drive
Amherst, New York 14228-2197

Published 1999 by Prometheus Books

Inquiries should be addressed to
Prometheus Books, 59 John Glenn Drive, Amherst, New York 14228–2197.
VOICE: 716–691–0133, ext. 207.
FAX: 716–564–2711.
WWW.PROMETHEUSBOOKS.COM

03 02 01 00 99   5 4 3 2 1

Library of Congress Cataloging-in-Publication Data

Men and power / edited by Joseph A. Kuypers.
     p.   cm.
    Includes bibliographical references.
    ISBN 1–57392–796–4 (cloth : alk. paper)
    1. Men. 2. Masculinity. 3. Sex role. 4. Control (Psychology)
I. Kuypers, Joseph A.
HQ1090.M4283   1999
305.31—dc21   99–41269
                                                      CIP

Printed in the United States of America on acid-free paper

Contents

SECTION II: EXTENSIONS

Introduction
Joseph A. Kuypers

If there is any one single concept that organizes the passions and actions of men as a gender, I would propose that power is a likely candidate. From the private fantasies of boys becoming men and later of men acting out their internal scripts, being powerful and having power takes a high position. Seldom is powerlessness a preferred and admired quality in the male. Power holders expect the use of power to be unidirectional: to exert power if circumstances seem to demand it. In the absence of real and valued alternatives to power, the expectation becomes both a beacon and a plague. As a beacon, power directs action and organizes thought; it sets out how things ought to be. The equation appears simple and straightforward. As a response to threat, in the pursuit of progress, as a means to maintain order and conserve what is owned, power is the answer. As a plague, however, the quest for power becomes an incessant drive and unattainable goal. For those who cannot satisfy the expectation (and that logically must include all of us who come in second), the struggles with failure are deep. Many men live with the shame that they are not powerful enough. Given little alternative to living out the images of power, many men know only to addictively try harder, with ruinous consequences: in the abuse and oppression of those who cannot or will not operate from the power position, in the creation of legions of victims, in the unwillingness to soften power with compassion, and in the entrenched compromise of basic human and social justices.

Historical accounts leave no doubt that we already know about power abuse. And we already know how power organizes societies and is justified and glamorized. What we may not yet know as well is the unique relationship men as a gender have with power. This book asks: how are men in general raised to relate to power and with what consequences? What is unique in the male connection to power and how is this connection related to wider questions of male health, relationship health and social health? The promise in this inquiry is that it may help us better understand the men/power connection, and therefore more easily go beyond the glib resignation that power corrupts, to more precisely identify what men can do to transform their quest for power in healthy ways.

In the burgeoning field of men's studies, where both men and women are attempting to examine how gender organizes action and thought, the role of power is not yet settled. Perhaps it never can be. Some see men as the beneficiaries of social and personal power which is given or appears to be attached to them by virtue of their biology. This view proposes it is "natural" that men are powerful and that men inhabit positions of power. Some justify while other reject the legitimacy of that power. Alternatively, it is argued that men are operating out of powerlessness. From this perspective men are seen to be imprisoned in social roles which provide no real power. Men are in harness and denied the power that is expected by or due to their gender. The divide between these two positions is wide. The distance between them appears to help fuel the heat and anger attached to some of the rhetoric on this topic. Is the view that men are powerful an illusion? Is this a belief that serves a political agenda? Or does this view simply reflect ignorance of the inner struggles men have with being men? Is it that men need to deny their real power in order to keep it? Or is it that the power men do have is experienced differently from the inside and the outside? What appears to be power may not be experienced as power. Some men claim that women hold the "real" power and these men use this claim to minimize their own power. Is this a convenience for men who have trouble admitting their abuse of power? Or does the other side always seem more advantaged when it comes to power? Apparently untroubled by this conundrum are the men who acknowledge that they do have power and who claim its usefulness in settling conflict, organizing commerce, and driving progress and achievement.

Beyond the curiosity of how people are able to see this male/power connection so differently lie serious questions of ethics and safety. For example, the differences in how people see the fundamental nature of the man/power connection are mirrored by similar differences in how men's violence is viewed. As an expression of men's power, male violence is argued to be the institutionalized extension of their privilege or of their biology. As an expression of men's powerlessness, however, men's violence is, at root, a compensation for experienced failure or frustration to attain the power that is expected and so highly valued. Depending on which side of the divide one chooses, the route to less male violence is through either increasing or decreasing men's power.

How are these positions to be reconciled? Or can they be? What is healthy power for men? What does it look like and is it different from healthy power for women? The questions abound. Together they present the challenge of this volume: to explore the complex and often murky territory that is the man/power connection. An analogy to the root structure of a tree is appropriate. Collectively the authors in this book are attempting to reveal something of the root structure of the men and power connection. Some authors may reveal what they consider to be a tap root: an element central to understanding men and power. Others may explore a multiple root structure with many arteries and show the connections between aspects of male power. These may include sexuality, intimacy, equity, male identity, pornography and more. All the authors hope to lay bare how these connections and relationships generate both the problems and potential functions of power as it connects to men.

This project is a variation on a favourite fantasy that many may share: to gather great thinkers throughout history in one place and time and engage them in serious discussion about serious questions of the ages. In this case, ten men, already placed together in time, were enlisted to seriously discuss the man/power connection. The creation of the author list for this book followed a unique process. Traditionally, an editor assumes a central position in selecting authors. Like the hub of a wheel, the editor reaches out to many people to create the set of voices, each connected to the editor and each guided by his or her vision of purpose and form. In this case, a process was developed which linked authors together in series. Each author chose the next in line. Each author reached out to find a voice he respected and wanted to engage in the analysis of male power. My role as editor was to start the chain (by choosing the person I most wanted to hear from on this topic, John Stoltenberg) and to organize the development of the chain. We authors are linked, therefore, by respect for one another and by the desire to learn from each other.

Initial instructions to all of us were the same: we were to explore the connection between men and power. Nothing was said about the form the exploration should take, whether poetic, academic or other-wise, although personal reflections were encouraged. Care was taken not to suggest any particular theoretical orientation in the work or to require attention to particular themes. Authors were free to decide how and what they explored. Although this process could result in a some-what formless final product, it also promised a dynamic and creative outcome. Only male authors were sought, reflecting this editor's belief in the need for men to engage each other in serious discussions about their understandings of and struggles with such issues as power and violence.

The authors in this volume represent considerable diversity of background and perspective. With authors from the United States, Canada and Australia, with theoretical lenses including philosophy, social action, sociology and transpersonal psychology, with some writing from a mid-life platform and others as young men, with per-spectives from inside the experience of being socially marginalized by race or by sexual preference, with some explicitly attached to feminist scholarship, the author list promises a rich range of perspectives and insights.

The chapters that follow are divided into two groups. The first five chapters under the heading Connections are each focused directly on the man/power connection. Some deal more specifically with the issue of power, some more with the concept of masculinity, but each attempts to tease out how these two are connected. The next five chap-ters are Extensions of the man/power connection into other areas of inquiry. One author deals specifically with male power over women and how this extends to both the physical body and pornography. Three authors decry the failure of men, whether straight or gay or whether in contemporary relationships which are committed to gender equity, to successfully adopt a non-dominance model of relationships. They speak to the difficulty of developing and living an alternative sexual ethic. Collectively these authors expected more in terms of adopting gender equity from their gender and are struggling to understand the failure. Another author reveals how, for young men becoming adults, the power model is both seductive and ruinous. While the chapters are not intended to be sequential, the arguments in Section I provide background to the issues raised in Section II.

Note: The reader should know that the serial author referral system did not unfold completely as planned. For various reasons, the chain broke and required a restart with other referrals. Authors already on the list were consulted and additional names were identified. Consequently, John Stoltenberg made two referrals and I made three. As well, the volume's publisher, Errol Sharpe, became an intellectual partner in the venture, giving not only concrete commitment to the project before the authors list was known, but proposing names for consideration. Errol's courage and unqualified support are special and continue to be highly prized.

Section I

Connections

1

The Paradox of Men's Power

Joseph A. Kuypers

Postscriptus Prologue: In writing this chapter, the evolution of my thinking, disjointed as it was, rested on the thoughts in the following two paragraphs.

The problem with power lies in the fact that we men demand that our gender strive for an inherently unhealthy state of affairs: control over one another. As we achieve this kind of power, and use it for unhealthy acts, we suffer its errors and terrors, including abuse and corruption, guilt, dissatisfaction and alienation, to name a few. And we leave in our wake a social system locked into self-protection and entrenched injustices. We learn to deny the negative consequences, including our own guilt, of what our power does.

But, when we do not achieve such power, we suffer the equally devastating consequences of failure, including self-loathing, victimization by others who are more powerful, addictive striving and rejection by our own gender. At best, exerting power and control over another person is a trade off and a poor one at that. Any apparent benefits, when balanced against on-going abuses of power, appear to serve self-interest far more than justice. And to the degree that the quest for power is a condition of manhood, we continue to produce unhealthy men. To produce healthy men, the quest needs to be directed to other

15

qualities in men. The list of qualities is long: initiative, inventiveness, ability to solve problems, alertness to danger, loyalty, cooperation, project management, and more.

ON IMAGES AND ACTIONS

Peter the Great
Saturday morning professional wrestlers
    Howard Hughes and the Karate Kid
    Corporate warriors and men who abuse their partners
        These operate out of the *Power Mode*.
        They construct barriers, edges and walls,
        They imagine attack and defend with power.
    Atlas and the pointed gun
    Military parades and politicos flanked by body guards
    Gritty teethed linemen on three points
    Black leather astride motorcycles
        These are *Power Images*.
        Suggestions of violence ready to explode
            (given the "proper" circumstances).
            Suggestions of caution and alertness.
            Warnings.
    Overpowering the enemy, setting the ambush
    Dirty tricks, corporate raiding
    Bluffing, forcing the issue, having the last word,
    Shouting down, terrorizing, cautioning with a fist:
        These are *Power Plays*.
    We men know these well.
        They are tactics for our sex
        Proof that we can play this game that takes away.
        Proof that we qualify, man to man.
    But we of the "FOR MEN ONLY CLUB" must protect our lie
        As we pretend to ethics
        As we claim to serve the greater good.
    For we know as deeply as we know anything
    That our quest for power is beyond the pale
    We can see the pain and fear

We can smell the damage
We can hear the protest
If we only will

MY PROJECT

My personal project in writing this chapter is to discover just what I think and feel about power. In some respects this push to clarify the matter for myself is an extension of my previous work on men and their violence (Kuypers 1992). I have not written specifically about power before, so the following piece is not a practiced or even finished line of thought. The text is organized by the time line of my explorations, with intermittent attempts to connect and integrate pieces.

This chapter is my version of a process I think all men should undertake: I examine my thinking about and engagement with what I would call the *male power imperative*, and put that self-discovery out for public reaction. It is a call to men to willingly look at the gendered uses and abuses of power, the premise being that to the extent that power rules and ruins and that we men have a unique hold on power, we also have a unique responsibility to correct our own mistakes.

GANDHI, HITLER AND ME:
SOME EARLY LESSONS

As a white, North American male, I have lived in a world where male power and the privileges that go with it have often been handed to me. And so I can only have an indirect knowledge of the depth of the fears, resentments and angers of people who have lived continuously with oppression. I am fortunate to be from a family where power seeking was not valued. My mother was a poet and my father a musician. They introduced issues of social welfare, common cause and compassion for suffering in our collective family discussions. They questioned the justice and absolutism of power; they helped me become and remain sensitive to the impact power abuse has on recipients of that abuse.

But I was also a product of the tough American mentality that glorified the power images of the day: soldiers, sports heroes, governments fighting for freedom around the world. The images and stories in my youth were ever present and the pressures to adopt them as models incessant, if not explicit. The models of power seemed uniquely male. From the preferred father images to the preferred warrior, or to the underground and dark side heroes (Al Capone and all the nameless bad guys in Hollywood films), all were images of power. They did what they had to, for some claimed benefit, and left their casualties behind. While some wore white hats and some black, they each embodied a shared ethic—to use their practised power to settle things.

As a young boy growing up in the often belligerent and intolerant American heartland, reconciling these power images with compassion for their victims was not so easy. The public script rewarded and admired the powerful men whose actions usually championed some worthy cause. Victim suffering was often ignored and dismissed as the "just" reward for failure at the game of power. Compassion seemed then, as it often does now, inconsistent with the standard images of male power. In learning the political difference between having and expressing feelings, I also learned how to avoid becoming a target myself. It was clear (although not something I was fully conscious of) that by not at least adopting the pretences of power and by not staying quiet in front of men's power plays, I risked ridicule and violence. I learned there was safety in pretence. I learned, as all boys must learn, how useful it was to be a pretender to power and to ignore the victim's pain. Call it a charade or call it taking on a masculine mask, but also call it a solution. The solution was to avoid being denied acceptance into the *for men only club*. For many boys and men the posturing becomes obsessive. It became a reflex geared to convince the threatening male audience that we are "in line," that we are inside the equation that connects maleness with power.

But for me the case was not settled by this pretence. How could it be when, in addition to the gift of my family's ethics, I witnessed the global struggle between evil power over others and its apparent opposite, between Hitler and Gandhi. My inner struggles were written on a world level, and perhaps the larger drama took over my smaller one. Would the embodiment of evil power dominate? Or would Gandhi, this meek and barefooted man, with no army to enforce his word and no territory to defend. With none of the pretences of power, would he demonstrate that principle and compassion were real forces that could fight real and big battles? The cast of my life would be forever framed by this struggle. As a child I knew that Hitler lost. But so did Gandhi. Both failed. And the duality they represented then seems as sharp today.

So I survived childhood carrying both a disquieting incompleteness about this drama and a deep distrust of power itself. Why should we trust powerful people, let alone groups, countries, armies or businesses! Why should we tolerate the authority and control achieved on the basis of violence and the threat of violence? These questions and cautions are the background against which I attempt to further my understanding of the man/power connection.

Two sections follow. The first looks at power without reference to gender. The goal is to examine why power qua power is so problematic. The second section focuses on power as it connects to men. Here the goal is to reveal why some men seek gender health by disconnecting from the power imperative.

ON THE "NATURE" OF POWER

What it is, what it is not

Is power the strength or impact of an experience ("I saw a powerful movie"), or is it the ability to do work ("we had the power to build a bridge")? Is it a feeling of capacity and confidence ("I feel so powerful, I could do the impossible"), or is it directing and focusing efforts of an organized labour force? In general usage, power has these meanings and more: the force of an initiative, the potential for control, the strength of an engine and the feeling of oneness with the world. For the purposes of this discussion, the term is limited. In this chapter, I am not talking about power as achievement such as the power to invent the internet, or about power as an adjective used to grossly describe the intensity of an experience. I am talking about power as encompassed in actions which involve the *enhancement of the rights and freedoms of one person over another*. This power is a statement of relationship. It exists because of what it does to someone. An act has power if it limits the freedoms and security of another person. The threat or possibility of similar acts gives the power-holder power over another person.

The dynamics of one having power over another creates patterns of action between people which, when normalized, define basic free-doms and rights. Those holding power-over claim a set of rights and prerogatives not accorded the other, including the right to hit another person, the right to greater mobility, the right to force the actions of the other, the rights to punish and jail, and many other rights of "higher" authority. Those so positioned control resources and achieve greater reward. The powerless must endure, trapped and prevented from leaving their position. So while power may at times seem to serve some necessary purpose of defense, or public health, it is also always a dynamic which reduces the fundamental freedoms and privileges of someone else.

This view of power sees violence and the threat of violence as an elemental tool in the pursuit and maintenance of power. In this respect, problems with violence are, at root, problems with power. This use of power includes both killing to silence dissent and killing to serve justice. It includes using a straightjacket to protect the public good and requiring immunizations for public health reasons.

On the utter necessity of power

There appears to be a universally accepted and seldom examined belief that power is a natural part of the order of things. Power organizes our public and private lives. It determines who gets ahead, who is on top and who is in charge. It is fundamental to our judgments of each others' worth. It settles conflicts, maintains borders, and appears to be the irreducible core of self-defense. Power is both a way of looking at the world and a way of organizing action. Borders are defined and defended, enemies are constructed (real or imagined), and power becomes the necessary commerce of defense and expansion—of survival and self-interest. Power is a core element of human nature. It lies outside the domain of human choosing and rests firmly in the nature of things. Or so it seems!

Given this elemental positioning of power in human affairs, and its apparent naturalness, problems with power are difficult to see. It is possible to identify abuses of power, but these are likely to be visioned as exceptions, aberrations or regrettable but understandable side products of a more fundamental necessity, such as to be powerful or die. For many, the choice of whether to use power or not is unimaginable.

At the moment of threat or attack, the consideration becomes decidedly pragmatic and power seems to be the only alternative. For many, the case is closed. Power is proven to be essential, inherent and logical. Its utter necessity is indisputable.

How people like to see power

As people live with a belief in the utter necessity of power, they develop favourite ways of understanding and justifying its inevitability. Consider the following: for many who contemplate the logic of power, it appears somehow to be "in" nature. It is a system defined and positioned to be essential to border sharing and the dynamic that maintains unit separation and integrity. This is the *Power is Inherent* position. The logic is seductively simple and attracts many. When entity meets entity (amoeba or otherwise), the question is whether one will incorporate the other or whether they will maintain their separate forms, side by side. In either case, to secure stable borders or to incorporate and grow larger, power is the medium of exchange. It is at the point of contact between entities that power meets power. An entity driven by the imperative to protect its fundamental form must meet several conditions, each of which is designed to enhance the entity's ability to resist intrusion and to increase its own power to intrude. It must be able to detect danger and threat before it is too late, it must have the power to resist the force of an intruder, and it must be able to advance without increasing its own vulnerability. Vigilance, defense, attack and even cooperation with allies to increase effectiveness: these are the dynamics that maintain order and assure survival. Power operates with the explicit logic that selfhood, family survival and any other element of "us-ness" are central. Power, therefore, maintains identity.

An alternative view of power is that it is simply useful. It works, nothing more, nothing less. This is the *Power is Pragmatic* position and it attracts many, as well. Here the logic is that power over another exists and persists simply because it accomplishes things and does so efficiently. Although power may become firmly fused and connected to various areas of human encounter, it remains essentially a tactical choice. In this view, power is not intrinsic to human sexuality, for example, but an element within the sexual realm which achieves certain desired ends (for some). Nor is power an absolute requirement for

organizing business and corporate affairs. But it is a highly prized feature of commerce, because it works so well. Furthermore, in this view
of power, masculinity is not an inherent expression of power (and vise
versa), but a valued attribute that somehow becomes attached to men
in particular ways. This position holds that there are positive expressions of power and that power can serve desirable ends. To attain these
ends it is necessary that society examine how power is used and take
responsibility for examining its own abuses of power.

However, one might suspect that power is not so benign. Beyond
being simply useful or central in maintaining identity, it may be fatally
flawed. This is the *Power (Naturally) Corrupts* position. It assumes a
more pernicious and suspicious truth about power. This view under-
stands power as a dynamic force carrying a high and unique risk of
becoming like a cancerous growth. Power appears to inevitably become
excessive and out of control. It eventually destroys itself and its host.
Unlike some other human qualities which appear to move naturally to
positive ends, power cannot be trusted to do so. People are not victims
of too much understanding or too much cooperation, but they are victims of too much power. If people accept that power is not so benign,
then social goals around power seem to shift from attentive support to
strengthening safeguards against it and developing alternatives to it.

These views on power (as naturally "in" the situation, as simply
useful, or as fatally flawed) are usually combined, often with telling
consequences in their overlapping outcomes. Each combination appears
to seal the same end: that power is not disposable in the human condition, making serious attraction to the Gandhi option difficult. For
example, if "inherent" and "useful" are combined, a logic of pragmatic
determinism follows that justifies power as both a means and an end.
Enter pragmatic determinism. "So what's your choice in this dog-eat-
dog world?" If power is cancerous but useful, then cognitive dissonance
forces choice since a healthy disease is hard to imagine. When "useful"
wins out, power's failures are isolated and argued to be exceptions.
When "cancer" wins out, damage control is called for. But if power is
seen as an inherent cancer, then fatalism and resignation in the face of
abuse seem logical. "Yes it is an ugly world out there," as the saying
goes, leaves little choice but to use power's tools, despite the warnings.
For those who believe this latter view, a trap is set which offers little
chance of escape. A power imperative develops: operate out of a posi-

tion of power or be controlled by others! Develop power-play skills or lose the battle. Defend or be invaded. Be powerful or be weak.

But suppose that power *really* is negative growth and a dangerously risky proposition. Suppose it is not simply a matter of what we believe power to be but more a matter of what power is inherently. If power were a benign dynamic, concern would be unwarranted. But the evidence suggests otherwise. There is a toxic element here and warning bells are sounding. Consider the causalities of power. In the hands of men, much of the world's terror and torture, war and shrinking of economies stems from power use or abuse. And often the distinction between the two is not clear.

Consider the addictive nature of power seeking. Many men appear to pursue power as a quest with no end. They intensify their pursuit even in the face of its obvious contradictions: it breeds discontent and fear, insecurity and self-doubt in those who have it. Despite the romantic vision of glory and happiness that some attach to power, it appears to create the opposite. Why do these men not learn the lessons of power's failures? I return to this question in the following section where I examine the man and power connection. For now the curious question is why so many men willingly collude with the argument that power is an elemental and inherent dynamic in human affairs, in the face of its obvious abuses. Partial answers may be found in how they justify power's place in the scheme of things.

Justifications

There is a series of justifications for power which confirms in the minds of many that there is no real and effective alternative to the power imperative.

As an act of controlling another person's rights, the use of power is fundamentally an ethical judgment. At the moment of such control, the loss of rights of the victim or target is weighed against the gains made by exerting the control in the first place. The prisoner is shackled to protect the innocent, the child is slapped to "teach" a vital lesson or the city is bombed to "end" the war. In this respect, while some may agree that power is pernicious, or that power is not the goal itself, it may be seen as *a necessary means to the greater good*. The suffering and loss of rights of one element are played off against the rights, securities and rewards of another. Power use is given ethical justification. It may be true that in the mind of the power-holder, all acts of power over another person (as with all acts of violence) are for the greater good. The logic may be twisted or drastically out of sync with the public perception, but the one with power, nonetheless acts out his or her power as a moralist. The morality appears self-evident as well as being self-serving.

The unrelenting lesson of yesterday's heroes

Obviously the lessons of history are used to justify the continuing use and glorification of power. The impact of our history making, where heroes amass wealth, command armies, steal from the rich and in other wondrous ways employ their power for reasons both good and bad, is that power is the only game in town. Period!

Failures of "soft" power

Short of discarding the option of power over another person, some people advocate a softer, more compassionate expression of that power. This approach to power remains sensitive to and gives real authority to the victims of power abuse. It requires a "principled" use of power that goes beyond self-interest and considers matters such as collective well-being, justice and equity. As well, it tries to reduce its power use when conditions allow. The approach can shift from an adversarial to cooperative position, from using "hard" power to "soft" power.

When effective, expressions of an ethical and compassionate power may go a long way toward curbing the risks of power abuse. There is always the option of considering the wider consequences of using whatever power seems necessary to achieve a particular limited end. When a parent chooses not to discipline a child or not to use corporal punishment but instead explores explanation and consensus building, power is softened and transformed. When businesses develop joint ventures or institute environmental protection or equity policies, power is softened by promoting alternative values. Or, when a person who is physically threatening disarms himself or herself and listens carefully to the fears of his or her partner, power can begin to be replaced by caring.

Yet this soft power, if history is any lesson, is insufficient. When confronted with hard power, it is overruled, proving that ultimately soft power fails. The sword always wins over the pen. Despite compassionate analysis or moral persuasion, the will to silence dialogue with force settles the matter and ends the search for alternatives. This may not be fair, it may not lead to justice, and it may not ultimately achieve the original purpose, but invoking power silences choice. For those who believe this "justifies" the use of power, a common resolution emerges: to cooperate, *maintaining the threat of "hard" power*. "Negotiate from strength," "speak softy and carry a big stick," "hit first and ask questions later"—these reflect the popular view that cooperation, understanding and compassionate power can only be achieved once the threat of a silencing power is established and believed. But this view upholds the original premise that, given the proper circumstances, power is the last, first and only resort. Real non-power options do not exist. At the moment of "truth," power operates, practically, to reduce the likelihood that cooperation (and compromise and empathic reaching out) will be attempted, unless prior agreement to do so is reached by both parties in a dispute. Unless both agree and both can be trusted, hard power predominates—always.

Proponents of game theory have constructed a "prisoners dilemma game" which operates by the now familiar "logic" of power (Poundstone 1992). Among other things, this game that justifies power was used to rationalize U.S. cold war armament policies. Do we need reminding that this period saw two world powers poised with the capacity to totally destroy each other, since no other alternative could be imagined? The game did not allow alternatives.

As the two person game is played, three options are available: 1) both parties cooperate, 2) both fight, or 3) one cooperates while the other fights. If both parties cooperate and play by the rules, then both survive and achieve a modest reward. If both parties fight, each merely survives with little reward (stalemate, cold war, mutual assured destructiveness). However, if one party chooses to fight and the other chooses to cooperate, the fighter is given the greatest reward and the cooperator is eliminated—the sucker play. Advocates argue that this game merely *reflects* reality. It is seldom asked whether the game *creates* it as well.

In the logic of power, the game highlights the risk in choosing wrong. If an approach is made with trust, but one party catches the other by surprise and changes the rules (and therefore cannot be trusted), the rule breaker is in line to gain the most for himself or herself at the expense of other higher values—like cooperation. On the other hand, if one party anticipates that the other will use force (which is likely after a violation has occurred), the initial party's only choice is to meet this force with force, and thereby avoid complete failure. The reality? Once a party has used power, meeting fire with fire is the only option—unless a party can con its opponent into thinking that it can be trusted and the opponent lays down its arms, in which case the former can go for The Kill. In this game the greatest personal reward is achieved if one's opponent can be conned into cooperation (a strategy that can only work once, since distrust will be established, leading to the inevitable survival choice, e.g., both fight). This game "proves" that cooperation does not work by demonstrating the high risk of guessing wrong. Survival requires the power option.

While the prisoner's dilemma justifies power it also, curiously, reveals something of the costs of the power imperative. The game is played by bluff and stealth. It stabilizes over time to the lowest level of abstraction (survival) and yields minimal (but assured) results. The game also suggests an interesting dilemma: the greater gains of cooperation (which are "known" to be a real possibility since they are in the rules of the game) are tied closely to the issue of how one deals with vulnerability. It reveals that cooperative options promise the most while they simultaneously increase vulnerability the most. For those who might want to challenge the self-evident truths about power, two daunting tasks are presented. The first is to *distrust the apparent successes of the power imperative*. The second is to not recoil from *the apparent vulnerability of the cooperative approach*.[1]

CONDITIONED MEN

It seems true that the power imperative has a particularly strong grip on the male psyche. In most cultures in most of recorded history, men are assigned a unique position and responsibility when it comes to the power imperative. As warrior, chief, king, boss, head, enforcer, the male is the primary carrier of power. Some would argue, as I do, that boys becoming men have little choice in this matter since the logic for power is so unidirectional and the consequences of failure are so severe.

The "construction" of masculinity itself is infused with power images and demands. Power is expected and valued. Power is rewarded and glorified. And power failures are treated harshly in men's judgments each other. Few men are impervious to the social stigma that awaits them if they fail to maintain the threat of power. The labels are strong and go deep: weak, cowardly, incompetent, afraid, sexually suspect. Success becomes fused with power, so as men (and women as well) judge men, not having power results in social and personal devaluation.

The trap is there and it is designed to catch men. Faced with a power imperative which allows no real consideration of alternatives, demands participation in a process which is substantially unhealthy for both the doer and the victim, and punishes failures by challenging the core of their being (gender security), it is not surprising that so many men are caught. These men must do what they can to assure some peace with their gender. They play out their role and suffer the consequences. Given the context of the trap and the unrelenting pressures of power's logic, men must accomplish some drastic mind games. Some men do not or refuse to see the trap at all, some accept being bribed by its benefits, some willingly advance its case, and many deny its destructiveness.

The apparent paradox of power

Examination of the dominant arguments concerning the connections between men and power reveals an interesting and troublesome contradiction. In public discourse, men are often seen as powerful, for better or worse, but privately many men often express feelings of powerlessness (Brod & Kaufman 1994; Kaufman 1993).

On the one hand, men are argued to be, relative to women for example, organizers and beneficiaries of positions of power. From the bedroom to the boardroom, so the argument goes, men take the power position, claiming greater authority and control over the lives and welfare of women, in particular. This view holds that the organization of society is based on a male power model, where men position each other in hierarchies organized by power, and consistently place women, as a group, in the "disempowered" position. Men hold tenaciously to these power positions and use various methods, including their greater capacity for violence, to secure them.

The arguments in support of this view are well documented. For example, few would dispute that throughout the world, in armies, in policing bodies, in businesses, and in governments, men's hold on positions of power, legitimate or otherwise, is disproportionate to their percentage of the population. Nor would many dispute that the dominant model in families, world wide, is patriarchal, with men claiming many versions of the male prerogative. This claim is not benign: witness wife battering, setti, sexual assault, denial of women's right to vote and participate in the political process, barriers to financial independence for women, and more.

Not only do men have and hold power, they eagerly use power to define rules of conduct—man to man. Men direct their actions and define their organizations by it, make rules and judgments by it, and organize their politics and economies on a reward structure that reveres those who have it. They embed their sense of justice on the authority demanded by power. They make mythic the men and armies who embody the revered forms of power. Men keep order, secure property, close deals and express their sexuality by it. We position each other, either up or down, by the measure of who has more of it. Given this massive pressure to adopt a power model and mystique, it is likely that men will adopt the first view of power which holds that it is inherent and somehow "in" the situation.

However, many men do not feel powerful. They do not perceive themselves as operating in the power mode over women, for example, and they claim that arguing that men are beneficiaries of the power imperative is a myth (see Farrell 1993 and any issue of *The Backlash*). For those who view male power as a myth, male powerlessness is a more important issue to analyze. As with the men-are-powerful position, the men-have-no-power argument is amassing its own documentation. A central claim is that, while men may be positioned in hierarchies (and that hierarchies may be good), all but a few are in "power down" positions. Men are harnessed to work at unrewarding jobs, awarded little if any authority over their working conditions, and suffer the whims of superiors and economic shifts with little protection. They feel like powerless cogs in a larger system that denies them any real influence and control.

Furthermore, the "myth of male power" arguments observe that men around the world are forced to fulfil the dirty and dangerous jobs of society, from garbage collector to soldier. "It's a man's job" is the rallying cry, and the male who would protest is given little sympathy. The boy who refuses military duty, for example, may risk incarceration if not ridicule. From one angle the military may appear to comprise men inhabiting power positions, but from another it is men being coerced into sacrificing their bodies, without question. It requires that men consider the welfare of others over their own, without question. It is conditioning men to accept, without question, the legitimacy of orders from above. In the name of duty and preferred masculinity, men are conned into powerlessness. From this perspective, the various ways that men are trained to follow orders, in sports and business and policing forces, are all of the same cloth. They illustrate the many ways that men are raised into choiceless and powerless positions, where self-sacrifice and even death are the expectations. Many men ask: Where is the power in this?

For the political right, the goal is to restore a lost but legitimate power. Hierarchy of man over man and man over woman is defended. On the left, hierarchy may be challenged yet the call is still for men to find their lost power, perhaps by achieving freedom from control by other men or by reconnecting with their lost inner selves.

The political consequences of these two positions on men and power are fundamentally different. In the first instance (men have power), problems reside in men having too much power which leads to intolerable abuse and social injustice. The logical goal is, therefore, to find effective means to correct the injustice by, for example, correcting gender inequity or learning the arts of power sharing, compromise and cooperation.

In the second instance, the goal is just the opposite: to find ways for men to regain their lost power or to achieve meaningful power in their personal and work lives. Depending on how the reasons for male powerlessness are argued, the focus of how to gain this power differs. For some men-are-powerless believers, the cause rests in poor, weak or absent fathering, with the result that generations of weakened men are produced (Bly 1990). From this weakness are sown the seeds of discontent, violence and ineffectualness. The correction for this socialized "weakness" lies in helping men recover their unique rituals for teaching and learning about male power. Clearly the focus is on failures of how men socialize men. Other men-are-powerless believers blame women and the social systems which they perceive as favouring women's rights over men's rights. Women's advances are tied to men's losses and powerlessness (see any issue of *The Backlash*). Policies for redressing gender inequities and legal systems which adjudicate divorce and childcare disputes are cited as evidence of how men are denied their rights and positions of power. The logical consequence for corrective action based on this analysis is to fight women and social systems which further the assault on men.

Clearly, then, just as there are core differences in the conceptions of power, there are also fundamental differences in how men and power are connected. Is it that men do not have power but are supposed to? Or is it that they do have power, but are denying that they do? If the latter is true, is this a political convenience? Or perhaps men do have power but simultaneously do not feel powerful. Perhaps no one can have sufficient power to meet the expectations of the power imperative. And maybe what men do have can never satisfy them. For men to be powerful means, because of the nature of power, always being at war with themselves.

From my vantage point, the problems with power lie ultimately with the paradox of power itself: that men are trapped in an imperative that leaves no alternative but to strive for (and never attain) an inherently unhealthy condition of power over another. Power is negative growth and having power exacts a heavy price. While it appears to confer some benefits, it also prompts men to be and feel victimized by it. Power breeds resentment toward those who appear to have more of it, anger at those who deny it, fear of those who might take it away, and insecurity in the face of the threat of other men's power. Power twists and contorts values such that men try to be what one cannot be: both loving and controlling, both powerful over other people and loved by them. It is true that men are in power positions which exclude women's full participation. It is also true that men never have enough power, and that having it leaves them alone and fearful. It is true that men, as a gender, are addicted to power and do not know that they are. Let us look more carefully at this addiction.

THE ADDICTION ANALOGY

One apparent problem with power is that it is fundamentally *dissatisfying*. Men are taught to believe that power is an end in itself and that attaining power will resolve and settle things. The promise is great, if inexplicit: achieve personal power and be happy, secure and successful. But perhaps the primary goal of happiness has little to do with power. On a more elemental level, men's search may be for love or security or acceptance, but through socialization to manhood, power has become the substitute. It is a poor substitute, since, by achieving control over others, the primary goal itself is denied. Yet, in spite of dissatisfaction with power, its pursuit cannot be easily abandoned because the original premise, that men's logical quest lies in the power imperative, still remains. As with other addictions, the experience of dissatisfaction and failure leads people simply to try harder. Their commitment to the power imperative becomes stabilized and intensified. Ultimately this incessant search for power becomes disconnected from and perverts the character of the primary object, so that those so addicted lose sight of their more primary need for love and intimacy.

A second problem with power is that it is fundamentally alienating. The power that controls another person's freedom is, essentially, oppositional, pitting one person's ability to control against another. In this defense/offense positioning, walls and barriers are erected and maintained. A key element is that compassionate consideration of the plight of the victims must be disconnected from the power imperative. To do otherwise would compromise border maintenance. The victim voice must be silenced and discounted. The power imperative, therefore, acts to de-escalate ethical considerations and to devalue empathy for the other. Defense and attack, not empathy and sensitivity to pain, are essential elements in the act of holding power over another. It is interesting to note, in this regard, how young boys, through sports and other male organized activities, are taught to ignore their own pain and, eventually, the pain of others. This serves the power imperative well. And so, once in the power position, the power broker finds that apparent success built on isolation and disconnection breeds the same. "It is lonely at the top," so the saying goes. Once again, apparent power successes are, on another level, failures. The power player is now both dissatisfied and alienated, yet still firmly committed and/or addicted to the pursuit of power as the preferred pathway.

A third problematic feature of power is that its quest *has no end*. There is no ultimate target. What is the ideal state of having just the right amount of power? What is the proper balance of such power with other elements of relationships such as trust, cooperation and the ability to compromise? In the absence of answers to these questions, the pursuit of power becomes its own goal, unchecked by higher and softer values. The power imperative, therefore, provides no rest from the quest. A corollary to this pursuit-without-end is that the power imperative *lacks internal safeguards* against its own abuse and run-away. It is an engine without a governor or a computer programmed to expand itself to unspecified limits.

A fourth and final consideration is that the conditions of the power imperative seem decidedly *unstable*. Once having attained some level of control over others, staying alert to counterattack, retaliation or revolution is basic to the equation. Borders shift, alliances realign, and new methods of control emerge. All the players must prepare for the impermanence and instability of their power. In this context, each player carries a persistent feeling of anxiety, vulnerability and unease.

The conditions for power addiction now seem complete. In a social context that requires men in particular to participate in the power imperative, and provides few valued options when problems develop, men are caught in a process that is flawed and subject to runaway. The process becomes a quest that neither satisfies personally nor advances ethically. So conditioned, men pursue the goal without end, ensnared in the lie of all addictions: that lasting success and happiness will be the reward. The power seeker, disconnected from his deeper needs and unaware of what he is seeking in the first place, is required to be on constant watch—tireless, alert, wary and afraid.

This analysis concludes that the power imperative is a pathway to failure. Further, it assumes that the fundamental problem with power itself is that it operates ultimately to destroy itself. Yet the field cannot be abandoned as the paradox remains. Men cannot solve their disquiet by seeking more power, especially if that power involves controlling others. However, men cannot easily turn their power quest off, for many reasons. The risks—vulnerability and devaluation—are anything but inviting.

THE WAY OUT

When it comes to believing in real power options, the paradox of power and the logic that justifies it are difficult to overcome. Yet this appears to be exactly what is required, if warnings are to be taken seriously. The challenge for men is daunting, but crucial. For this work of overcoming the power imperative, the following conclusions may be useful.

1. Justification for power can be limited to clear, rare and exceptional circumstances. Alternatively, the belief that power is absolutely necessary in certain circumstances does not mean that it is necessary in all circumstances. I would call this the *limited test* standard.
2. While men may be committed to some power options, we can also be committed to apology, victim healing and redistribution as a means of continuously undoing the abuse of power. I would call this the *welfare test* standard.
3. It is possible to revision power as never good. It may be seen as necessary, but never healthy in a wider frame. In so believing, we may discover a myriad of ways to deal with real threats to our survival without normalizing power's failures. I call this the *health test* standard.
4. And finally, we men need to remind ourselves of the following. It is convenient for those who hold power at the moment to claim the absolute necessity of their power. It is useful for those who strive for more, to justify the quest. And obviously, for those who are face to face with their suffering victims, it is essential that they have a way of viewing the world (and consequently their actions) that supports their abuse and distances themselves from their victims, otherwise they would have to stop.

NOTE

1. It is not at all surprising, therefore, that two of the central issues facing the emergent men's movement are how to stop playing the deadly serious "game of winning" and how to allow emotions, including vulnerability, into a healthy male equation.

2

How Power Makes Men
The Grammar of Gender Identity
John Stoltenberg

Most folks assume that the words *men* and *power* point to things that exist in the objective, material world, rather like tables and chairs. *Men* and *power* are normal nouns, people believe. You can say "Over there are the men" the way you can say "Over there is the furniture." And you can say of those men that they have "power" just as you can say of a table or chair that it has legs.

By this ordinary, everyday grammar, the assertion "Men have power" becomes rebuttable. All tables do not have legs. Some are cubes with solid sides; some are jerry-built from crates and planks. Thus if but one man can be found who feels powerless, the statement "Men have power" fails to be true.

Similarly, the assertion "Men have more power than women do" must be tossed on the trash heap of illogic if but one woman can be found who has more power than some man. Grammatically, we assume, the statement *could* be true—the way the statement "Chairs have more legs than tripods" could be true. But if just one three-legged chair turns up, there goes the premise out the window—whence it lands, presumably, on an assortment of unstable seats.

So is it true that "men do not have power" and "men do not have more power than women"? Well, no; summary negation does not get us out of our nominal dilemma.

The fact is, ordinary, everyday talk of men and power inevitably becomes illogical, because our ordinary, everyday grammar has played a trick on us. To see how, let us look closely at the word *power*.

In the sentence "Men have power," the word *power* is not a normal noun. We are not talking about "power" by analogy to electrical power or horsepower or even muscle power. What we are talking about is a kind of noun that never just is; it exists only in some action. On close inspection this peculiar noun does not point to something one has but to something one does.

We can recognize this distinction in the following sentence:

Men do not have power unless they do power.

This sense of the word *power* is distinct from various meanings used in religious, human-potential or recovery circles—spiritual power, inner power, the power of faith and such. In the sentence above, the word *power* refers to its concrete and root sense of "ability or capacity to act or exercise control or authority." A close synonym might be *might*.

Our everyday language treats this odd noun form in an ordinary way, but the thing it points to does not behave like an ordinary thing.

This sense of power is manifested in verbs, in acts that happen because they are committed; and it is transitive—there is a doer and a done-to. No such credible power exists apart from the actions that assert it. To conceive of power otherwise—as a free-standing, self-sufficient entity, for instance, or a subjective state of awareness—is to miss the particular power denoted here, which is made manifestly real in and through how it functions.

Of course there is much power in the world that just is—it charges through high-tension electric lines; it's in your pocket when you have money to spend; it's the combined force of momentum and muscle that hurls a track-and-field athlete over a high bar. But the power named in the sentence "Men have power" is different. In this specific sense, the state of being powerful does not occur apart from some act that expresses and effectuates itself. We know the thing because it does, and we do not know it otherwise. This noun is nothing without a verb.

Now let us look at the word *men*.

It turns out that *men* is not a normal noun either. People assume that men are free-standing, self-sufficient entities, like furniture. Alas, they are not. Tables and chairs do not have to do anything in order to be tables and chairs. Leave some tables and chairs in a room for a few minutes or a half hour and when you return they will likely still be there: tables and chairs. Their intrinsic tendency to still be there makes these nouns thingish—as thingish as nouns can be. But for a human being who aspires to belong to the category "men," that is not the case. The human being has to work at it.

The category "men" is not a static one, and it therefore behaves grammatically in an unusual way. It has no definitional, intrinsic existence in the worlds of mental or material objects apart from the doings and deeds that are recognizable as "how men act." To fail to act that way can mean falling outside the category "men" into its logical opposite, "not-men." This prospect is terrifying for almost all aspirants to the category; therefore efforts of various sorts must be expended. Acting like men act is what must be done, spasmodically, at intervals. Lucky the furniture that need only collect dust! Men's existence as men, by contrast, is not thingish at all. Leave them alone in a room for a few minutes or a half hour and you never know what they might do next to stay real.

Note that the collective noun *men* is neither presumed nor ordained by the adjective *male*. Even in everyday speech this disjunction is understood: Being born a male human does not guarantee being one of the men. Nor is the plural noun form *males* synonymous with the collective noun *men*. That is because the adjective *male*, when applied to a human being, is simply a descriptor synonymous with *penised*; it names a trait customarily eyeballed after birth (lately sonogramed before). Grammatically *male* is parallel to adjectives for other physiological traits, such as *curly-haired, left-handed*—all of which may be deemed noteworthy by and by. "A male" refers literally to a human whom we presume to be penised. It always remains for said penised human to qualify for the category "men" by acting like men act, according to the grammar of gender identity:

Unless males do power,
they do not experience themselves as men.

Unless males do power, they may not be perceived as men.

Doing power is what men do.

Men are recognizable and identifiable
by the power that they do.

Note that here we have two trick nouns, *men* and *power*, the meanings of which come into being through action. Also note that in each of the above four sentences, replacing the word *females* for *males*, and *women* for *men*, fails our commonsense test of veracity. Try it and see: "Unless females do power they may not be perceived as women" is counterintuitive.

Why do these four sentences appear to make sense if about "men" but become nonsense if about "women"? Nowhere in these sentences is information that specifies genital or reproductive "sex" as an anatomical binary; yet we read in them some binary logic of social gender, one that pertains mainly, if not exclusively, to the category "men."

To make these sentences say something meaningful about "women," we could perhaps replace "do power" with some other verb expression. Straining to assert some basic and biological binary difference, for instance, we might try "Unless females have babies, they may not be perceived as women." But this sentence too fails our common sense. Being childless rarely disqualifies a female human from the category "women," not these days in secular Western society anyway—and certainly not to the extent that a penised human can be bumped at any moment from the category "men" for not acting "like men act." Moreover, especially in commercial-sex contexts, a female human body can be counted out of the category "women" precisely because it has been gravid.

Flip-flopping these four sentences to be about "women" is easier said than done. Evidently "doing power" cues how we interpret the meaning of the category "men" but not how we interpret the meaning of the category "women." Many people wish that gender were parallel, bipolar, analogous and impartial—with "men" getting constructed and interpreted this way; "women," that (hence the huge bestseller *Men are from Mars, Women Are from Venus*).[1] But grammatically the collective noun *men* comes into being completely differently from how the collective noun *women* does.

Often in everyday life we infer that the grammar of gender identity is oddly lopsided, but we are not in the habit of noting its underlying nonanalogous logic. Among aspirants to the category "men," for example, passivity and inaction are often construed as "emasculating." Certain penised folk may not feel they have been properly introduced until what they "do" (i.e., for a living) has been disclosed. And many are said to feel out of sorts just "being" rather than "doing"—during sex, for instance. A male toddler gets praised upon exclaiming, "Look what I just did!" while a female sibling is told, "How pretty you look!" We are all familiar with a vast fund of such everyday experiences, and we track them according to the tacit grammar of gender identity. As if intuitively, we parse their gendering meaning:

Unless men do, they may not be men.

How the collective noun *women* comes into being is beyond the scope of this chapter—but far more contingent upon how the collective noun *men* comes into being than most people realize. To a remarkable extent, for instance, the category "women" becomes real transactionally by enabling the category "men" to become real. Thus the collective noun form *women* seems to occur in helping verbs.

Because of this grammatical anomaly, we err when we manipulate the nouns *men* and *power* conceptually as if they reside in metaphysical reality unverbed and undone. And we compound the confusion when we attempt to compare and contrast "men's power" with "women's" as if power were an acquisition, an attribute or a quantifiable, material possession. Such misreading not only fails to reckon with the power in question, which is a transaction, a transitive and dynamic doing; it fails to take into account how "doing power" makes "men":

To be, men must do power.

This way of framing the problem of men and power originates in a radical view of gender politics, which treats the category "men" functionally as a *Gegenidentität*—a German word meaning "identity against," an identity that can be experienced only via negation of that which it anathematizes.[2]

This way of framing the problem of men and power is not how these notions are commonly conceived of, either in real life or in academic discourse (a true either/or). That is a pity, because looking at how power makes men is a very practical way of analyzing what a funk some of us find ourselves in as would-be men. For one thing, it explains why so many men feel powerless.

Among academics, the notion that gender is socially constructed has become widely accepted as a virtual truism. Roles, identities and sexualities are said to be conditioned and socialized, signed and performed ad nauseam; yet there is a tendency to avoid pursuing why the social construction of "men" is nonanalogous to the social construction of "women." Students and scholars of so-called men's studies, for instance, determined to assert bipolar difference in a parallel universe, typically treat the collective noun *men* as an eternal theme with variations—like chairs now built this way, now upholstered that.[3] But the category "men" never exists on a ground of being. So the earnest academicians of men's studies, lacking a serviceable analytic frame for their discipline, stay stuck doing field work, taking taxonomic notes on "masculinities," yet failing, fundamentally, to perceive the operative dynamic, or grammatical syntax, whereby the category makes conceptual sense. "Look at what a wondrous variety of trees there are," they seem to exult, "all grown up from strapping seedlings and saplings!" But if asked, "Why is there a forest?" they cannot provide a clue.

We must ask how and why the category "men" comes into being. As the millennium approaches, the category "men" is being socially constructed in developed nations in a way that cannot be sufficiently explained by looking to long ago, evolution, human anatomy, cellular biology or aboriginal cultures. Many of the religious, economic and legal institutions that once demarcated the category "men" are now waning in their credibility as fortifiers of gender, making now a good time to observe, in ever sharper relief, the particular pattern and process by which the category "men" comes into being transactionally. And I submit that we can usefully detect the interior logic of that event through the metaphor of framing social gender as a "grammar":

To be, men must do power—and that power must be done to.

The power by which the category "men" comes into being is interactional, relational and transitive; it exists when a doer does it to a done-to. This genderizing power can operate one on one, some against one or some toward some. Anyone who grows up aspiring to belong to the category "men" learns its grammar viscerally. Even though individuals' biographies differ greatly, the grammar of gender identity that gets learned is remarkably unitary and paradigmatic.[4]

At its most basic, the grammar of gender identity goes like this, one on one:

Picture two human beings. And imagine that each wishes fervently to belong to the category "men," because not to—to lapse into the category "not-men"—would be repugnant. The category "not-men" is usually thought of as "female"—and the cultural fear and loathing of "female" is fundamentally what codes it repugnant—but grammatically the category "not-men" is not limited to "female"; it can also contain penised people who are not construed as belonging to the category "men." To illustrate, let us say that between the aforesaid two human beings, both aspiring to belong to the category "men," a contest or a competition or a challenge erupts between them, because the first somehow alleges that the second is not a member in good standing.

Recall that the noun *men* is not normal. It exists when it *does*; thus the imputation of nonmembership in the category always has grammatical validity. Calling someone a wuss or a wimp or a fairy or a girlie functions as slang and slander in a syntax where "men"-ness is never a settled matter; qualification for membership in the category "men" is constantly contestable. The noun form *men* is loosey-goosey that way.

Say of something, *"That's* not a chair!" and one need only attempt to sit down on the thing to see whether it is. The answer will be forthcoming, without any input from the thing. But say, or even hint, to someone who fervently desires to be one of the men, "You're not!" or "You don't cut it as a category member!" (or crueller words to that effect) and the situation gets dicey. The grammar of gender identity kicks in.

The basic transactional unit of this grammar occurs between two aspirants to the category "men." All other permutations of this grammar derive from a dyadic dispute: one would-be member of the category "men" communicating a threat or challenge or insinuation to another: "I belong but you don't."

Linguists remind us that *gender* really only means "kind." French and German each have three genders, called masculine, feminine and neuter. English has lost its genders except in some third-person pronouns and archaic remnants like *priest* and *priestess*, *aviator* and *aviatrix*, which are falling into disuse. Some languages have as many as sixteen genders,[5] because linguistically gender is only tangentially associated with sexual or reproductive anatomy. Grammatically, gender is simply a sorting system.

And systematic sorting is what is going on when someone's membership in the category "men" is being impugned: Someone, it is being suggested, is not the men sort, not the men kind. This sorting occurs transactionally between two would-be belongers to the kind, and the distinguishing feature of this transactional grammar is that a power play always prompts it. Someone does power to another would-be belonger to the kind—the power to impugn membership credentials, to cast out of the kind, to delimit who belongs and who does not. It is a power made manifest at the point of the challenging action. The challenging action is what gives the power whatever credibility it has. And the power does not exist unless it issues such challenges now and then.

A skeptic or a biological determinist might argue here that many living species engage in combat. From watching two bull moose in the wild ram horns to win the right to rut, for instance, an anthropomorphizing observer might conclude that dominance and competition among penised humans is also linked to a reproductive gambit. It is not. The moose may indeed be instinctually jockeying for conceptional presence in the moose gene pool—who knows?—but they are definitely not impugning one another's conceptual mooseness. Only Homo sapiens, the languaged animal, repetitively does gender sorting by doing power.

In the grammar of gender identity—the sub-rosa rules by which the meaning of the noun *men* comes into being—the gender "men" is reified when one human aspirant issues a challenge to another human's membership in it. The concept "men" only exists in and through an instance of verb-doing power, which is fundamentally an act of sorting—the power to include within or exclude from the category. Thus:

Men are the humans who act out the power
to sort other humans into, or out of,
the category "men."

The category "men" is maintained by all such acts of sorting.

Without such acts of sorting,
the category "men" could not be sustained.

Without such acts of sorting,
there would be no category "men."

Fencing out "female" from the category "men" would seem to be the primary purpose of the grammar of gender identity. Indeed it does that, by the binary logic of men/not-men. Discriminating against humans as "female"—including by doing violence—delivers the message "You are not one of us" with unmistakable vehemence and effect. But if the category "men" arose distinctively from nature or anatomy or material reality in any credible way, why should any effort be required to keep anyone out of it?

And why does the fencing out not stop at "female"? Aspirants to the category "men" engage in so many power plays against "female"— to delimit the category and certify their membership in it—that they seem to get carried away; they cannot seem to quit. Their *Gegenidentität* sorting maneuvers, ostensibly for the purpose of sorting out "female," seem to know no bounds; anyone remotely "not-men" could be sorted out next; hence everyone desirous of belonging among "the men" knows the relative risk they run of being sorted out. To stay on the safe side, aspirants to the category "men" have been known to fortify themselves with muscles or money, anger or armaments, a secular myth of the male archetype or a religious myth of God's plan for His (*sic*) penised people; yet by the grammar of gender identity, would-be men are really safe only in sorting out someone to the not-safe side.

The fact that so much fencing out goes on is evidence that what is operative and dispositive is the grammar of gender identity, not human anatomy.

We think in terms of its syntax all the time. We get taught it in childhood through an elaborate and individuated process of rewards and punishments, trial and error. We experience its being acted out episodically, and some of us incessantly. We abide by its grammatical rules without even knowing consciously what they are. All we know is: We could be sorted out next.

Why are we not inquisitive about the underlying rules we are following (particularly if we be academics)? Why the aura of taboo? Why not bring to light the grammar of gender identity and expose the ethics by which gender is socially constructed?

To observe the values in the conduct that keeps the category "men" aloft, we must look closely at the dramatic moment when one human aspirant has contested another's membership in it. Human 1 has just issued a challenge, threatening to sort human 2 out of the category "men." So what happens next?

The answer, in the grammar of gender identity, is one of three outcomes.

The first possible outcome is that human 1 successfully manages to sort human 2 out of the category. Since the collective noun *men* is evanescent and insubstantial, nothing without a verb, this sorting action may take any number of forms: from a humiliating taunt to a fist to a segregation policy to a bazooka. And though the effect on human 2 may be temporary or long-term (stinging only a moment or stigmatizing for a lifetime), the instant sorting action is what is key: the act of doing that power which becomes meaningful by excluding another gender aspirant from being perceived as having full-fledged membership in the category.

The second possible outcome is that human 2 turns the event around and sorts out human 1. This is the "Don't mess with me; *I* exclude *you*" approach. Again its effect on another aspirant may be momentary or momentous, and again the sorting action may take any number of forms, from insult to injury. What is constant is the grammar of gender identity. Between any two humans whose gender-anxiety buttons are pushable because both aspire to the category "men," the validity of their claim to the noun *men* is constantly contestable, but only transiently and transactionally attainable.

*Men are the humans who act out the power
to sort other humans into, or out of,
the category "men."*

The power to sort other humans
into or out of the category "men" is honoured
whenever any human attempts to sort another out.

Honouring the power to sort out
respects the grammar of gender identity
and keeps "men" a category
that humans can be sorted out of or into.

Western societies throughout recorded history have devised various moral norms according to which the grammar of gender identity may permissibly be transacted. No such modern society has yet rejected the grammar outright. Instead, Western cultures have attempted to make the best of a bad lot, sustaining the category "men" yet ameliorating, however possible, the human toll that would result if aspirants followed the grammar of gender identity out the window. Without some restraint, their insistent sorting actions would become a bloodbath.

Thus, for instance, in many Western societies it is generally okay to impugn someone's membership in the category "men" by demarcating differentials in stature, muscle mass, wealth, skin pigment and such, but generally not okay by means of murder or anal rape. Managing the fallout and controlling damage from contests among aspirants to the category "men" is a full-time undertaking of Western civilization.

The grammar of gender identity is nothing if not simple and systematic. Understanding its syntax, one can parse an infinite number of human events—from playground tiffs to father-son feuds to teenage gang warfare to international relations (both in strife and in truce). It also offers a unified theory of oppression. Both racial animosity and homophobia, for instance, are not only linked to the grammar of gender identity but driven by it: Excluding someone on account of race or sexual orientation is a sorting action that makes real a noun category ("white," "heterosexual") that is otherwise as porous as "men."

To maintain the meaning of the collective noun *men*, to keep this subject category valid, a culture must maintain a level of us/them, included/excluded and winners/losers, which fundamentally mitigates against any comprehensive ethic of fairness, equality, harmony, empathy and egalitarianism. Some sorting actions must always be valid. Some would-be doers must always be done to. There must always be direct objects. Some folks must always be one-upped, kept out, put down, wiped out.

If Marxism can be said to explain why capitalism requires a population of people kept poor, the grammar of gender identity can be said to explain why maintenance of the category "men" requires—like nobody's business—persistent sorting actions among aspirants.

But wait. It gets worse.

Recall that in the grammar of gender identity there can be three outcomes after a sorting challenge. We have looked at two: human 1 sorts out human 2, or human 2 sorts out human 1. It is the third that is the doozy.

Humans 1 and 2, in order to credential each other for membership in the category "men"—in order not to have to mess with or rough up each other to do so—jointly sort out someone else. Humans 1 and 2 both become subjects in a grammatical sentence in which the direct object of their sorting power, human 3, is someone they both agree to be outside the category "men," someone self-evidently scornable, mockable, excludable.

And who is human 3? To humans 1 and 2 it might matter a whole lot; but by the grammar of gender identity, the qualities or traits or behaviours that might distinguish any given human 3 are malleable and irrelevant. What is syntactically key is that a sorting action be effected whereby there is not a binary logic of win/lose between aspirants but rather a binary logic of men/not-men between those collegial aspirants and some sorted-out third party. By positing that human 3 is outside the category "men," humans 1 and 2 can both belong, painlessly and simultaneously and comradely. According to the grammar of gender identity, two or more category aspirants can thus do power together without risking the price of doing power to one another. For any category aspirants who jointly fence out the same third party, this is a win-win.

Human 3 may be an individual or group fenced out as "female" or an individual or group that is simply younger, weaker, poorer, queerer, darker, less abled, whatever. The grammar of gender identity does not specify any particular traits for the sort-status "not-men." The only specified placeholders in its syntax are "the men who do the power to sort." The status "not within the 'men' category" is relative to some action by would-be sorters acting individually or in consort. The various "identities" that seem to arise by contrast—the various groupings of people over and against whom "men who do power" form alliances (such as people of colour, homosexuals, poor people, exploited workers)—come into meaningful being only to the extent that "men who do power" successfully bring the identity "men" into meaningful being. And the *Gegenidentität* "men" does not arise by contrast to any particular inherent features or characteristics of the sort-status "not-men." Except for humans permanently fenced out as "female," humans fenced out of the category "men" in one instance may turn around and claim membership in the category by fencing out someone else. That is the genius of the grammar of gender identity: It is an infinitely replicable syntax that has only a prescribed subject, not a predefined direct object. Doers of the deed must be "the men who do power to sort," and doers of the deed *become* "the men who do power to sort" by the act of doing the power—but whom they sort out could be anyone.

Loyalty to the concept of the category "men" prevents people from scrutinizing the actions and deeds that sustain it. These actions and deeds are systematic because they are grammatical: They follow the same rules; they adhere to the same ethics; they reify the same paradigmatic power to sort; they maintain the sort-status by maintaining the sorting system.

A human 1 and a human 2 might successfully transact a sorting action against a human 3 in one instance, but nothing in the grammar of gender identity prevents humans 1 and 2 from being turned into third parties in a sorting action conducted by other claimants to the sort-status "men." Two aspirants to the category "men," for instance, may perform a sorting action against some third party who is less "heterosexual"; meanwhile those same aspirants may be sorted out of the category "men" on account of being less "white." The permutations of this transaction are endless. The constant is its grammar, whereby the noun *men* gets verbed into meaning.

An aspirant to the sort-status "men" who is episodically the butt of some other penised folks' sorting action always has the option to reclaim affiliation among "the men who do the power to sort" by fencing out anyone as "female." The grammar of gender identity sorts "female" as "not men" with conspicuous consistency, more often than any other "other." Consequently an aspirant to the category "men" who has been sorted out as "fag," for instance, together with an aspirant who has been sorted out as "nigger" may transiently reclaim membership in the sort-status "men" simply by some mutual act that jointly ejects someone as "cunt." The permutations of this transaction too are endless. But the constant is not any intrinsic feature or characteristic that goes by the affirmative name of "queer" or "Black" or even "female." The constant is the grammar whereby the noun *men* gets verbed into being by doing the power to sort out.

This explains why would-be men so frequently "feel powerless": Even as men do power to women, men do power to other men. They have to, for there to be men. And this explains why huge male-only public gatherings are all the rage: Fencing out all women is sometimes sufficient to allay, at least for an ephemeral time, would-be men's impulses to do power to one another—and would-be men's dread that power will surely be done to them next.

I believe it makes great personal and political sense to interrogate the category "men" as an ethical and political construct—a project I have pursued in my non-fiction work on sexual politics for the past twenty years. The problem with men's studies as an academic field, however, is that it fundamentally accepts gender as a meaningful sorting system—even applauds it—without inquiring into the systematic sorting by which the concept "men" is literally made up.[6]

While it may be informative to focus on the various identities that seem to arise among subgroupings of humans 3 who are endlessly disenfranchised or excluded on account of not qualifying for the category "men," it is not *transformative*. Looking only at groupings of people classified by category of "oppression" fails to subvert the transactional dynamic of oppression. We need to explain usefully how and why many humans 3 also episodically *qualify* for the category "men," by means of the power they do to sort out others, especially anyone female. We need also to provide for penised folks a practical analytic frame with which they, in their day-to-day lives, can comprehend for themselves why they are sometimes put down and sorted out even as they sometimes sort out and put down. Such an analytic frame would link the dynamics of racism, homophobia and sexism interactionally so that it can be pragmatically applied to each penised individual's particular life, everyday experience and ethical choice-making.

Recognizing that there are only three possible outcomes to a sorting challenge provides exactly such an analytic frame—easily accessible and immediately applicable. Once a penised individual realizes that these three outcomes are inevitable and predictable, and are all premised on belief in the validity of the sorting challenge, the sorting challenge itself can be recognized for what it is—a maintenance maneuver for the category "men"—and conscientiously interrupted.

To inspire individuals for lives of conscientious resistance to all such sorting challenges, we must seek out the us/them grammar, the *Gegenidentität* program, the "dis"-operating system that shuts out all disidentified-with groups in order to construct meaning for the noun *men*. This means recognizing how exposed everyone is, how vulnerable anyone is, to being cast into a shut-out sort-status so that two or more aspirants to the collective noun "men" may posit, at least momentarily, their bona fide membership in it.

Attempts by men's studies academicians to reconceptualize the category "men"—to "transgress" it, for instance, or to "redefine masculinity"—will not work. Such efforts, noodling with an inherently indeterminable noun form, bypass the real problem; they do not address the prior and fundamental grammar. If one stakes one's claim to societal change on redeeming and redefining the category "men" (whether by trying to be among the "good" men, the "enlightened" men or even the "profeminist" men), one is still at risk of being targeted as a third party in some other would-be men's pact, and one's buttons are still pushable in any challenge to one's membership in the sort-status "men"—perhaps all the more so for having vouchsafed personal and political defense of the category "men" as one's talisman. Trying to retool the meaning of the noun *men* is therefore both retro and futile. However sincerely one may wish to reconfigure that noun form (and indeed, what thinking person would not?), one cannot effectively do so without subverting the underlying us/them grammar that operationally now delineates the category as a *Gegenidentität*.

Only when we take apart the grammar of gender identity completely—rejecting and replacing both its structural rules and its inexorably unjust ethics—will anyone on earth be safe from the power that "the men who do power" do in order to be men. To accomplish this revolution in the language of our lives, our conduct must endeavour to accord with a different grammar, based in an I–Thou ethic, which functions transactionally not to maintain "men" but to honour our common humanity and create justice.[7]

NOTES

1. This book by John Gray (1992) popularizes the essentialist notion of gender dimorphism, extolling it as an evenhanded split in the human species. He casts the notion into what could be dubbed "planet parenthood"—men from one, women from another—and uses it to explain and justify a duplicitous moral double standard. He lectures women (Venusians) on what sorts of annoying behaviour to accept from men (Martians), for instance, because that is the way Martians "are." Gray's spacey message has wide appeal, but philosophically he has the problem exactly backward. In fact, Western civilization's male-supremacist ethical double standard is what creates and justifies people's belief in the faulty notion of gender bipolarity, as I have argued in "Rapist Ethics" in *Refusing to Be a Man* (Stoltenberg 1990) and elsewhere.

2. The late German author Heiner Müller was widely known for his critique of postwar German nationalism and for his view that Germany as a political construction exists only in opposition to something else. I draw a related social and political parallel between "the idea of the male sex" and "the idea of an Aryan race" in "How Men Have (a) Sex" in *Refusing to Be a Man*: "[P]enises exist, the male sex does not. The male sex is socially constructed. It is a political entity that flourishes only through acts of force and sexual terrorism" (Stoltenberg 1990:30). In a personal conversation several years ago, John Goetz, a U.S. journalist in Germany who knew Müller, Goetz coined the word *Gegenidentität* to name the similarity between Müller's observation and mine.

3. For example Harry Brod, a prominent framer of the field, writes that "the subject matter of men's studies is the study of masculinities and male experiences in their own right as specific and varying social, cultural, and historical formations" (1993:264).

4. Boys are taught the grammar of gender identity by means of varying amounts and intensities of childhood trauma and perks, as I have elaborated in *The End of Manhood* (Stoltenberg 1994a). If one thinks of all the men one has met in one's lifetime and if one could flash back to each of their childhoods, one would see a vast gradation in how violently or abusively (or lovingly and justly) they each were raised. This variable is perhaps the most significant in men's biographies. I believe it accounts, for instance, for how some men learn to eroticize violence and why for other men violence is antierotic.

Even someone with a kind, supportive, completely nonviolent childhood background can grow up obsessed with the grammar of gender identity. That obsessional subjective state—that drive to make real one's membership in the category men—is penised people's common "conditioning," and I intend my ethical dissection of that obsessional state to contribute to the growing literature on gender politics. At minimum, I submit, framing gender as a grammar suggests important lines of inquiry for social science research into correlations between early-childhood learning experiences and subsequent antisocial violence.

5. As linguist Joan Bresnan has written of Kivunjo, a Bantu language spoken in Tanzania (cited in Pinker 1995:27).

6. For example: "I like gender, and I like gender difference," writes Michael S. Kimmel, a pre-eminent men's studies academician; "in difference is heat. . . . It's in our jeans . . . not in our genes" (Kimmel 1993:66).

7. For a fuller discussion of the everyday ethics of selfhood affirmation as an alternative to manhood proving, see *The End of Manhood*, especially my discussion of Martin Buber's conception of "I and Thou" (Stoltenberg 1994a:301–38).

3

Integrating Love and Power
Reflections on Power, Helplessness, Nurture and Male Identity
Walter Isaac

It's dinnertime, Tuesday evening. Diane has cooked an appetizing dinner: orange roughy with saffron rice and asparagus. The three of us, Diane, Murray and I are at the dinner table ready to eat. I'm feeling nervous, awkward, uncomfortable, but at the same time happily excited. I'm thinking, "What am I so worked up about? This is a commonplace act I'm about to perform, but I feel as if I'm about to dive into some very unfamiliar waters." Diane and Murray are both looking at me expectantly. She gives me a warm smile and Murray has a mischievous twinkle in his eye, letting me know that the humour of my predicament is by no means lost on him.

It's time to take the plunge. I reach over, pick up Murray's fork, break off a bite sized piece of orange roughy and lift it from his plate. Eyes still twinkling, he opens his mouth. As I gently place the forkful of food into his waiting mouth a great wave of tenderness washes over me. I'm thrown off balance by the power of this feeling. Tears well up in my eyes. I notice Murray's eyes are also moist and for a moment we seem about to melt. We share a long moment of intimacy and closeness beyond anything we have touched in the seven years we have known each other. I place his fork back on the table and pick up my own. Murray chews and swallows with pleasure. Tuesday night dinner has begun. We'll be here having dinner with Murray every Tuesday night until he dies. That will be seven months from now. Murray is thirty-three years old. He has ALS (amyotrophic lateral sclerosis or Lou Gehrig's disease). Below the level of his head and neck, Murray is unable to move.

This experience of feeding Murray for the first time contains the seeds of my exploration into the themes that I address in this chapter: the nature of authentic power, the relationship of power to helplessness, and the importance for men of developing their capacity for nurturing.

As human beings we experience an unusually prolonged period of infancy during which we are helpless and vulnerable. We later fear a return to this early helplessness. My initial discomfort with bringing the first forkful of food to Murray's lips arose partly from the fear of fully facing the profundity of his helplessness. His vulnerability was a mirror of my own: I too was once unable to feed myself and in some future, near or far, I will once again be similarly helpless. I recall that in my twenties and thirties my greatest fear was of losing my ability to move and becoming physically dependent. My plan, in the event of such a fate, was to take my own life rather than endure the horror of total dependency. After a few Tuesday evening dinners with Murray this old fear dissolved.

Murray, through enlisting the support of a network of friends and helpers, managed, in spite of his condition, to live at home during the last, most debilitating year of his disease. Not only did he survive during this difficult period, but he lived it with great joy, humour and creativity. He was a powerful inspiration to those of us that were part of his care giving team. He faced and accepted his helplessness and, finally, he transcended it. His lack of fear in the midst of his vulnerability enabled us, his care givers, to face our own fears. The model he embodied pointed toward possibilities and futures more hopeful than those we had envisioned on the basis of our own fear. Being around him during this time never felt like being around a sick person. The disease was not the dominant theme of his life. The dominant theme was a deep, compassionate interdependence.

Murray's funeral was, for most of us on his "team," not solely a time of sadness, but also a time of great joy, gratitude and triumph. We had taken on a dark, difficult situation and discovered its hidden blessings. We had all stretched ourselves beyond our previous limits. We had experienced what human beings at their very best are capable of. We had done it right. Murray's ability to transform a potentially dark and hopeless situation into a triumph of human love, cooperation and creativity is for me an example of authentic human power at it's very highest and best. Authentic power, as I see it, is not a power based in competition, but rather in compassion; not a power that divides, but rather one that unites.

In retrospect, I believe that my discomfort at the prospect of feeding Murray had a second source. Lifting that fork to Murray's mouth just did not quite feel "manly." In spite of my having spent years in a nurturing role as a massage therapist and bodyworker, this form of nurturing somehow felt like female rather than male territory. Of course this should come as no surprise. Men in the Western world generally experience themselves as recipients, not sources, of nurturing. This is especially evident when one considers who is the source of most infant and early childhood nurturing. I will explore some of the causes of the gender disparity in regard to nurturing. It is, in my view, a most unfortunate disparity. For it is through the deepening of compassion in the act of nurturing that men become capable of facing and transcending their helplessness and vulnerability. And until men become capable of facing our helplessness, authentic power will elude us. These are the themes I address in the material that follows.

My approach is personal and informal. I believe I can best express my ideas by telling my personal stories as honestly and well as I can. Aside from my use of some of Dorothy Dinnerstein's ideas, what I have to say does not come out of the literature that addresses issues of men and power: it is simply my attempt to make some sense of my own experience. I ask the reader to be tolerant of my tendency to over generalize at times, saying "men" when "most men" would be more accurate. I am well aware that there are significant exceptions to the generalizations I make and the conclusions I draw. I have at times omitted qualifying statements because they either seem to be implicitly understood, or would disrupt the informal tone of the piece. What I am writing here is, after all, perhaps more a confession than an argument.

My approach to power is an introvert's approach. I have never been particularly interested in the kind of power games that are played out in the public arena. Political power, for example, is not the kind of power I have much interest in. As an introvert, I am more concerned with the power issues of self-mastery and inner strength. For me, the quality of the inner experience counts more than external appearances. The external manifestations are of course important, but to an introvert they count only in so far as they provide validation of the inner experience. My hope is that discussing power from this perspective will provide some balance to the extroverted points of view on power that prevail in society.

POWER AS ABILITY VERSUS POWER AS DOMINATION

More power. What would that mean, more independence, more freedom, more territory, or more speed? Having mastery of space, time and movement? Acquiring a single item from this shopping list would surely magnify one's personal power. What would it mean to attain them all in a single extraordinary act of balance and daring? Sounds too good to be true? No, not at all. Paradoxically, such extraordinary acts of power are commonplace. All of us, by virtue of being human, have performed such acts. We did so when we learned to walk, to ride a bicycle, to drive a car or to read a book.

The power inherent in these commonplace acts is simple, innocent and wholesome. This power is not power over another. This is power as ability: "power to." There are no hurt, resentful losers here, no winners of hollow victories tinged with guilt. Although I use the word power in this sense, it is not the way the term is most often used. Discussions of power usually deal with more complex situations involving competition, status and the social pecking order. This power seeks to dominate and control others. If power as ability is "power to," then power as domination is "power over."

It is not uncommon to hear widely differing kinds of power spoken of interchangeably and indiscriminately. Because the various uses of the word power are often not clearly separated and defined, much confusion and misunderstanding results. For example, one speaks of the love of power and the power of love. Small shifts of word order create enormous shifts in meaning. Often I experience a sense of uneasy, hard to penetrate ambiguity in discussions of power. My game plan is to begin by examining a simple, common example of power to help to dispel the fog of ambiguity and confusion.

RIDING A BICYCLE: AUTHENTIC POWER VERSUS REACTIVE POWER

Vancouver, Canada, 1950. A summer afternoon. I've crash landed on a neighbour's lawn. I'm frustrated, but not defeated. I've fallen from the bicycle again. I am eight and a half years old.

I get up, mount the bicycle and try once more. I've borrowed the bike from a kid up the street. I've got it all to myself for a few hours. This is my chance finally to learn to ride. The pressure to master bike riding is big. It's an embarrassment learning to ride at eight and a half, when four and five year olds on the street are already riding. I'm fiercely determined, single minded, focused.

Now I'm sitting on the bike balancing with my legs stretched out, toes touching the grass. (I'm not ready for the sidewalk yet; I'm still falling off too often.) I push off with both feet, glide a short distance, struggling to stay balanced. I do this over and over, building confidence. Finally, just as the bike is in mid-glide, my feet go for the pedals. But they're a moving target and my feet miss the mark. In the struggle with the pedals I lose my balance. Another crash landing on the lawn.

I'm not getting much better at staying up. What I am getting better at is falling. I'm learning how to fall and not get hurt. Soon there's no more fear of falling; the crash landings become part of the game. As I relax more, time slows down. Details of the art of balancing come more sharply into focus. My feet find the pedals more often after the push off. I learn to move the handlebars to compensate for shifts of my body weight.

Soon the sidewalk becomes the runway for my test flights. Everything moves faster. Falling becomes more dangerous and hurts more when it happens. But I find to my surprise that balance becomes easier with speed. I'm getting more and more excited as the crash landings grow fewer and I stay up longer and longer.

There comes a point when my body just knows how to do it. It knows, but I don't know that it knows. I can't simply trust it yet so I get in my own way by trying too hard. I need to surrender control and let my body take over. But this is difficult! It requires a 180 degree turnabout in attitude. What has got me this far now stands in my way. I have to give up effort and struggle and just trust my body. To reach a higher level of control, I must give up the hard won control I've achieved.

As I struggle with this paradox everything gets worse. I'm falling all the time again. Onto the sidewalk now. I'm getting bruised; my knees and elbows are scraped raw. Nothing works. I sit on the sidewalk and stare helplessly at the wretched bike, beyond knowing what to do. Frustration and bewilderment build and hit a peak. Then, gradually, the momentum of effort and determination finally winds down. I give up trying. I don't care anymore what happens. I pick the bike up, get on, and just go.

I find myself riding the bike. I'm watching my body do it. There's nothing to it. I've got it! I've got the knack. I experience lightness, freedom, speed and power. The sidewalk that I ride along, the houses, lawns and trees shimmer with aliveness.

There was great power in learning to ride that bicycle. The old limits of time and space dissolved. My world on foot—limited to a few square blocks—now expanded to include the entire city. The possibilities for exploration and adventure became endless. Socially, I passed through an initiation that brought me closer to my peers: I gained the power of belonging. Personally, I learned the power of perseverance, tapped the hidden power of my body and felt the unexpected power and freedom that came with letting go.

The way to this power had been beset with difficulties: the awkward helplessness of loss of balance; the embarrassment of falling; the humiliation of my failures being witnessed by children younger than myself, children who had mastered that with which I struggled. There is no way around these difficulties. Learning to stand, to walk or to ride a bicycle requires that we give up the safe and the familiar. We have to give up the exercise of powers already in our grasp before reaching out toward those not yet our own. We have to leave behind our safe and solid footing on the ground when we face the uncertain balance up on the bicycle seat. Awkwardness, helplessness and humiliation have to be endured and passed through before the new power is attained. This is the way of authentic power.

The temptation to resort to false, reactive power is always at hand. It is easy to imagine the boy who was me falling from the bicycle and, at the height of his frustration, picking himself up then giving the bike a few hard kicks. The helplessness and humiliation feel too overwhelming to absorb. They are pushed away and then projected onto the bike. "Stupid bike!" As he turns to leave he spots a small boy watching him from across the street. The boy is laughing. He runs down to the younger boy, throws him roughly to the ground, then storms off.

Reactive power is, of course, not real power at all. There is no enlargement of ability, confidence or self-knowledge. It is an illusion of power that serves the function of keeping hurt and helplessness at bay. The boy who passes through the trial of his helplessness and masters the bicycle will never lose the skill and power he gained. That power cannot be taken away by others. The boy who is overcome by the temptation to use reactive power stands on a shaky foundation of fear and doubt. Through splitting himself off from his helplessness he becomes fragmented. Instead of trusting himself and connecting to his depths and discovering his inner strength in times of stress and difficulty, he must work harder to wall off what has been denied. He has lost his center and fears what others might be thinking of him. No longer in possession of himself, yet in continual need to prove himself, the temptation to fall into reactive power grows ever stronger.

Reactive power is a strategy people use for self-preservation and face saving when we are either unable or unwilling to deal directly with our helplessness. The greater the helplessness the stronger the temptation to resort to reactive power. The helplessness and frustration we encounter as we work toward mastering a vital new skill can be intense. But this kind of helplessness is tempered by the fact that we can choose to step out of the learning situation at any time and head for the exit door. We can get down from the bike and call it a day. Most often we stay on the bike. In fact, knowing there is an exit door helps keep us from needing to use it. There are, however, other life situations where the exit door does not exist, where there is little choice and where the helplessness into which we fall is of a different order altogether.

CRAB SOUP

In the early 70s, when I was in my late twenties, I wrote the following poem:

Crab Soup

At low tide crabs would lurk in their dark hideouts
    under loose stones.
And we would walk along the beach like little gods
    kicking over likely stones in a deadly game of hide and seek.
Sometimes, stiff legs moving all at once,
    they'd scramble backwards in a blur.
Sometimes they would twitch just once
    then freeze
    black shiny pinhead eyes dazzled by a blast of sunlight.
We felt their terror
    felt their bewildered eyes
    watching our moving hands;
Hands that would lift them nervous and delicate
    as needled claws pinched at the air;
Hands that would drop them
    one by one
    into the rusted tin cans . . .
With thick blunt sticks gripped tightly in our fists
    we mashed them to a pulp
    pounding the sticks down again and again . . .
"Crab soup!" "Campbell's Cream of Crab Soup!"
    And then we'd laugh and laugh
    our devil's laughter rising louder
    until it drowned the gentle murmur of the sea.

This poem emerged fully formed during a high school creative writing class I was teaching. I was surprised by the emotional intensity of the poem and the memory it was based in—a memory that had lain buried for over fifteen years. The crab soup incident had a ritualistic quality about it. I had a vague sense at the time of writing that I had done this more than once. Perhaps several times. And that was all I remembered.

It was not until twenty years after writing the poem that a deeper dimension of the crab soup incident revealed itself. I was sorting through some old papers and ran across a copy of the poem. When I reread it, its larger context came into focus. What I now realized was this: the last time I enacted the crab soup ritual was on the day of my father's funeral. The two experiences, the killing of the crabs and the funeral, their relationship to each other long buried and forgotten, suddenly fused and illuminated each other. The dark forces driving the seemingly wanton violence stood out clearly. I now knew what was driving that boy to pound a stick into a rusty tin can full of crabs.

My father died suddenly, of a heart attack, on June 9, 1956. He had not felt well after dinner and had gone up to bed to lie down. I remember my mother's panicked voice shouting to me from their bedroom. I sprinted upstairs where I found my father gasping for breath, his chest heaving and his face contorted. I sent my mother downstairs to phone for an ambulance while I remained with him. Clumsily, not really knowing what to do, I pumped his chest in a futile effort to keep him breathing. He broke out into a cold sweat. Then all motion stopped and he was gone. It was all finished in a matter of minutes. I was in shock. It could not be. My world was shattered. All seemed unreal. I was fourteen.

Seven years earlier my parents and I emigrated from Europe leaving family and friends behind. Now, my mother and I were alone. To make matters worse, over the year or two prior to my father's death, she had grown obsessively frightened and suspicious. Later, when I was sixteen, she would be diagnosed paranoid schizophrenic. I felt helpless and alone, burdened with a mother who was mentally disturbed and barely able to cope.

After the funeral there was a reception at our home. I found the event unbearably oppressive. Together with my best friend, I managed to slip out of the house. I knew where I needed to go. We headed down to the ocean, a three minute walk from the house. The rocky expanse of beach was deserted. The tide was out. The gloomy mood of the funeral reception gave way to a strange hilarity. We were like a pair of convicts on the loose, revelling in a kind of crazy fleeting freedom. At the same time, underneath the wild, manic emotional release ran a dark, dense current of grief and rage. I could not have named it that then, but I felt its threatening presence. There was a kind of power in our manic craziness, a power that could hold the grief and rage at bay. And right then, that was the power I needed. This was the frenzied energy that drove the crab soup ritual. I needed the crab soup a great deal more than I needed the tea and sandwiches and consolation of the adult world we had left behind.

Before I remembered what happened on the day of the funeral, I dismissed the violence and cruelty of the wanton killing as a regrettable action common to young boys. My adult self understood the cruelty of my younger self in terms of compensation for a kind of general powerlessness. The powerless child takes out his or her frustrations on a weaker creature lower down the biological pecking order.

Set in the context of my father's funeral, the act of killing the crabs desperately proclaimed, *I have control over life and death*, when life and death were the very things over which I had no control. I was reacting to a helplessness too painful and overwhelming for my fourteen-year-old self to face. That helplessness needed to be projected onto those unfortunate crabs and squashed.

When I wrote "Crab Soup" I read it out to the creative writing class. We ended up discussing acts of childhood cruelty. While most of the boys recalled doing similar things, the girls had no such memories. They found these acts of cruelty disgusting and disturbing. The boys remembered them with a mixture of embarrassment and uneasy humour. The class's attempts to explain this gender disparity boiled down to the usual conclusion that "boys will be boys."

What would a fourteen-year-old girl have done under the circumstances? I have no doubt she would have handled her helplessness differently. Sneak away from her father's funeral reception with a girlfriend, then cruelly kill the nearest available creatures? Unthinkable. She likely would have stayed at the funeral reception, wept profusely and accepted comfort from the adults who loved her. The care and support thus offered would have reminded her that while she had lost her father, she had not lost her community. Rather than desperately grabbing onto illusions of power, I expect she would have let herself experience her helplessness.

When one's helplessness cannot be experienced and dealt with, the pull toward reactive power strengthens. Men are not very good at facing their feelings of helplessness. It is more difficult for men than women even to admit that they need help. In my work as a massage therapist and bodyworker, over seventy percent of the clients I see are women. This is hardly surprising as women generally tend to seek help more frequently than men do. They are also usually more comfortable in admitting that they need help.

Usually these gender disparities are explained by differences in socialization. From an early age boys are taught not to behave like babies. They learn the manly stance of self-reliance and self-control. Any emotional expression that might reveal an unmanly weakness must be held in check. For girls, on the other hand, crying and other expressions of vulnerability are not regarded as unfeminine.

Consequently, when faced with a situation in which she feels helpless, a woman can more easily admit to and express what she is experiencing without compromising her identity as a female. A male in the same position, even if he succeeds in hiding his feelings from others, will likely feel ashamed of himself for being unmanly. Women, in the midst of their vulnerability and feelings of powerlessness, are freer to express what is troubling them and to seek help. Men are less able to do likewise without compounding their helplessness with shame and self-doubt.

These kinds of social pressures make it difficult for most men to face the places of vulnerability inside themselves. What cannot be faced and challenged is unlikely to be integrated and outgrown. The authentic power that would result from such growth is missed. When the pressures of anxiety and helplessness are great and the avenues to genuine emotional expression and authentic power are blocked—as they were for me on the day of my father's funeral—males often will, as a last resort, turn to reactive power.

The foregoing socialization-based explanations can help one understand the particular difficulties men have in dealing with helplessness and reactive power. They do not, in my opinion, account for the sheer intensity of the emotional charge surrounding these difficulties. When men enter directly into states of helplessness during body-work, the emotional intensity often reaches survival levels: what is going on feels like a matter of life and death. In addition to the sheer emotional intensity, there is often a sense of having touched a primitive, pre-verbal level of experience. In short, I believe the complexities of reactive power cannot be fully accounted for by the familiar socialization explanations.

A deeper and more challenging investigation of these and related issues appears in Dorothy Dinnerstein's *The Mermaid and the Minotaur: Sexual Arrangements and The Human Malaise* (1977). Dinnerstein's book is an eloquent and courageous attempt to understand the root causes of the pathological stance the human species has adopted toward nature and toward itself. Although the scope of her thesis is

larger than problems of male helplessness and reactive power, I believe
her book offers valuable insights into these issues.

The "sexual arrangements" to which Dinnerstein refers in her sub-
title all revolve around one key fact: the physical and emotional early
childcare of both male and female children is provided almost exclusively by women. The "human malaise" refers to the pathologically
self-destructive and nature-destructive aggression with which we have
become all too familiar. Her book goes a long way toward uncovering
the roots of what I have here termed reactive power.

In *The Mermaid and the Minotaur*, Dinnerstein reminds readers
that we humans must endure a longer period of helplessness than our
fellow creatures in the animal kingdom. To further intensify and complicate this predicament, a large portion of this period of dependency
and vulnerability is experienced while our awareness has already been
enriched and extended through the use of language. Thus, not only do
we feel the helplessness of the moment, but through the inner representations of language, we project our present vulnerability into the
future, compare ourselves with others whom we envy for their greater
power, and so on.

During this long period of dependency, the powerful, seemingly
god-like Other who looks after the majority of our needs is nearly
always a woman. This woman becomes our source of nourishment,
warmth, stimulation, comfort, guidance and support. To the extent that
even the most skilled, loving and dedicated mother cannot perfectly
anticipate or fulfil all of her child's needs, she also becomes the source
of discomfort, pain, frustration and rage.

The fact that for both male and female children this powerful, primary nurturing human presence is usually a woman can explain a great
deal about why men have such a hard time dealing with their helplessness. The explanation in turn sheds light on the forces that drive men
toward reactive power.

Dinnerstein's point that both male and female children are nurtured by women and grow up seeing women as the sources of nurture
produces different results. Girls generally see themselves as being
essentially like mother and are reinforced in the assumption that like
mother, they too will become sources of nurture. Boys, on the other
hand, come to understand that they are essentially unlike mother. As
such, they have every reason to regard themselves as recipients, not

sources, of nurturing. The girl's perception that she is like mother is reinforced through play and other forms of socialization. Boys, on the other hand, are not trained to become nurturers. Their play and socialization reinforce aggression rather than nurturing. Their fantasy figurines are not doll-babies that cry and wet, but rather fighters and soldiers that shoot to kill. The emphasis is not on empathy and compassion for what is vulnerable in themselves and in others; the emphasis is on a fantasy of invulnerability. The path to reactive power is paved and waiting.

Because of these prevailing child-rearing arrangements, men tend to see women as the sole sources of nurture. They are likely to be unaware that these resources reside within themselves as well. This means that in order to get the nurturing he needs, a man has to secure a female source of this special quality he lacks. But the pressure to find a female source of nurturing care is in conflict with the pressure toward manly self-sufficiency. Even once he has secured a level of perceived control over a female source of nurturing, he can only go so far in receiving the care and support now available to him. For in opening himself to receive what the woman can offer he must let his manly guard down and allow himself to feel. At this point, his situation begins to trigger uncomfortable resonances with his vulnerability as an infant: the time when he was totally dependent on the first god-like female presence that provided for him. The wordless feeling-memory substratum of early infancy holds both ecstasy and terror. He does not want to move too far into this dimension of his being. It is too frightening. When faced with his vulnerability and dependence, a man is trapped by the pressures of his socialization and cut off, by his perception of his identity as a man, from his own deeper resources of caring and compassion. He has become boxed into a very cramped and lonely place indeed.

On the other hand, a man who has been nurtured in his infancy and early childhood not only by his mother but by his father as well, would grow up more connected to the sources of nurturing power within himself. For such a man, nurturing would not be a scarce commodity available only through women. Also, the nurturing available from others, both men and women, could be more safely and more deeply received. Then, when life presents him with its many opportunities for experiencing vulnerability he would have more options and resources at his disposal. He would have the tools he needed for working his way through helplessness toward the rewards of authentic power.

I will put this in the form of an example. A man loses his job. He feels vulnerable, frightened and useless. His job, the symbol of his manly role of self-reliant provider, has been stripped from him. Receiving support from his female partner, especially if she is employed, becomes difficult because he is now completely dependent on her. Disturbing resonances with the situation of early infancy surface. Because he has little capacity for self-nurturing, all he can do with his intense fear and rage is bottle it up. He is cut off from himself and his shame keeps him isolated from the help and support of others. The stage is set for an explosion of reactive power.

A man in the same situation but with his connection to his inner resources of compassion intact, is in a much stronger position within himself. He judges himself less severely. His dependence on his female partner feels less total and therefore more tolerable. His compassion extends out to others in the same boat as himself. He is moved to help those others and is more able to receive their help. So although his situation is still difficult and frightening, his capacity to bear it is far greater than if he had little self-nurturing capacity. The pressures on him that could erupt into reactive power—that manifests as abuse and family violence—are far more manageable.

The ability to see oneself as a source of nurturing reduces the pressure to misuse power. At the same time it also makes such misuse more difficult to justify. A person in touch with his or her sources of nurturing can more easily empathize with those who are weaker or more vulnerable than he or she is. In one's relations with weaker others, the others are perceived to be essentially like oneself. The motivation is not to exploit, but to protect. When one is cut off from the ability to empathize, the weaker other becomes the projection screen for the despised weakness within oneself. The other is then turned into something subhuman—fair game as a target for false, reactive power. My fourteen-year-old self could sense the terror of the crabs. But because I had lost my connection to my own vulnerability and compassion I turned the crabs into inconsequential creatures that I had every right to destroy.

The healing journey from the shattered teenager making crab soup on a lonely beach to the adult I became has been long and rich and strange. There were many gifts along the way that gave me the inspiration and the courage to take the "road less travelled." The following was one such gift.

A FOOT IN THE DOOR

In the summer of 1973, when I was thirty, a friend led me through a door into a realm of experience that would change my life. The key that opened the door was a foot massage.

I was tired, stiff and out of sorts that day. A friend offered to massage my feet. Because massage was new to me then, her offer was unexpected and seemed a bit odd. But my resistance was low and, besides, what did I have to lose? I removed my socks and lay down on the living room rug. None of my previous experiences in the realm of touch prepared me for what happened next. Lovingly, with exquisite sensitivity and creative variety of pressure and movement, her hands led me through a long forgotten door into the realm of healing touch. As my linear mind let go its grasp, I rediscovered the holographic nature of touch. Moving rivulets of feeling and sensation flowed through my feet and up into my legs, abdomen, chest, head and face. My attention slipped out of my busy, distracted thinking mind and entered the eternal present of my body.

Fifteen minutes (or was it fifteen hours) later, I arose refreshed. I was restored to my senses and to my humanity. My stiffness, tiredness and disgruntled mood had vanished. There was a power in the touch that I had experienced. It was neither the power of bulging muscles nor roaring engines. Nor was it the separative power that seeks superiority through competition and winning. It was not the "power over" that preys on the weakness of others. This was a power far more gentle and profound. I resolved to make it my business to find out everything I could about it.

In 1975, two years after that foot massage, after having been a high school English teacher for eight years, I decided to become a massage therapist. Looking back twenty-one years later, I see that my work as a massage therapist has played a transforming role in my experience of myself as a male. Secondarily, it has transformed my way of exercising power in the world.

Much of the early nurturing children receive is transmitted through touch. So it seems fitting that touch became the key that awakened the nurturing power lying dormant in me. In practising massage therapy I assumed the role of nurturer. The nurturing abilities that I gradually developed through this work opened possibilities beyond what my fourteen-year-old self could ever have imagined. What I learned became especially important to me at the time of my mother's death.

BEYOND CRAB SOUP

I woke up suddenly and sat bolt upright in bed. I knew in that moment that my mother was dead. There had been no dream as such to inform me of this, only the absolute certainty I felt that she was dead. I wondered what to do. I looked over at the clock. It was 3:00 a.m. I decided to wait and go check on her in the morning. When I arrived at the personal care home in which she was staying, she was, to my surprise, still very much alive. I was puzzled.

It took me some time to understand that both realities were true: my mother was alive, and at the same time she was dead. My mother's health had been slowly deteriorating for years. She had become bedridden. Her once busy, energetic personality had grown stagnant and dull. The mother I had once known was no more. While her body remained, *she* was no longer here. In effect, the experience of waking up in shock and realizing that my mother was dead was my emotional recognition of this fact.

Visiting her, as I did for an hour each week, was becoming painful and frustrating for me. We would greet each other, then fall into a strange silence. Her eyes would close and she would drift off into a troubled sleep. Then she'd awaken, looking surprised to find me there. Often she didn't recognize me. This made me furious. "It's me, Walter!" I would half-shout in Russian. "I've been here half an hour." She'd stare back at me blankly. Then her eyes would close up like shutters and she'd disappear somewhere inside herself where I couldn't follow.

I would sit at her side, fury running rampant, desperately trying to collect myself and calm down. The anger would protest, "Why am I coming here to visit her? She doesn't even know I'm here. Doesn't she know how busy I am?" The more reasonable side would reply, "Take it easy. She's not ignoring you on purpose just to push your buttons. She can't help being sick and demented. She's *dying* for God's sake! The last thing she needs is your anger." I'd settle down some, then leave, depressed and disgruntled, deeply ashamed of myself.

This little drama went on for months. As she faded further away, my anger grew worse. Try as I might to be kind to her, a single blank look from her and I'd be furious. I was at my wits end. Out of control. I wasn't at all sure what was happening to me. I could understand being annoyed at her. But the degree of my fury made little sense. My shame was growing. How could I be helping strangers with their pains and their problems and have so little patience with my dying mother?

When the breakthrough finally came, it took me by surprise. On an impulse, I went to Thunder Bay to visit my spiritual teacher and friend Ella Fern. I had no idea at the time why I felt drawn to visit her. On the second day of my visit we were chatting over tea. I noticed a strange, unsettling feeling arising in me. I asked her to bear with me while I went inside myself to check out what this was. We stopped talking, closed our eyes, went inside and waited.

Something big and very powerful inside me grew louder. I felt somehow that this was the reason I had come here. This was where I needed to be to see it through. I centred myself in my breathing and in my heart centre. Immediately, I felt safer. As I let my guard down the threatening feeling intensified. Now I recognized what it was. Fear. An enormous fear. Ella Fern and I looked at each other. From the concern on her face I could see she sensed the magnitude of the fear arising in me. I felt ready to release control and ride out the storm that was brewing. She nodded her support.

For an endless half hour we just breathed with the fear, watching it go through its paces. It grew bigger in size and intensity, expanding out through my body, until the two of us, the room and finally the entire house all were encompassed by it. Thinking disappeared. All that remained of my mind was a wordless knowing: *I was a being that could choose.* I could choose where I placed my attention. From years of meditation, and later through massage therapy and bodywork practice, I had learned the power of placing my attention in my breathing and my heart centre. The heart centre is the felt location in the area of the chest where we experience love and compassion. The act of keeping one's attention in the heart centre, even if nothing much is sensed there, can have the effect of calming fear. After a few minutes of focusing my attention in this way, my fear of the enormous fear moving through me left. The energy of the big fear remained, but it no longer threatened me. What I felt was just an enormous energy and power.

Finally, like a great storm, the feeling passed. It had rattled the windows and shaken the walls of my entire being. In its passing, something had lifted from within me and I was no longer the same. I felt calm and clear and free.

I finally knew what the big fear was about. My mother was about to die. When she died, because I had no other family, the memories that I shared with her would now exist in my mind only. There would be no one left to validate them. These memories formed the foundation of my being, or so I thought. My early childhood, which I could know only through her, would be lost altogether. I was being cut adrift, left helpless and alone once again. Yes, some of this fear belonged to a lost fourteen year old. And some of it felt ancient; it arose out of a part of me that had no words, perhaps out of the infant for whom mother is the whole of life, the source of being.

Everything made sense: the fear, the anger at my mother's inability to recognize me and, finally, my coming here to be with Ella Fern. Her presence served to connect me to something deeper and more real than what I was losing. She gave me a place to stand that was bigger than the fear. Without that, I could not have endured it.

On visiting my mother when I returned to Winnipeg, I found that the anger with which I'd struggled was gone. It no longer mattered that she was unaware that I was there, that she couldn't recognize me. Now, when I went to see her in the nursing home, I would sit with her and meditate, expecting nothing, happy just to be there. Often when I'd get there, she'd be lost in a troubled, agitated sleep. I would meditate on her breathing, following her erratic breath rhythms, matching hers with my own. After a while, I seemed to sense her inner mood. Then, remaining emotionally in tune with her, I would gradually resume my own breathing rhythm. My intention was just to support and accept her, wherever she was and whatever she was feeling. Soon I would calm right down, and so invariably would she. Then I would leave, at peace with her and with myself, knowing that at some level, we had connected.

When my mother's body passed away a year later, I felt no grief or fear. I had already done my grieving and I'd finished with the fear that afternoon in Thunder Bay. All that remained was a deep feeling of relief and freedom.

Learning to ride a bicycle expanded my territory externally. Transforming the big fear created a similar expansion internally. After passing through the latter experience, I felt as if there was nothing inside of me that I could not face, nothing that I needed to protect myself against by building inner walls. The power of that fear, transformed, in time became my power. For years I had somehow contained that enormous fear deep within myself. I could see now that if I had the strength to contain the fear then surely I could, with that same strength, confront and transform it.

From my meditation practice I had learned to remain heart centred during difficult times. This ability helped me face many of my fears. However, I was still hesitant to claim the power that was available to me once those fears had been confronted and transformed. What prevented me from claiming this power was lack of self-trust. I knew from experience that I was capable of giving in to the seductive trap of reactive power. How could I be sure that I could handle power without misusing it? It seemed better to stay away from power altogether.

I resolved this dilemma through discovering and developing my nurturing abilities. Massage therapy and bodywork became my training ground. I found myself relating primarily through touch to people of all ages, shapes, sizes and colours. If I became stuck in my personal prejudices and judgments I was in trouble. Things would get highly uncomfortable. In order to achieve the equanimity I needed to survive, I learned to keep centred in my heart, no matter what.

I discovered a handy little trick to use when faced with personalities or bodies that triggered negative reactions in me. I would imagine the troublesome person growing younger and younger until he or she reached the point where the judgments dropped away and the flow of compassion was restored. The hardest cases would, in my mind's eye, eventually be lying on the massage table in diapers.

At first it was a revelation to me that I could choose to centre myself in a place of loving kindness. It was a revelation that love could be a choice, not just a state into which I haphazardly fell. There was great power in this discovery. The capacity to generate love by choice made me much less dependent on others, especially women, for love and nurturing. I became freer and less manipulative in my relationships.

Centring myself in a place of compassion during bodywork grounded and deepened my connection to the heart centre that had begun to develop through meditation. As the heart centre focus became more stable and consistent through working with others, it became possible for me to transform deeper and more intense anxieties. Love and compassion are inseparable from trust. And trust dissolves fear. In my bodywork practice I became a kind of co-pilot for others who were ready to move through their fear and anxiety.

Perhaps the greatest gift that came after the nurturer inside me was awakened and set free was that of self-trust. Through spending hours of each day centred in the generation of compassion, I began to believe more and more in the innate goodness of human beings. I began to see possibilities beyond the self-centred, brutally competitive models of the human being I had encountered in Freud's theory of the Id and Darwin's concept of the survival of the fittest. I began to see that the human qualities of self-centredness and deadly competition were balanced by our capacities for cooperation and compassion. With the emergence of this new kind of self-trust I no longer had to hide from my own power out of the fear of misusing it.

Years before my mother's death, when I was nearing the end of my massage therapy training in 1976 in Toronto, I had the following dream. The dream struck me at the time as a "big dream," one that marked a turning point, a new life direction. The path I have travelled for the past twenty years, in a very real sense, had its origins in this dream. The ideas I am writing about in this chapter also had their beginnings there. The dream suggested a possibility that I had been unable to conceive of or imagine: it suggested that power and compassion could be integrated.

A DREAM OF LOVE AND POWER

I am in a grove of oak trees. I look up into the tree beside me. It is filled with orioles. I reach out my hand and one of the orioles flies over to me. I spread out my arms, the bird spreads out its wings and we embrace. I feel its feathers and its beating heart. Love, warmth—but it is a new and unfamiliar kind of love that I am just learning to accept. It is like an old song played in a new key and thereby radically transformed. When the beautiful but alien quality of the feeling becomes too much, I end the embrace. And that is all right. It will take time to tune the instrument for the new songs.

I look away from the oak tree down to the ground. There I see the single leg, foot and talons of what would have been an impossibly large bird, had the creature been whole. The fragment is alive! It moves like the arm of a great powerful man. It reaches for my hand. I fearfully approach it. I ask it not to hurt me, to remember it is much more powerful than I. A trembling moment of contact—then I awaken.

Upon awakening I feel I must go back into the dream and master my fear. I close my eyes and bring back the image of the bird-arm. I move toward it through the fear. I touch, embrace and merge with it. It spreads out into my countless millions of cells. I feel an enormous surge of power. My own long denied power. Power. The word has always sounded ugly. But I gain this insight: what I disown, what I thereby fragment, turns ugly. When I face and accept what I have denied and fragmented, I open toward healing and wholeness. The princess kisses the frog; beauty kisses the beast—transformation.

The orioles of the dream embody a pure, spiritual form of love: beautiful, delicate, not quite of this earth. My earthly human body is not at all accustomed to this kind of love. I long for it but when it actually touches me, I cannot tolerate it for long.

The grotesque leg, feet and talons suggest something powerful but fragmented. The bird leg is about the size of a human arm. It is lying on the ground, suggesting a lower order of life and energy than the orioles. Yet the creature, if it were whole, would be a bird of some kind, perhaps a huge eagle. This suggests a possibility of flight, of reaching beyond the earth. But, in its fragmented state the bird leg is grounded.

The beautiful, delicate oriole is love bereft of power, while the grotesque bird leg is power bereft of love. The dream presents me with the challenge of integration. The work I do with the dream images upon awakening gives me a taste of what is possible. Fully living what I have tasted is a distant goal I strive for but may never reach.

CONCLUSION

Late one afternoon, not long before he died, Murray, Diane and I were cooking and chatting in Murray's kitchen. I was absentmindedly nibbling at some olives from a dish on the kitchen table. Murray caught my eye, tilted his head back slightly and opened his mouth; this was his way of saying, "I'd like one too." I popped an olive into his mouth. He smiled in appreciation. I started looking for some tissue or a paper towel to put under his chin so he could spit out the pit. He caught my eye again and shook his head, "No." Then, still holding my eyes he spit the olive pit clear across the room. It hit the floor and skipped across the kitchen tiles like a stone across a pond. And then he laughed, his face glowing with an aura of freedom and delight. Before long all three of us were laughing.

There was no need for words to complicate the moment. All three of us knew what the laughter was about. The old Murray, at the height of his physical powers, would have been horrified. That Murray, immaculately dressed in his tailored clothes and fancy Italian shoes, caught in the grip of the demon of perfectionism, could never have spit that pit across the floor. But for this Murray, physically more helpless than an infant, laughing with a bright glint in his eye, it was an act of power and freedom. Not the power of a Mike Tyson crushing his opponent in the first round to the roar of a blood thirsty crowd. Rather, the power of a man winning a victory over himself in the last round, with two friends cheering him on. And perhaps, looking in from another time, a young boy, who once skipped stones across a pond. And perhaps his soul looking on from the sidelines, with the clock running down, with the final lessons now done. Looking on. Smiling.

4

Men, Feminism and Men's Contradictory Experiences of Power

Michael Kaufman

In a world dominated by men, the world of men is, by definition, a world of power. That power is a structured part of our economies and systems of political and social organization; it forms part of the core of religion, family, forms of play and intellectual life. On an individual level, much of what so many cultures associate with masculinity hinges on a man's capacity to exercise power and control.[1]

But men's lives speak of a different reality. Although men hold power and reap the privileges that come with it, that power is tainted. There is, in the lives of men, a strange combination of power and privilege, pain and powerlessness. Men enjoy social power, many forms of privilege and, often-unconsciously, a sense of entitlement by virtue of being male. But the way men have set up that world of power causes immense pain, isolation and alienation not only for women, but also for men. This is not to equate men's pain with the systemic and systematic forms of women's oppression. Rather, it is to say that men's worldly power—as we sit in our homes, walk the street, apply ourselves at work or march through history—comes with a price for us.[2] This combination of power and pain is a hidden story in the lives of men. It is a story of contradictory experiences of power.

The idea that men endure contradictory experiences of power does not simply suggest that there is both power and pain in men's lives.

75

Such a statement would obscure the centrality of men's power and the roots of pain within that power. The key, indeed, is the relationship between the two. As we know, men's social power is the source of individual power and privilege, but as we shall see, it is also the source of the individual experience of pain, fear and alienation. That pain has long been an impetus for the individual reproduction—the acceptance, affirmation, celebration and propagation—of men's individual and collective power. Alternatively, it can be an impetus for change.[3]

The existence of men's pain cannot be an excuse for acts of violence or oppression perpetrated by men. After all, the overarching framework for this analysis is the basic point of feminism, and here I state the obvious, that almost all humans currently live in systems of patriarchal power which privilege men and stigmatize, penalize and oppress women.[4] Rather, knowledge of this pain is a means to better understanding men and the complex character of the dominant forms of masculinity.

The realization that men's experiences of power are contradictory also allows us to better understand the interactions of class, race, sexual orientation, ethnicity, age and other factors in the lives of men; this is why I speak of contradictory experiences of power in the plural. It allows us to better understand the process of gender acquisition for men. It allows us to better grasp what might be thought of as the *gender work* of a society.

An understanding of men's contradictory experiences of power, enables both women and men, when possible, to reach out to men with compassion, even as they are highly critical of particular actions and beliefs, even as they challenge the dominant forms of masculinity. This concept can provide one means to understanding how good human beings can do horrible things, and how some beautiful baby boys can turn into horrible adults. And it can help people understand how the majority of men can be reached with a message of change. It is, as I illustrate in subsequent pages, the basis for men's embrace of feminism.

This chapter develops the concept of men's contradictory experiences of power within an analysis of gender power, of the social-psychological process of gender development, and of the relation of power, alienation and oppression. It looks at the emergence of pro-feminism among men, seeking explanations for this within an analysis of men's contradictory experiences of power. It concludes with some thoughts on the implications of this analysis for the development of counter-hegemonic practices by pro-feminist men that can have a mass appeal and a mainstream social impact.

MEN'S CONTRADICTORY EXPERIENCES OF POWER

Gender and power

Theorizing men's contradictory experiences of power begins with two distinctions. The first is the well-known, but too often glossed over distinction between biological sex and socially-constructed gender. Derived from that is the second, that there is no single masculinity although there are hegemonic and subordinate forms of masculinity. These forms are based on men's social power but are embraced in complex ways by individual men who also develop harmonious and non-harmonious relationships with other masculinities.

The importance of the sex/gender distinction in this context is that "gender" is a basic conceptual tool which suggests how integral parts of our individual identity, behaviour, activities and beliefs can be a social product, varying from one group to another, and often at odds with other human needs and possibilities. Our biological sex—that small set of absolute differences between all males and all females—does not prescribe a set and static natural personality.[5] The sex/gender distinction suggests there are characteristics, needs and possibilities within our potential as females or males that are consciously and unconsciously suppressed, repressed and channeled in the process of producing men and women. Such products, the masculine and the feminine, the man and the woman, are what gender is all about.[6]

Gender is the central organizing category of our psyches. It is the axis around which people organize their personalities, and around which distinct egos develop. I can no more separate "Michael Kaufman–human" from "Michael Kaufman–man" than I can talk about the activities of a whale without referring to the fact it spends its whole life in the water.

Discourses on gender have had a hard time shaking off the handy, but limited, notion of sex-roles. (See Carrigan, Connell and Lee 1987 for a critique of the limits of sex-role theory.) Certainly, roles, expectations and ideas about proper behaviour do exist. But the central thing about gender is not the prescription of certain roles and the proscription of others; after all, the range of possible roles is wide and changing and, furthermore, roles are rarely adopted in a non-conflictual way. Rather, perhaps the key thing about gender is that it is a description of actual social relations of power between males and females and the internalization of these relations of power.

Men's contradictory experiences of power exist in the realm of gender. This suggests there are aspects of men's gendered experiences that are conflictual. Only part of the conflict is between the social definitions of manhood and possibilities open to us within our biological sex. Conflict also exists because of the cultural imposition of what Bob Connell calls hegemonic forms of masculinity (Connell 1987). While most men cannot possibly measure up to the dominant ideals of manhood, these ideals maintain a powerful and often unconscious presence in our lives. They have power because they describe and embody real relations of power between men and women, *and* among men: patriarchy exists as a system of men's power over women, and of hierarchies of power among different groups of men and between different masculinities.

The dominant ideals vary sharply from society to society, from era to era and, these days, almost from moment to moment. Each subgroup, based on ethnicity, class, age, sexual orientation or whatever, defines manhood in ways that conform to the economic and social possibilities of that group. For example, part of the ideal of working-class manhood among white, North American men stresses physical skill and the ability to physically manipulate one's environment. Part of the ideal of their upper-middle-class counterparts stresses verbal skills and the ability to manipulate one's environment through economic, social and political means. Each dominant image bears a relationship to the real-life possibilities of these men and the tools at their disposal for the exercise of some form of power. (See Brod and Kaufman 1994 for a discussion of the issue of different masculinities.)

Power and masculinity

Power, indeed, is the key term when referring to hegemonic masculinities. As I argue at greater length elsewhere (Kaufman 1993), the common feature of the dominant forms of contemporary masculinity is that manhood is equated with having some sort of power.

There are, of course, different ways to conceptualize and describe power. Political philosopher C. B. Macpherson points to the liberal and radical traditions of the last two centuries and tells us that one way we have come to think of human power is as the potential for using and developing human capacities. Such a view is based on the idea that people are doers and creators able to use rational understanding, moral judgment, creativity and emotional connection (Macpherson 1973). Most people possess the power to meet their needs, the power to fight injustice and oppression, the power of muscles and brain, and the power of love. All men, to a greater or lesser extent, experience these meanings of power.

Power, obviously, also has a more negative manifestation. Men have come to see power as a capacity to impose control on others and on our own unruly emotions. It means controlling material resources around us. This understanding of power meshes with the one described by Macpherson because, in societies based on hierarchy and inequality, it appears that all people cannot use and develop their capacities to an equal extent. You have power if you can take advantage of differences between people. I feel I can have power only if I have access to more resources than the next person. Power is seen as power over something or someone else.

Although men and women all experience diverse forms of power that either celebrate life and diversity or hinge on control and domination, the two types of experiences are not equal in the eyes of men for the latter is the dominant conception of power in our world. The equation of power with domination and control is a definition that has emerged over time in societies where various divisions are central to the way people have organized their lives: one class has control over economic resources and politics, adults have control over children, humans try to control nature, men dominate women and, in many countries, one ethnic, "racial," or religious group, or group based on sexual orientation, has control over others. Whatever the forms of inequality, in all cases these societies' relations of power are structured into social, cultural, political and economic institutions. There is, though, a common factor to all these societies: all are societies of male domination. The equation of masculinity with power is one that developed over centuries. It conformed to, and in turn justified, the real-life domination of men over women and the valuation of males over females.

Individual men internalize all this into their developing personalities because, born into such a life, we learn to experience our power as a capacity to exercise control. Men learn to accept and exercise power this way because it gives us privileges and advantages that women and children do not usually enjoy or, simply, because it is an available tool that allows us to feel capable and strong. The source of this power is in the society around us, but we learn to exercise it as our own. This is an internalization of social power. The collective power of men rests not simply on transgenerational and abstract institutions and structures of power, but on the ways we internalize, individualize and come to embody and reproduce these institutions, structures and conceptualizations of men's power.

Gender work

The way in which power is internalized is the basis for a contradictory relationship to that power.[7] The most important body of work that looks at this process is, paradoxically, that of one of the more famous of twentieth century intellectual patriarchs, Sigmund Freud. In spite of his miserable, sexist beliefs and confusions about women's sexualities, he identified the psychological processes and structures through which gender is created. The work of Nancy Chodorow, Dorothy Dinnerstein and Jessica Benjamin and, in a different sense, the psychoanalytic writings of Gad Horowitz, make a important contribution to our understanding of the processes by which gender is individually acquired (Chodorow 1978; Dinnerstein 1977; Benjamin 1988; Horowitz 1977).

The development of individual personalities in line with "normal" manhood is a social process within patriarchal family relationships.[8] The possibility for the creation of gender lies in two biological realities: the malleability of human drives and the long period of dependency of children. Upon this biological edifice, a social process is able to go to work for the simple reason that this period of dependency is lived out within a society. Within different family forms, each society provides a charged setting in which love and longing, support and disappointment become the vehicles for developing a gendered psyche. The family gives a personalized stamp to the categories, values, ideals and beliefs of a society in which one's sex is a fundamental aspect of self-definition and life. The family takes abstract ideals and turns them into the stuff of love and hate. As femininity gets represented by the mother (or mother figures) and masculinity by the father (or father figures) in both nuclear and extended families, complicated conceptions take on flesh and blood form: I am no longer talking of patriarchy and sexism, masculinity and femininity as abstract categories. I am talking about your mother and father, your sisters and brothers, your home, kin and family.[9]

By five or six years old, before children have much conscious knowledge of the world, the building blocks of their gendered personalities are firmly anchored. Over this skeleton is built the adult as we learn to survive and, with luck, thrive within an interlocked set of patriarchal realities that includes schools, religious establishments, the media and the world of work.

The internalization of gender relations is a building block of our personalities; that is, the individual elaboration of gender, and our own subsequent contributions to replenishing and adapting to institutions and social structures, wittingly or unwittingly preserves patriarchal systems. This process, when taken in its totality, forms what I call the gender work of a society. Because of the multiple identities of individuals and the complex ways they all embody both power and powerlessness—as a result of the interaction of their sex, race, class, sexual orientation, ethnicity, religion, intellectual and physical abilities, family particularities and sheer chance—gender work is not a linear process. Although gender ideals exist in the form of hegemonic masculinities and femininities, and although gender power is a social reality, when we live in heterogeneous societies, we each grapple with often conflicting pressures, demands and possibilities.

The notion of gender work suggests there is an active process that creates and recreates gender. It suggests that this process can be an ongoing one, with particular tasks at particular times in our lives, and this allows us to respond to changing relations of gender power. It suggests that gender is not a static thing that we become, but is a form of ongoing interaction with the structures of the surrounding world.

My masculinity is a bond, a glue to the patriarchal world. It is the thing which makes that world mine, which makes it more or less comfortable to live in. Through the incorporation of a dominant form of masculinity particular to my class, race, nationality, era, sexual orientation and religion, I gained real benefits and an individual sense of self-worth. From the moment when I learned, unconsciously, that there were not only two sexes but a social significance to the sexes, my own self-worth became measured against the yardstick of gender. As a young male, I was granted a fantasy reprieve from the powerlessness of early childhood because I unconsciously realized I was part of that half of humanity with social power. My ability not simply to incorporate the roles, but to grasp onto this power—even if, at first, it existed only in my imagination—was part of the development of my individuality.

The price

In more concrete terms, the acquisition of hegemonic masculinities (as well as many forms of masculinity that are devalued and subordinate) is a process through which men come to suppress a range of emotions, needs and possibilities, such as nurturing, receptivity, empathy and compassion, which are experienced as inconsistent with the power of manhood. These emotions and needs do not disappear; they are simply held in check or not allowed to play as full a role in our lives as would be healthy for ourselves and those around us. We dampen these abilities and emotions because they might restrict our capacity and desire to control ourselves or to dominate the human beings around us upon whom we depend for love and friendship. We suppress them because they come to be associated with the femininity we have rejected as part of our quest for masculinity.

There are many things men do to have the type of power men associate with masculinity. We have to perform and stay in control. We are supposed to conquer, be on top of things and call the shots. We have to tough it out, provide and achieve. Meanwhile we learn to beat back our feelings, hide our emotions and suppress our needs.

Hegemonic masculinities, although associated with power can also be the source of enormous pain. Because the associations are, ultimately, childhood visions of omnipotence, they are impossible to obtain. Surface appearances aside, no man is completely able to live up to these ideals and images. For one thing we all continue to experience a range of needs and feelings that are deemed inconsistent with manhood. Such experiences become the source of enormous fear. In our society, this fear is experienced as homophobia or, to express it differently, homophobia is the vehicle that simultaneously transmits and quells the fear.

Such fear and pain have visceral, emotional, intellectual dimensions—although none of these dimensions is necessarily conscious—and the more we are the prisoners of the fear, the more we need to exercise the power we grant ourselves as men. In other words, men exercise patriarchal power not only because we reap tangible benefits from it. The assertion of power is also a response to fear and to the wounds we have experienced in the quest for power. Paradoxically, men are wounded by the very way we men have learned to embody and exercise our power.

A man's pain may be deeply buried, barely a whisper in his heart, or it may flood from every pore. The pain might be the lasting trace of things that happened or attitudes and needs acquired twenty, thirty, or sixty years earlier. Whatever it is, the pain inspires fear for it means not being a man, which means, in a society that confuses gender and sex, not being a male. This means losing power and ungluing the basic building blocks of our personalities. This fear must also be suppressed for it is inconsistent with dominant masculinities.

As every woman who knows men can tell us, the strange thing about men's attempt to suppress emotions is that it leads not to less, but to more emotional dependency. By losing track of a wide range of our human needs and capacities, and by blocking our need for care and nurturance, we dampen our emotional common sense and our ability to look after ourselves. Unmet, unknown and unexpected emotions and needs do not disappear but rather spill into our lives at work, on the road, in a bar or at home. The very emotions and feelings we have tried to suppress gain a strange hold over us. No matter how cool and in control we appear, these emotions dominate us. I think of the man who feels powerlessness who beats his wife in uncontrolled rage. I walk into a bar and see two men hugging each other in a drunken embrace, the two of them able to express their affection for each other only when plastered. I read about the teenage boys who go out gay-bashing and the men who turn their sense of impotence into a rage against Blacks, Jews or any who are convenient scapegoats.

Alternatively, men might direct buried pain against themselves in the form of self-hate, self-deprecation, physical illness, insecurity or addictions. Interviews with rapists and batterers often show not only contempt for women, but often an even deeper hatred and contempt for themselves. It is as if, not able to stand themselves, they lash out at others, possibly to inflict similar feelings on another who has been defined as a socially acceptable target, possibly to experience a momentary sense of mastery (Levine and Koenig 1980; Beneke 1982).

Men's pain can be said to have a dynamic aspect. We might displace it or make it invisible, but in doing so we give it even more urgency. This blanking out of a sense of pain is another way of saying that men learn to wear a suit of armor; that is, we learn to maintain an emotional barrier between ourselves and those around us in order to keep fighting and winning. The impermeable ego barriers discussed by feminist psychoanalysts simultaneously protect men and keep us locked in a prison of our own creation.

Power, alienation and oppression

Men's pain and the way we exercise power are not just symptoms of our current gender order. Together they also shape our sense of manhood, and this sense of masculinity has become a form of alienation. Men's alienation is our ignorance of our own emotions, feelings and needs, and of our potential for human connection and nurturance. Our alienation also results from our distance from women and our distance and isolation from other men. In his book, *The Gender of Oppression*, Jeff Hearn suggests that what we think of as masculinity is the result of the way our power and our alienation combine. Our alienation increases the lonely pursuit of power and reinforces our belief that power requires an ability to be detached and distant (Hearn 1987).

Men's alienation and distance from women and other men take on strange and rather conflicting forms. Robert Bly and others in the mytho-poetic men's movement have made a lot out of the loss of the father and the distance of many men, in dominant North American cultures anyway, from their own fathers. Part of their point is accurate and reaffirms important work done over the past couple of decades on issues around fathers and fathering. (For numerous sources on fatherhood see Lamb 1981; Cath, Gurwitt and Ross 1982; Yogman, Cooley and Kindlon 1988; Osherson 1986.) Their discussion of these issues, however, lacks the richness and depth of feminist psychoanalysis which holds, as a central point, that the absence of men from most parenting and nurturing tasks means that the masculinity internalized by little boys is based on distance, separation and a fantasy image of what constitutes manhood, rather than on the type of oneness and inseparability that typifies early mother–child relationships.

The distance from other men is accentuated, in many contemporary heterosexual men's cultures at least, by the emotional distance from other males that begins to develop in adolescence. Men might have buddies, pals, workmates and friends, but they seldom experience the level of complete trust and intimacy enjoyed among many women. The depth of our friendships is limited by the reduced empathy that becomes the masculine norm (Rubin 1984; Nardi 1992). As a result most heterosexual men (and even many gay men) in the dominant North American culture are extremely isolated from other men. In fact, as I have argued elsewhere, many of the institutions of male bonding—the clubs, sporting events, card games, locker rooms, workplaces, professional and religious hierarchies—are a means to provide safety for isolated men who need to find ways to affirm themselves, find common ground with other men and collectively exercise their power (Kaufman 1993; Burstyn forthcoming). Such isolation means that each man can remain blind to his dialogue of self-doubt about making the masculine grade. Virtually all adolescent males consciously experience these self-doubts that are later consciously or unconsciously experienced as adults. In a strange sense, this isolation is key to preserving patriarchy: it increases the possibility of all men colluding with patriarchy, in all its diverse myths and realities, since their own doubts and sense of confusion remain buried.

It is not only other men from whom most men (and certainly most straight men) remain distant. It is also from women. Here another important insight of feminist psychoanalysis is key: Boys' psychological separation from their mothers or mother figures means the erection of more or less impermeable ego barriers and an affirmation of distinction, difference and opposition to those things identified with women and femininity. Boys repress characteristics and possibilities unconsciously and consciously associated with mother/women/the feminine. Thus Bly and the mytho-poetic theorists have it all wrong when they suggest that the central problem with contemporary men (and by this they seem to mean North American middle-class, young to middle-aged, white, straight urban men) is that they have become feminized. The problem, as suggested above, is the wholesale repression and suppression of traits and possibilities associated with women (Kimmel and Kaufman 1993, 1994; Kimmel 1995).

The above factors suggest the complexity of gender identity, gender formation and gender relations. It appears that we need forms of analysis that allow for the contradictory relationships that exist between individuals and the power structures from which they benefit. It is a strange situation when men's very real power and privilege in the world hinge not only on that power, but also on an experience of alienation and powerlessness which is rooted in childhood experiences but reinforced in different ways as adolescents and then adults. These experiences (in addition to the obvious and tangible benefits) become a spur for individual men to recreate and celebrate the forms and structures through which men exercise power.

But, as mentioned earlier, there is no single masculinity nor one experience of being a man. The experience of different men, their actual power and privilege in the world, is based on a range of social positions and relations. The social power of a poor white man is different from that of a rich one, a working class Black man from that of a working class white man, a gay man from a bisexual man from a straight man, a Jewish man in Ethiopia from a Jewish man in Israel, a teenage boy from an adult. Within each group, men usually have privileges and power relative to the women in that group, but in society as a whole, things are not always so straightforward.

The emergent discourses on the relation between oppression based on gender, ethnicity, class and social orientation are but one reflection of the complexity of the problem. These discussions are critical in the development of a new generation of feminist analysis and practice. The tendency, unfortunately, is often to add up categories of oppression as if they were separate units. Sometimes, such tallies are even used to decide who, supposedly, is the most oppressed. The problem can become absurd for two simple reasons: one is the impossibility of quantifying experiences of oppression; the other is that the sources of oppression do not come in discreet units.

For example, think of an unemployed Black gay working-class

man. We might say this man has been economically exploited by owners and controlled by bosses (as a working-class man), yet he has also enjoyed certain workplace privileges as a man vis-à-vis women. He is oppressed and stigmatized as a gay man, oppressed and the victim of racism because he is Black, suffering terribly because he is out of work (and is more likely to be unemployed than are Black women), and is demeaned and possibly gains strength from the dominant images of his supposed hypersexual masculinity, but we are not going to say, oh, he is oppressed as a man. Of course he is not oppressed as a man, but I worry that the distinction is rather academic because none of the qualities used to describe him is completely separable from the others. After all, his particular sense of manhood, that is, his masculinity, is in part a product of those other factors. "Man" becomes as much an adjective modifying "Black," "working class," "out of work" and "gay" as these things are modifiers of the word "man." Our lives, minds and bodies simply are not divided up in a way that allows us to separate out the different categories of our existence. This man's experiences, self-definition(s) and locations in the hierarchies of power are co-determined by a multitude of factors. Furthermore, since the reality of different masculinities includes within it relations of power among men, and not between men and women, a man with little social power in the dominant society, and whose masculinity is not of a hegemonic variety may be the victim of tremendous social oppression. At the same time, he might wield tremendous power in his own milieu and neighbourhood vis-à-vis women of his own class or social grouping or other males, as in the case of a school-yard bully or a member of an urban gang who certainly does not have structural power in the society as a whole.

Our whole language of oppression is in need of an overhaul for it is based on simplistic binary oppositions, reductionist equations between identity and social location, and unifocal notions of the self. What is important to recognize is that while men, as a group, have social power, some men, within their subgroups, tend to have considerable power. However, at the same time there are different forms of structural power and powerlessness among men. Similarly, it is important not to deny the structural and individual oppressions of women as a social group. Rather we must recognize, as expressed above, that there is not a linear relationship between a structured system of power inequalities, the real and supposed benefits of power, and one's own experience of these relations of power.

MEN AND FEMINISM

An analysis of men's contradictory experiences of power gives one useful insights into the potential relation of men to feminism. The power side of the equation is not anything new and, indeed, men's power and privileges form a very good reason for men to individually and collectively oppose feminism. But an increasing number of men have become sympathetic to feminism (in content if not always in name) and have embraced feminist theory and action (although, again, often more in theory than in action). There are different reasons for this acceptance of feminism. It might be outrage at inequality, it might result from the influence of a partner, family member or friend, it might be a man's own sense of injustice at the hands of other men, it might be a sense of shared oppression, say because of his sexual orientation, it might be his own guilt about the privileges he enjoys as a man, it might be horror at men's violence, it might be sheer decency.

While the majority of men in North America would still not label themselves pro-feminist, a strong majority of men in Canada and a reasonable percentage of men in the United States would sympathize with many of the issues as presented by feminists. As we know, this sympathy does not always translate into changes of behaviour, but, increasingly, ideas are changing and in some cases, behaviour is starting to catch up. What are the reasons for this increase in the number of men who are supportive of feminism and women's liberation (to use that term which was perhaps too hastily abandoned by the end of the 1970s)? Except for the rare outcast or iconoclast, there are few examples from history where significant numbers of a ruling group supported the liberation of those over whom they ruled and from whose subordination they benefited.

One answer is that the current feminist wave—whatever its weaknesses and whatever backlash might exist against it—has had a massive impact during the past two and a half decades. Large numbers of men, along with many women who had supported the status quo, now realize that the tide has turned and, like it or not, the world is changing.

Women's rebellion against patriarchy holds the promise of bringing patriarchy to an end and, in the meantime, dramatically reducing the differential power of men and women. Although patriarchy in its many different social and economic forms still has considerable staying power, it seems to me that an increasing number of its social, political, economic and emotional structures are proving unworkable. Some men react with rearguard actions while others step tentatively or strongly in the direction of change.

This explanation of men's support for change only catches part of the picture. The existence of contradictory experiences of power suggests there is a basis for men's embrace of feminism that goes beyond swimming with a change in the tide. The rise of feminism has shifted the balance between men's power and men's pain. In societies and eras where men's social power went largely unchallenged, men's power so outweighed men's pain that the existence of this pain could remain buried, effectively denied because it was amply compensated for. When you rule the roost, call the shots, and are closer to God, there is not a lot of room left for doubt and pain, at least for pain that appears to be linked to the practices of masculinity. But with the rise of modern feminism, the fulcrum between men's power and men's pain has been undergoing a rapid shift. This is particularly true in cultures where the definition of men's power had already moved away from tight control over the home and tight monopolies in the realm of work. (For a fascinating account of total patriarchal control of the home, see Mahfouz 1956.)

As men's power is challenged, those things that came as a compensation, a reward or a life-long distraction from any potential pain are progressively reduced or, at least, called into question. As women's oppression becomes problematized, many forms of this oppression become problems for men. Individual gender-related experiences of pain and disquietude among men have become increasingly manifest and have started to gain a social hearing and social expression in widely diverse forms, including different branches of the men's movement ranging from reactionary anti-feminists, to the Bly-type mythopoetic movement, to pro-feminist men's organizing.

In other words, if gender is about power, then as actual relations of power between men and women, and between different groups of men (such as straight and gay men or Black and white men) start to shift, then our experiences of gender and our gender definitions must also begin to change. The process of gender work is ongoing and includes this process of reformulation and upheaval.

Rising support and looming pitfalls

The embrace of feminism by men is not, surprisingly, entirely new. As Michael Kimmel argues in his insightful introduction to *Against the Tide: Profeminist Men in the United States 1776–1990. A Documentary History* (Kimmel and Mosmiller 1992), pro-feminist men have constituted a small, but persistent feature of the U.S. socio-political scene for two centuries. What makes the current situation different is that pro-feminism among men (or at least acceptance of aspects of feminist critiques and feminist political action) is reaching large-scale dimensions. Ideas that were almost unanimously discounted by men (and indeed by most women) only twenty-five years ago, now have widespread legitimacy. When I lead workshops in high schools, colleges and workplaces, men—even those who either on the surface are upset by the pace of change in gender relations or feel slighted or put-down—will give a list of the forms of power and privilege that men are still accorded and women still denied, and they will suggest without prompting that women are right to be concerned about these disparities.

Of course it does not help to overstate the progress that has been made; many males and females remain staunchly pro-patriarchy and most institutions remain male-dominated. But changes are visible. Affirmative action programs are widespread, many social institutions controlled by men—in education, the arts, professions, politics and religion—are undergoing a process of sexual integration even though this usually requires not only ongoing pressure but often women adapting to masculinist work cultures. In various countries the percentage of men favouring abortion rights for women equals or outstrips support by women. Some male-dominated governments have accepted the need to adopt laws that have been part of a feminist agenda. (One of the most dramatic instances was in Canada in 1992 when the Conservative government completely recast the law on rape following a process of consultation with women's groups. The law states that all sexual relations must be explicitly consensual, that "no means no" and that it takes a clearly-stated and freely-given "yes" to mean yes. Also in Canada, one thinks of the way that feminist organizations insisted on their presence, and were accepted as key players, at the bargaining table in the 1991 and 1992 round of constitutional talks.) All such changes were a result of the hard work and impact of the women's movement; this impact on institutions controlled by men shows the increased acceptance by men of at least some of the terms of feminism, whether this acceptance is begrudging or eager.

For those men and women interested in social change and speeding up the type of changes described above, some serious problems remain: While there are ever-increasing sympathies among men for the ideas of women's equality, and while some institutions have been forced to adopt measures promoting women's equality, there is still a lag between the ideas accepted by men and changes in their actual behaviour. And while many men might reluctantly or enthusiastically support efforts for change, pro-feminism among men has not yet reached mass organizational forms in most cases.

This brings me to the implications of the analysis in this article for the issue of pro-feminist organizing by men. Stimulated by the ever-widening impact of modern Western feminism, the past two decades have seen the emergence in countries around the world of something that, for lack of a better phrase, has been called the men's movement. For the purposes of this discussion, there have been two major currents to the men's movement.[10] One is the mytho-poetic men's movement which came to prominence in the late 1980s, in particular, with the success of Robert Bly's *Iron John* (1990). This movement is an expression of an approach dating back to the 1970s that focuses on the pain and costs of being men. It is also the continuation of a masculinist politic dating back almost one hundred years that sought to create homosocial spaces as an antidote to the supposed feminization of men.[11]

A second has been the less prominent pro-feminist men's movement (within which I count my own activities) which has focused on the social and individual expressions of men's power and privileges, including issues of men's violence.

Unfortunately, the dominant expressions of these two wings of the men's movement have developed with their own deformities, idiosyncrasies and mistakes in analysis and action. In particular, each has tended to grapple primarily with one aspect of men's lives—men's power, in the case of the pro-feminist movement; men's pain, in the case of the mytho-poetic. In doing so, they not only miss the totality of men's experience in a male-dominated society, but miss the crucial relationship between men's power and men's pain.[12]

The pro-feminist men's movement starts from the acknowledgment that men have power and privilege in a male-dominated society. Although I feel strongly that this must be our starting point, it is only a beginning for there are many challenging issues. For instance, how can men and women build mass and active support for a change in gender relations and gender identity among men? How can we encourage men to realize that support for feminism means more than supporting institutional and legal changes but also requires personal changes in our own lives? How can we link the struggles against homophobia and sexism and realize in practice that homophobia is a major factor in promoting misogyny and sexism among men?

Within these questions are a set of theoretical, strategic and tactical problems. I would suggest men need to take such questions very seriously, particularly if our goal is not simply to score academic or political debating points, or to feel good about our pro-feminist credentials, but rather, alongside women, to actually effect the course of history in a positive direction.

For me, several points emerge from this analysis. Whether a man assumes that his most pressing concern is to work in support of women's equality and challenge patriarchy, or to challenge homophobia and encourage a gay- and lesbian-positive culture, or to enhance the lives of all men, or to challenge the racism that is linked to gender oppression, our starting point as men must be a recognition of the centrality of men's power and privilege and a recognition of the need to challenge that power. This is not only in support of feminism, but is a recognition that the social and personal construction of this power is the source of the malaise, confusion and alienation felt by men in this era as well as being an important source of homophobia.

The more people realize that homophobia is central to the experience of men in most patriarchal societies, that homophobia and heterosexism shape the daily experiences of all men, and that such homophobia is central to the construction of sexism, the more we will be able to develop the understanding and the practical tools to achieve equality. The pro-feminist men's movement in North America, Europe and Australia has provided a unique opportunity for gay, straight and bisexual men to come together, work together and dance together. And yet, I do not think that most straight pro-feminist men see confronting homophobia as a priority or, even if a part of a list of priorities, as something that has a central bearing on their own lives.[13]

The notion of contradictory experiences of power, in the plural, provides an analytical tool for integrating issues of race, class, age and ethnicity into the heart of pro-feminist men's organizing. It allows people to sympathetically relate to a range of men's experiences, and to understand that men's power is non-linear and subject to a variety of social and psychological forces. It suggests forms of analysis and actions that understand that the behaviour of any group of men is the result of an often contradictory insertion into various hierarchies of power. It belies any notion that our identities and experiences as men can be separated from the identities and experiences that are based on the colour of our skin or our class background. The notion therefore suggests that struggling against racism, anti-semitism and class privilege, for example, are integral to a struggle to transform contemporary gender relations.

Perhaps, the very nomenclature I am using is a problem. I, along with others, have repeatedly referred to "pro-feminism." This term situates the focus from beginning to end as one of men supporting women's struggles and challenging men's power over women. But the analysis in this chapter suggests that while this support and challenge are indeed fundamental, they are not the sole issues or problems for men. Nor do they comprise the only path to demolishing patriarchy and creating a society of human equality and liberation. Once men include an analysis of the impact of a male-dominated society on men ourselves, then the project becomes not just "pro-feminist," but something that is "anti-sexist" (with a focus on how sexist ideas and practices affect men), "anti-patriarchal" and "anti-masculinist" (while being clearly male-affirmative, just as it is female-affirmative.)

Today, I believe the rewards of hegemonic masculinity are simply not enough to compensate for the pain in the lives of many men. For the majority of men who comply with North American culture, at any rate, the pain of trying to conform and live up to the impossible standards of manhood outweigh the rewards they currently receive. In other words, patriarchy is not only a problem for women. The great paradox of all patriarchal cultures (especially since experiencing significant challenges from feminism) is that the damaging forms of masculinity within male-dominated societies are damaging not only for women, but for men as well.

Various groups of men know this and understand this. For example, gay and bisexual men have developed both a new self-consciousness and cultural institutions, and have been organizing as men, in opposition to the hatred, fear and bigotry they encounter and to the dominant forms of masculinity (even as, at the same time, many gay men have embraced parts of the dominant vision and practice). They have long been aware of the pain inflicted on them by the current patriarchal society. Black men have developed their own cultures of resistance against structural discrimination and the hatred they experience from many men and women in the dominant, white society. Even though some of these forms of resistance include a reaffirmation of some of the worst features of patriarchal culture (one thinks of the sexism, homophobia and anti-semitism of the Nation of Islam; the brutality both reflected in, and reaffirmed by, gangsta rap; or the machismo of dominant sports culture in which Black male athletes are now at the pinnacle), there is also an affirmation of the intelligence of Black men, of masculine grace and of a distinct language, all of which were denigrated by the dominant culture and dominant forms of manhood. And, to give a short third example, young men of all races know that the likelihood of their acquiring the relative economic privileges enjoyed by their fathers and grandfathers has been dramatically diminished.

This is not to say that men within these groups, or even these men as a group, do not still enjoy certain forms of privilege and power. It is simply to point out that various groups of men have been struggling *as men* to reject at least some of the hegemonic ideas of manhood and some aspects of hegemonic male culture. The problem is that they have not necessarily done so within an analysis of gender and sexism, or in combination with a sympathy either for feminism or women, or with an understanding of the nature of men's social and individual power.

Nonetheless, all men might benefit from looking to the experiences of particular groups of men. And, within the particular experiences of these groups, they may find common cause, common concerns and common challenges. There is, indeed, a basis for men to organize as men and to organize on our own. This would be as part of a broader anti-patriarchal movement. It would be an anti-masculinist movement of men that would go hand-in-hand with feminism, but have its own raison d'être and its own clear issues and priorities.

In setting down this pathway, we must follow the lead of the women's movement in asserting not only the importance of both "personal" and "social" change, but of the relationship of the two. As men, we need to advocate and actively organize in support of a range of legal and social changes, from freedom of choice to childcare programs, from new initiatives that challenge men's violence to affirmative action programs at our workplaces. We must support and help build such changes not only at the level of macro-politics, but in our own workplaces, trade unions, professional associations, clubs, places of worship and communities. We must see these matters not simply as "women's issues" but issues that confront and effect all people.

This latter point is important if people genuinely hope to shape an anti-patriarchal politic that will embrace men as much as it does women. In the case of childcare, for example, men's agenda must not only support the visions of feminist women and the needs of mothers (although this support is an important part of what we do). It must also articulate childcare policies that will enhance the lives of boys and men and allow men to be better fathers, caregivers and nurturers. We must look at experiments in Sweden, for example, where public policy and government authority have been used, with both successes and failures, to reconstruct work and family life in such a way as to make possible healthier forms of fatherhood and motherhood.

One key to future child-centred social policies is a shortening of the work day. This has enormous implications for the lives of men (including those younger men and men-of-colour who have experienced huge amounts of discrimination in the job market). It has enormous implications for the self-identity of all men since work life, with all its emotional and physical hazards and tolls, has been such an integral part of masculine identity. For men to escape the painful constraints of painful masculinity we must, among other things, redefine the work of parenting and the world of work. This, in turn, opens up new possibilities for the largely middle-class organizations of anti-sexist men to bridge the chasm that sometimes separates us from the concerns and aspirations of working-class men.

All this is equally true for issues of men's health and safety. The very definitions of ruling forms of masculinity—we are always strong, we do not feel pain, we are never scared, etcetera—mean that by definition it is terrifying for men to seriously look at issues of our own health and safety. Even recognizing such issues seems to be a confession that we are not masculine. This is true within dangerous workplaces where men, in practice, seldom refuse unsafe work or refuse the overtime that will keep them away from their families and cause huge physical and emotional stress, even as it gives financial benefit.[14] Meanwhile generations of patriarchal societies have placed production, achievement and conquest over the needs of humans within an all-too-fragile environment. I think, for example, of the low sperm count of an increasing number of men the world over and of the increasing incidence of sexual dimorphism among newborn boys. It appears that a large part of the problem is caused by man-made chlorine compounds which mimic estrogen. These are issues that men do not talk about, but which have a huge impact on our lives. They are issues that men must and can address as men, in concert with similar concerns of women.

Such work not only involves providing verbal, financial and organizational support to the campaigns organized by women; it also requires that men that organize campaigns of men aimed at men. Efforts such as Canada's White Ribbon Campaign[15] are critical for breaking men's silence on a range of issues effecting the lives of women and subsequently the lives of men. This effort, which focuses on violence against women, has been surprisingly successful at encouraging men to identify with these concerns and to productively use the resources men have disproportionate access to. Such efforts must be carried out in dialogue and consultation with women's groups so that men do not come to dominate this work.

Like other groups of men working on issues of violence against women, the White Ribbon Campaign has been clear that men should not shrink back from taking up pro-feminist issues as our own. In many countries of the world, such as my own, the majority of men are not physically violent against women, but the majority have been silent about this violence. The campaign recognizes that men have a responsibility to speak to, and challenge, other men. It does not glibly say we were all responsible for incidents of violence, but rather that we have a shared responsibility for stopping it.

The campaign has also taken some steps to go beyond reacting to violence and talk about the patriarchal culture that has produced violent men. We have talked about the individual and social changes that are necessary to raise children without violence and to bring up a generation of men who will not resort to violence. In other words, as well as appealing to men's compassion, anger and concern about the experiences of the women we love, we also appeal to men's own best interests, encouraging men to find ways to lead healthier and happier lives.

Whatever our focus is in our work to challenge sexism and patriarchy, whether it be violence, sexual orientation, health, racism, childcare or workplace safety, for example, at the same time as we engage in social activism, we need to learn to scrutinize and challenge our own behaviour. We must understand that our contribution to social change will be limited if we continue to interact with women on the basis of dominance; it will be limited if we do not actively challenge homophobia and sexism among our friends and workmates and in ourselves. Change will be limited if we do not begin to create the immediate conditions for the transformation of social life, especially striving for equality in housework and childcare.

But this does not mean sinking into guilt or joining those men within the anti-sexist men's community who like the feel of a good hair shirt. After all, a diffuse sense of guilt (as opposed to specific remorse for particular actions) can be a profoundly conservative, demobilizing and disempowering emotion. For many of us active in pro-feminist, anti-patriarchal, anti-masculinist work, there are moments when we cease to be true to ourselves and worry more about attempting to please women or worry about what particular subgroups within the women's movement might think of our work. We sometimes feel guilty about our successes. Instead of such guilt, we should be saying that it is about time men were doing this work, we should be celebrating the fact that we are making a contribution to change, and we should know that our successes are, ultimately, about the successes of the women's movement in reaching men.

What is more, efforts to be "accountable to feminism and the women's movement" sometimes ignore the fact that there is not one feminism and that there are very real differences and debates within the women's movement: there is no way we can agree with everyone or adopt policies that will meet the approval of all feminists. (One only has to think about a number of issues, such as the issue of pornography, to realize there are many views within feminism, that is, many feminisms. See Kaufman, Chapter 6, 1993 and Kimmel 1990 on men's responses to the issue of pornography.)

Rather than feeling guilty about our successes in reaching other men or questioning our ability to come up with good ideas and initiatives to contribute, as equals with women, to an anti-patriarchal politic, men need to proudly assert that gender work is men's work as much as it is women's work. We must appeal to men's enlightened self-interest. This means not just supporting the efforts of women, but exploring and discovering ways that our interests truly coincide. Unless men organize to reach other men, men as a group will never stop propping up and perpetuating the patriarchal order. Why? Because, for the majority of men, it is the definition of masculinity by other men that matters more than anything. Part of the pathway of change is for men to act as examples and models for other men about how we can be fully male— that is, simply biological creatures who are male—without being masculinist. And in this project, in this celebration of maleness, straight men have a lot to learn from gay and bisexual men.

Men can proudly take our place—for respecting women's autonomy, capacities, priorities and the insights of feminism—as leaders in the anti-patriarchal, anti-sexist movement. To ultimately succeed at challenging and demolishing patriarchy and all its vestiges, we will all need men's unique contributions and insights alongside women's unique contributions and voices.

Part of this struggle for personal and social change by men is the need for men to reduce our isolation from other men. Although this isolation might be experienced most acutely by straight men, it is not simply a question of sexual orientation. This isolation is structured in our interactions with other men; breaking it down requires creating a true sense of safety and emotional intimacy with at least some other men.

Creating trust, safety and closeness among men is important because, in isolation, most men continue to accept as reality the uncontested assumptions about what it means to be a man. These act, as I have earlier pointed out, as a sort of collective hallucination within patriarchal society. It is as if millions of people have taken the same drug and are walking around knowing, with seeming certainty, the reality of what a man is, when, in fact, it is simply a gender construction. Any doubts we have as individuals are quickly dismissed because, in isolation from other men, we come to assume that only we have got it wrong, only we feel these differences. For many men, such doubts only confirm that they are not real men—and, after all, no man can actually live up to the ideals. The conflict between our own reality and what we have learned is supposed to be the real reality becomes a basic reason why individual men construct and reconstruct personalities shaped by patriarchy.

So, developing a social action approach is entirely consistent with, and perhaps ultimately requires, men's development of supportive organizations, support groups, and informal ties of intimacy and support among men. Such groups and individual practices allow us to look at our individual process of gender work, that is, how we have all been shaped by our patriarchal system. It allows us to examine our own contradictory relationships to men's power. It allows us to overcome the fear that prevents most men from speaking out and challenging sexism and homophobia. It can give us a new and different sense of strength.

In our public work, and in our challenges to sexism, homophobia, racism and bigotry in our daily lives, we must not shrink back from a politics of compassion. This means that men should never lose sight of the negative impact of contemporary patriarchy on ourselves even if our framework is centred around the oppression of women. It means looking at the negative impact of homophobia on all men. It means avoiding the language of guilt and blame and substituting it with the language of taking responsibility for change. Such a politics of compassion is only possible if we begin from the sex/gender distinction. If patriarchy and it's symptoms were a biological fiat then not only would the problems be virtually intractable, but punishment, repression, blame and guilt would seem to be the necessary corollaries. But if we start with the assumption that the problems are ones of gender—with gender referring to particular relations of power that are socially-structured and individually-embodied—then we are able to be simultaneously critical of men's collective power and the behaviour and attitudes of individual men *and* be male affirmative and say that demolishing patriarchy will enhance the lives of men. We can say that change is a win-win situation that requires men to give up forms of privilege, power and control.

On the psycho-dynamic level—the realm in which people can witness the interplay between social movements and the individual psyche—the challenge of feminism to men is one of dislodging the hegemonic masculine psyche. This is not a psychological interpretation of change because it is a social challenge to men's power and the actual reduction of men's social power is the source of change. What was once a secure relationship between power over others, control over oneself and the suppression of a range of men's own needs and emotions—is under attack. What had felt stable, natural and right is being revealed as both a source of oppression for others and the prime source of pain, anguish and disquietude for men ourselves.

The implication of all this is that the feminist challenge to men's power has the potential of liberating men and helping more men discover new masculinities which will be part of demolishing gender altogether. Whatever privileges and forms of power we will lose will increasingly be compensated for by the elimination of the pain, fear, dysfunctional forms of behaviour, violence experienced at the hands of other men, violence we inflict on ourselves, endless pressure to perform and succeed, and the sheer impossibility of living up to our masculine ideals.

Our awareness of men's contradictory experiences of power gives us the tools to simultaneously challenge men's power and speak to men's pain. It is the basis for a politics of compassion and for enlisting men's support for a revolution that is challenging the most basic and long-lasting structures of human civilization.

NOTES

1. This is a substantively revised version of an article that originally appeared in Brod and Kaufman 1994. For further information, see the following website: www.michaelkaufman.com.

2. Although it may be somewhat awkward for women readers, I often refer to men in the first person plural—we, us, our—to acknowledge my position within the object of my analysis.

3. My thanks to Harry Brod who several years ago cautioned me against talking about men's power and men's pain as two sides of the same coin, a comment that led me to focus on the relationship between the two. Thanks also to Harry and to Bob Connell for their comments on a draft of this article. I would particularly like to express my appreciation to Michael Kimmel both for his comments on the draft version and for our ongoing intellectual partnership and friendship.

4. Although there has been controversy over the applicability of the term "patriarchy" (see, for example, Michele Barrett and Mary MacIntosh's reservations in *The Anti-Social Family*, 1982), I follow others who use it as a broad descriptive term for male-dominated social systems.

5. Even the apparently fixed biological line between males and females—fixed in terms of genital and reproductive differences—is subject to variation, as seen in the relatively significant number of males and females with so-called genital, hormonal and chromosomal "abnormalities" that bend the sharp distinction between the sexes. These render men or women infertile, women or men with secondary sex characteristics usually associated with the other sex, and women or men with different genital combinations. Nonetheless, the notion of biological sex is useful as shorthand and to distinguish sex from socially constructed gender. For an accessible discussion, particularly on the endocrinology of sex differentiation, see Money and Ehrhardt 1972.

6. The sex/gender distinction is ignored or blurred not only by reactionary ideologues or socio-biologists (of both liberal and conservative persuasions) who want to assert that the current lives, roles and relations between the sexes are timeless, biological givens. At least one stream of feminist thought—dubbed cultural feminism or difference feminism by its critics—celebrates to varying degrees a range of supposedly timeless and natural female qualities. Similarly, some of those influenced by Jungian thought, such as Robert Bly and the mytho-poetic thinkers, also posit essential qualities of manhood and womanhood. Even those feminists who accept the sex/gender distinction often use the term "gender" when what is meant is "sex," as in "the two genders" and "the other gender" when in fact there are a multiplicity of genders, as suggested in the concepts of femininities and masculinities. Similarly, many feminist women and pro-feminist men refer erroneously to "male violence" rather than "men's violence" even though the biological category "male" (as opposed to the gender category "men") implies that a propensity to commit violence is part of the genetic mandate of half the species, a supposition that neither anthropology nor contemporary observation warrants.

7. Although I am referring here to men's contradictory relationships to masculine power, a parallel, although very different, discussion could also be conducted concerning women's relationship to men's power and to their own positions of individual, familial and social power and powerlessness.

8. This paragraph is based on text in Kaufman 1987 and 1993.

9. I am not implying that the nature of the relations or the conflicts are the same from one family form to another or, even that "the family" as such exists in all societies. (see Barrett and McIntosh 1982.)

10. A third is the anti-feminist and, at times, unashamedly misogynist, men's rights movement which is not highly relevant to this article.

11. In the 1970s and early 1980s, books and articles by men such as Herb Goldberg (1976) and Warren Farrell (1993) spoke of the lethal characteristics of manhood, particularly the ways it was lethal against men. By the time Robert Bly's *Iron John* made it to the top of the bestseller lists in the U.S. and Canada at the end of 1990, vague analyses had crystalized into a broad North American movement with a newspaper, *Wingspan*, as well as men's retreats, groups, drumming circles, regional newsletters, and a string of books that has yet to abate.

There are some positive and potentially progressive aspects to this approach and the work of the thousands of men who participate in some sort of men's group within this framework. One is the simple, but significant, acknowledgment of men's pain; another is the participation of men in men's groups and the decision by men (usually, but not always, straight men) to break their isolation from other men and seek collective paths of change.

On the other hand, as Michael Kimmel and I argue at length elsewhere (Kimmel and Kaufman 1993), the theoretical framework of this movement virtually ignores men's social and individual power (and its relation to pain), ignores what we have called the mother wound (following the insights of feminist psychoanalysis), crudely attempts to appropriate a hodge-podge of indigenous cultures, and pulls men away from the social (and possibly the individual) practises that will challenge patriarchy. My thanks to Michael for the formulation of masculinist politics creating new homosocial space.

12. Although categorizing these two wings of the men's movement is a useful tool for discussion, there are no hard and fast boundaries between the two. A number of the men (more so in Canada than the U.S.) attracted to Robert Bly and the mytho-poetic movement are actively sympathetic to feminism and the contemporary struggles of women. Meanwhile, most men pulled toward the pro-feminist framework are also very concerned about enhancing the lives of men. And men, particularly those in the latter category, are concerned with the impact of homophobia on all men.

13. My favourite story about the reluctance of many straight people to identify with the need to publicly challenge homophobia is told by a colleague who, in Toronto in the early 1980s, was teaching a course on social change. At the student pub after class one night, one of the students was lamenting that he did not live in another era. It would have been great to live in the 'thirties, he said, so he could have gone off and fought in the Spanish revolution. My colleague said, "Well you know, dozens of gay bathhouses were raided by the police this week and there have been big demonstrations almost every night. You could join those." The student looked at him and said, "But I'm not gay," to which my colleague responded, "I didn't know you were Spanish."

On the relationship of homophobia to the construction of "normal" masculinity see Pharr 1988; Kimmel 1994 and Kaufman 1993.

14. A number of years ago I worked briefly at a saw mill in British Columbia. One day, my low-seniority job had me dislodging jumbled up wood from chains that were carrying lumber from one saw to the next. My supervisor pointed across the vast room at a red button which would stop the moving chains before I ventured into their midst. He said it would halt the whole operation but made it clear that anyone who was not man enough to go into the moving chains should not be working there in the first place.

15. The White Ribbon Campaign focuses on men's violence against women. A small group of us began the campaign in late 1991 and within a week tens of thousands of men across Canada (hundreds of thousands a year later) wore a white ribbon for a week as a pledge they would not "commit, condone or remain silent about violence against women." The campaign, aimed to break men's silence and to mobilize the energy and resources of men, enjoys support across the social and political spectrum and has spread to the U.S., Australia, Norway, Russia, Mexico and many other countries. It now gives particular attention to working with boys and young men and has produced a range of educational materials for use by teachers and students. The White Ribbon Campaign may be contacted at 365 Bloor Street East, Suite 1600, Toronto, Ontario, Canada M4W 3L4, tel: (416) 920-6684; fax: (416) 920-1678, or email: whiterib@idirect.com or on the web at www.whiteribbon.ca.

5

Masculinity as Homophobia
Fear, Shame and Silence in the
Construction of Gender Identity[1]
Michael S. Kimmel

"Funny thing," [Curley's wife] said. "If I catch any one man, and he's alone, I get along fine with him. But just let two of the guys get together an' you won't talk. Jus' nothing' but mad." She dropped her fingers and put her hands on her hips. "You're all scared of each other, that's what. Ever' one of you's scared the rest is goin' to get something on you." John Steinbeck, *Of Mice and Men* (1937)

We think of manhood as eternal, a timeless essence that resides deep in the heart of every man. We think of manhood as a thing, a quality that one either has or does not have. We think of manhood as innate, residing in the particular biological composition of the human male, the result of androgens or the possession of a penis. We think of manhood as a transcendent tangible property that each man must manifest in the world, the reward presented with great ceremony to a young novice by his elders for having successfully completed an arduous initiation ritual. In the words of poet Robert Bly, "the structure at the bottom of the male psyche is still as firm as it was twenty thousand years ago" (1990:230).

In this chapter, I view masculinity as a constantly changing collection of meanings that we construct through our relationships with ourselves, with each other and with our world. Manhood is neither static nor timeless; it is historical. Manhood is not the manifestation of an inner essence; it is socially constructed. Manhood does not bubble up to consciousness from our biological makeup; it is created in culture. Manhood means different things at different times to different people. We come to know what it means to be a man in our culture by setting our definitions in opposition to a set of "others"—racial minorities, sexual minorities and, above all, women.

Our definitions of manhood are constantly changing, being played out on the political and social terrain on which the relationships between women and men are played out. In fact, the search for a transcendent, timeless definition of manhood is itself a sociological phenomenon—we tend to search for the timeless and eternal during moments of crisis, those points of transition when old definitions no longer work and new definitions are yet to be firmly established.

This idea that manhood is socially constructed and historically shifting should not be understood as a loss, that something is being taken away from men. In fact, it gives us something extraordinarily valuable—agency, the capacity to act. It gives us a sense of historical possibilities to replace the despondent resignation that invariably attends timeless, ahistorical essentialisms. Our behaviours are not simply "just human nature," because "boys will be boys." From the materials we find around us in our culture—other people, ideas, objects—we actively create our worlds, our identities. Men, both individually and collectively, can change.

In this chapter, I explore this social and historical construction of both hegemonic masculinity and alternate masculinities, with an eye toward offering a new theoretical model of American manhood.[2] To accomplish this I first uncover some of the hidden gender meanings in classical statements of social and political philosophy so that I can anchor the emergence of contemporary manhood in specific historical and social contexts. I then spell out the ways in which this version of masculinity emerged in the United States, by tracing both psychoanalytic developmental sequences and a historical trajectory in the development of marketplace relationships.

CLASSICAL SOCIAL THEORY
AS A HIDDEN MEDITATION OF MANHOOD

Begin this inquiry by looking at four passages from that set of texts commonly called classical social and political theory. You will, no doubt, recognize them, but I invite you to recall the way they were discussed in your undergraduate or graduate courses in theory.

The bourgeoisie cannot exist without constantly revolutionizing the instruments of production, and thereby the relations of production, and with them the whole relations of society. Conservation of the old modes of production in unaltered form, was, on the contrary, the first condition of existence for all earlier industrial classes. Constant revolutionizing of production, uninterrupted disturbance of all social conditions, everlasting uncertainty and agitation distinguish the bourgeois epoch from all earlier ones. All fixed, fast-frozen relations, with their train of ancient and venerable prejudices and opinions are swept away, all new-formed ones become antiquated before they can ossify. All that is solid melts into air, all that is holy is profaned, and man is at last compelled to face with sober senses, his real conditions of life, and his relation with his kind. (Marx & Engels 1848/1964:476)

An American will build a house in which to pass his old age and sell it before the roof is on; he will plant a garden and rent it just as the trees are coming into bearing; he will clear a field and leave others to reap the harvest; he will take up a profession and leave it, settle in one place and soon go off elsewhere with his changing desires. . . . At first sight there is something astonishing in this spectacle of so many lucky men restless in the midst of abundance. But it is a spectacle as old as the world; all that is new is to see a whole people performing in it. (Tocqueville 1835/1967:536)

Where the fulfilment of the calling cannot directly be related to the highest spiritual and cultural values, or when, on the other hand, it need not be felt simply as economic compulsion, the individual generally abandons the attempt to justify it at all. In the field of its highest development, in the United States, the pursuit of wealth, stripped of its religious and ethical meaning, tends to become associated with purely mundane passions, which often actually give it the character of sport. (Weber 1905/1966:182)

> We are warned by a proverb against serving two masters at the same time. The poor ego has things even worse: it serves three severe masters and does what it can to bring their claims and demands into harmony with one another. These claims are always divergent and often seem incompatible. No wonder that the ego so often fails in its task. Its three tyrannical masters are the external world, the super ego and the id. . . . It feels hemmed in on three sides, threatened by three kinds of danger, to which, if it is hard pressed, it reacts by generating anxiety. . . . Thus the ego, driven by the id, confined by the super ego, repulsed by reality, struggles to master its economic task of bringing about harmony among the forces and influences working in and upon it; and we can understand how it is that so often we cannot suppress a cry: "Life is not easy!" (Freud 1933/1966:77)

If your social science training was anything like mine, these were offered as descriptions of the bourgeoisie under capitalism, of individuals in democratic societies, of the fate of the Protestant work ethic under the ever rationalizing spirit of capitalism, or of the arduous task of the autonomous ego in psychological development. Did anyone ever mention that in all four cases the theorists were describing men? Not just "man" as in generic mankind, but a particular type of masculinity, a definition of manhood that derives its identity from participation in the marketplace, from interaction with other men in that marketplace—in short, a model of masculinity for whom identity is based on homosocial competition? Three years before Tocqueville found Americans "restless in the midst of abundance," Senator Henry Clay had called the United States "a nation of self-made men."

What does it mean to be "self-made"? What are the consequences of self-making for the individual man, for other men, for women? It is this notion of manhood—rooted in the sphere of production, the public arena, a masculinity grounded not in land ownership or in artisanal republican virtue but in successful participation in marketplace competition—this has been the defining notion of American manhood. Masculinity must be proved, and no sooner is it proved than it is again questioned and must be proved again—constant, relentless, unachievable, and ultimately the quest for proof becomes so meaningless that it takes on the characteristics, as Weber said, of a sport. He who has the most toys when he dies wins.

Where does this version of masculinity come from? How does it work? What are the consequences of this version of masculinity for women, for other men, and for individual men themselves? These are the questions I address in this chapter.

MASCULINITY AS HISTORY AND THE HISTORY OF MASCULINITY

The idea of masculinity expressed in the previous extracts is the product of historical shifts in the grounds on which men rooted their sense of themselves as men. To argue that cultural definitions of gender identity are historically specific goes only so far; we have to specify exactly what those models were. In my historical inquiry into the development of these models of manhood[3] I chart the fate of two models for manhood at the turn of the nineteenth century and the emergence of a third in the first few decades of that century.

In the late eighteenth and early nineteenth centuries, two models of manhood prevailed. The *Genteel Patriarch* derived his identity from land ownership. Supervising his estate, he was refined, elegant and given to casual sensuousness. He was a doting and devoted father, who spent much of his time supervising the estate and with his family. Think of George Washington or Thomas Jefferson as examples. By contrast, the *Heroic Artisan* embodied the physical strength and republican virtue that Jefferson observed in the yeoman farmer, independent urban craftsman or shopkeeper. Also a devoted father, the Heroic Artisan taught his son his craft, bringing him through ritual apprenticeship to status as master craftsman. Economically autonomous, the Heroic Artisan also cherished his democratic community, delighting in the participatory democracy of the town meeting. Think of Paul Revere at his pewter shop, shirtsleeves rolled up, a leather apron—a man who took pride in his work.

Heroic Artisans and Genteel Patriarchs lived in casual accord, in part because their gender ideals were complementary (both supported participatory democracy and individual autonomy, although patriarchs tended to support more powerful state machineries and also supported slavery) and because they rarely saw one another: Artisans were decidedly urban and the Genteel Patriarchs ruled their rural estates. By the 1830s, though, this casual symbiosis was shattered by the emergence of a new vision of masculinity, *Marketplace Manhood*.

Marketplace Man derived his identity entirely from his success in the capitalist marketplace, as he accumulated wealth, power and status. He was the urban entrepreneur, the businessman. Restless, agitated and anxious, Marketplace Man was an absentee landlord at home and an absent father with his children, devoting himself to his work in an increasingly homosocial environment—a male-only world in which he pits himself against other men. His efforts at self-making transform the political and economic spheres, casting aside the Genteel Patriarch as an anachronistic feminized dandy—sweet, but ineffective and out-moded—and transforming the Heroic Artisan into a dispossessed pro-letarian, a wage slave.

As Tocqueville would have seen it, the coexistence of the Genteel Patriarch and the Heroic Artisan embodied the fusion of liberty and equality. Genteel Patriarchy was the manhood of the traditional aris-tocracy, the class that embodied the virtue of liberty. The Heroic Artisan embodied democratic community, the solidarity of the urban shopkeeper or craftsman. Liberty and democracy, the patriarch and the artisan, could, and did, coexist. But Marketplace Man is capitalist man, and he makes both freedom and equality problematic, elimi-nating the freedom of the aristocracy and proletarianizing the equality of the artisan. In one sense, American history has been an effort to restore, retrieve or reconstitute the virtues of Genteel Patriarchy and Heroic Artisanate as they were being transformed in the capitalist marketplace.

Marketplace Manhood was a manhood that required proof, and that required the acquisition of tangible goods as evidence of success. It reconstituted itself by the exclusion of "others"—women, non-white men, non-native-born men, homosexual men—and by terrified flight into a pristine mythic homosocial Eden where men could, at last, be real men among other men. The story of the ways in which Market-place Man becomes American Everyman is a tragic tale, a tale of striving to live up to impossible ideals of success leading to chronic terrors of emasculation, emotional emptiness, and a gendered rage that leaves a wide swath of destruction in it wake.

MASCULINITIES AS POWER RELATIONS

Marketplace Masculinity describes the normative definition of American masculinity. It describes his characteristics—aggression, competition, anxiety—and the arena in which those characteristics are deployed—the public sphere, the marketplace. If the marketplace is the arena in which manhood is tested and proved, it is a gendered arena, in which tensions between women and men and tensions among different groups of men are weighted with meaning. These tensions suggest that cultural definitions of gender are played out in a contested terrain and are themselves power relations.

All masculinities are not created equal; or rather, we are all *created* equal, but any hypothetical equality evaporates quickly because our definitions of masculinity are not equally valued in our society. One definition of manhood continues to remain the standard against which other forms of manhood are measured and evaluated. Within the dominant culture, the masculinity that defines white, middle class, early middle-aged, heterosexual men is the masculinity that sets the standards for other men, against which other men are measures and, more often than not, found wanting. Sociologist Erving Goffman wrote that in America, there is only "one complete, unblushing male":

> a young, married, white, urban, northern heterosexual, Protestant father of college education, fully employed, of good complexion, weight and height, and a recent record in sports. Every American male tends to look out upon the world from this perspective. . . . Any male who fails to qualify in any one of these ways is likely to view himself . . . as unworthy, incomplete, and inferior. (1963:128)

This is the definition that we will call "hegemonic" masculinity, the image of masculinity of those men who hold power that has become the standard in psychological evaluations, sociological research, and self-help and advice literature for teaching young men to become "real men" (Connell 1987). The hegemonic definition of manhood is a man *in* power, a man *with* power and a man *of* power. We equate manhood with being strong, successful, capable, reliable, in control. The very definitions of manhood we have developed in our culture maintain the power that some men have over other men and that men have over women.

Our culture's definition of masculinity is thus several stories at once. It is about the individual man's quest to accumulate those cultural symbols that denote manhood, signs that he has in fact achieved it. It is about those standards being used against women to prevent their inclusion in public life and their consignment to a devalued private sphere. It is about the differential access that different types of men have to those cultural resources that confer manhood and about how each of these groups then develop their own modifications to preserve and claim their manhood. It is about the power of these definitions themselves to serve to maintain the real-life power that men have over women and that some men have over other men.

This definition of manhood has been summarized cleverly by psychologist Robert Brannon into four succinct phrases:

1. "No Sissy Stuff!" One may never do anything that even remotely suggests femininity. Masculinity is the relentless repudiation of the feminine.
2. "Be a Big Wheel." Masculinity is measured by power, success, wealth, and status. As the current saying goes, "He who has the most toys when he dies wins."
3. "Be a Sturdy Oak." Masculinity depends on remaining calm and reliable in a crisis, holding emotions in check. In fact, proving you're a man depends on never showing your emotions at all. Boys don't cry.
4. "Give 'em Hell." Exude an aura of manly daring and aggression. Go for it. Take risks. (1976)

These rules contain the elements of the definition against which virtually all American men are measured. Failure to embody these rules, to affirm the power of the rules and one's achievement of them is a source of men's confusion and pain. Such a model is, of course, unrealizable for any man. But we keep trying, valiantly and vainly, to measure up. American masculinity is a relentless test.[4] The chief test is contained in the first rule. Whatever the variations by race, class, age, ethnicity or sexual orientation, being a man means "not being like women." This notion of antifemininity lies at the heart of contemporary and historical conceptions of manhood, so that masculinity is defined more by what one is not rather than who one is.

MASCULINITY AS THE FLIGHT FROM THE FEMININE

Historically and developmentally, masculinity has been defined as the flight from women, the repudiation of femininity. Since Freud, we have come to understand that developmentally the central task that every little boy must confront is to develop a secure identity for himself as a man. As Freud had it, the oedipal project is a process of the boy's renouncing his identification with and deep emotional attachment to his mother and then replacing her with the father as the object of identification. Notice that he reidentifies but never reattaches. This entire process, Freud argues, is set in motion by the boy's sexual desire for his mother. But the father stands in the son's path and will not yield his sexual property to his puny son. The boy's first emotional experience, then, the one that inevitably follows his experience of desire, is fear—fear of the bigger, stronger, more sexually powerful father. It is this fear, experienced symbolically as the fear of castration, Freud argues, that forces the young boy to renounce his identification with mother and seek to identify with the being who is the actual source of his fear, his father. In so doing, the boy is now symbolically capable of sexual union with a mother-like substitute, that is, a woman. The boy becomes gendered (masculine) and heterosexual at the same time.

Masculinity, in this model, is irrevocably tied to sexuality. The boy's sexuality will now come to resemble the sexuality of his father (or at least the way he imagines his father)—menacing, predatory, possessive and possibly punitive. The boy has come to identify with his oppressor; now he can become the oppressor himself. But a terror remains, the terror that the young man will be unmasked as a fraud, as a man who has not completely and irrevocably separated from mother. It will be other men who will do the unmasking. Failure will de-sex the man, make him appear as not fully a man. He will be seen as a wimp, a Mama's boy, a sissy.

After pulling away from his mother, the boy comes to see her not as a source of nurturance and love, but as an insatiably infantilizing creature, capable of humiliating him in front of his peers. She makes him dress up in uncomfortable and itchy clothes, her kisses smear his cheeks with lipstick, staining his boyish innocence with the mark of feminine dependency. No wonder so many boys cringe from their mothers' embraces with groans of "Aw, Mom! Quit it!" Mothers represent the humiliation of infancy, helplessness, dependency. "Men act as though they were being guided by (or rebelling against) rules and prohibitions enunciated by a moral mother," writes psychohistorian Geoffrey Gorer. As a result, "all the niceties of masculine behavior— modesty, politeness, neatness, cleanliness—come to be regarded as concessions to feminine demands, and not good in themselves as part of the behavior of a proper man" (1964:56–7).

The flight from femininity is angry and frightened, because mother can so easily emasculate the young boy by her power to render him dependent, or at least to remind him of dependency. It is relentless: manhood becomes a lifelong quest to demonstrate its achievement, as if to prove the unprovable to others because we feel so unsure of it ourselves. Women do not often feel compelled to "prove their womanhood"—the phrase itself sounds ridiculous. Women have different kinds of gender identity crises; their anger and frustration, and their own symptoms of depression, come more from being excluded than from questioning whether they are feminine enough.[5]

The drive to repudiate the mother as the indication of the acquisition of masculine gender identity has three consequences for the young boy. First, he pushes away his real mother, and with her the traits of nurturance, compassion and tenderness she may have embodied. Second, he suppresses those traits in himself because they will reveal his incomplete separation from mother. His life becomes a lifelong project to demonstrate that he possesses none of his mother's traits. Masculine identity is born in the renunciation of the feminine, not in the direct affirmation of the masculine, which leaves masculine gender identity tenuous and fragile.

Third, as if to demonstrate the accomplishment of these first two tasks, the boy also learns to devalue all women in his society as the living embodiments of those traits in himself he has learned to despise. Whether or not he was aware of it, Freud also describes the origins of sexism—the systematic devaluation of women—in the desperate efforts of the boy to separate from mother. We may *want* "a girl just like the girl that married dear old Dad," as the popular song had it, but we certainly do not want to *be like* her.

This chronic uncertainty about gender identity helps us understand several obsessive behaviours. Take, for example, the continuing problem of the school-yard bully. Parents remind us that the bully is the *least* secure about his manhood, and so he is constantly trying to prove it. But he "proves" it by choosing opponents he is absolutely certain he can defeat: thus the standard taunt to a bully is to "pick on someone your own size." He cannot, though, and after defeating a smaller and weaker opponent, which he was sure would prove his manhood, he is left with the empty gnawing feeling that he has not proved it after all, and he must find another opponent, again, one smaller and weaker, that he can again defeat to prove it to himself.[6]

One of the more graphic illustrations of this lifelong quest to prove one's manhood occurred at the Academy Awards presentation in 1992. As aging, tough guy actor Jack Palance accepted the award for Best Supporting Actor for his role in the cowboy comedy *City Slickers*, he commented that people, especially film producers, think that because he is seventy-one years old, he is all washed up, that he's no longer competent. "Can we take a risk on this guy?" he quoted them as saying, before he dropped to the floor to do a set of one-armed push-ups. It was pathetic to see such an accomplished actor still having to prove that he is virile enough to work and, as he also commented at the podium, to have sex.

When does it end? Never. To admit weakness, to admit frailty or fragility, is to be seen as a wimp, a sissy, not a real man. But seen by whom?

MASCULINITY AS A HOMOSOCIAL ENACTMENT

Other men: We are under the constant careful scrutiny of other men. Other men watch us, rank us, grant our acceptance into the realm of manhood. Manhood is demonstrated for other men's approval. It is other men who evaluate the performance. Literary critic David Leverenz argues that "ideologies of manhood have functioned primarily in relation to the gaze of male peers and male authority" (1991:769). Think of how men boast to one another of their accomplishments— from their latest sexual conquest to the size of the fish they caught— and how we constantly parade the markers of manhood—wealth, power, status, sexy women—in front of other men, desperate for their approval.

That men prove their manhood in the eyes of other men is both a consequence of sexism and one of its chief props. "Women have, in men's minds, such a low place on the social ladder of this country that it's useless to define yourself in terms of a women," noted playwright David Mamet. "What men need is men's approval" (cited in the *New York Times* 1993, Jan. 3). Women become a kind of currency that men use to improve their ranking on the masculine social scale. (Even those moments of heroic conquest of women carry, I believe, a current of homosocial evaluation.) Masculinity is a *homosocial* enactment. We test ourselves, perform heroic feats and take enormous risks all because we want other men to grant us our manhood.

Masculinity as a homosocial enactment is fraught with danger, with the risk of failure and with intense relentless competition. "Every man you meet has a rating or an estimate of himself which he never loses or forgets," wrote Kenneth Wayne in his popular turn-of-the-century advice book. "A man has his own rating, and instantly he lays it alongside of the other man" (1912:18). Almost a century later, another man remarked to psychologist Sam Osherson that "by the time you're an adult, it's easy to think you're always in competition with men, for the attention of women, in sports, at work" (Osherson 1992:291).

MASCULINITY AS HOMOPHOBIA

If masculinity is a homosocial enactment, its overriding emotion is fear. In the Freudian model, the fear of the father's power terrifies the young boy to renounce his desire for his mother and identify with his father. This model links gender identity with sexual orientation: The little boy's identification with father (becoming masculine) allows him to now engage in sexual relations with women (he becomes heterosexual). This is the origin of how we can "read" one's sexual orientation through the successful performance of gender identity. Second, the fear that the little boy feels does not send him scurrying into the arms of his mother to protect him from his father. Rather, he believes he will overcome his fear by identifying with its source. We become masculine by identifying with our oppressor.

But there is a piece of the puzzle missing, a piece that Freud, himself, implies but does not follow up.[7] If the pre-oedipal boy identifies with mother, he *sees the world through mother's eyes*. Thus, when he confronts father during his great oedipal crisis, he experiences a split vision: He sees his father as his mother sees his father, with a combination of awe, wonder, terror *and desire*. He simultaneously sees the father as he, the boy, would like to see him—as the object not of desire but of emulation. Repudiating mother and identifying with father only partially answers his dilemma. What is he to do with that homoerotic desire, the desire he felt because he saw father the way that his mother saw father?

He must suppress it. Homoerotic desire is cast as feminine desire, desire for other men. Homophobia is the effort to suppress that desire, to purify all relationships with other men, with women and with children of its taint, and to ensure that no one could possibly ever mistake one for a homosexual. Homophobic flight from intimacy with other men is the repudiation of the homosexual within—never completely successful and hence constantly re-enacted in every homosocial relationship. "The lives of most American men are bounded, and their interests daily curtailed by the constant necessity to prove to their fellows, and to themselves, that they are not sissies, not homosexuals," writes psychoanalytic historian Geoffrey Gorer. "Any interest or pursuit which is identified as a feminine interest or pursuit becomes deeply suspect for men" (1964:129).

Even if we do not subscribe to Freudian psychoanalytic ideas, we can still observe how, in less sexualized terms, the father is the first man who evaluates the boy's masculine performance, the first pair of male eyes before whom he tries to prove himself. Those eyes will follow him for the rest of his life. Other men's eyes will join them— the eyes of role models such as teachers, coaches, bosses or media heroes; the eyes of his peers, his friends and workmates; and the eyes of millions of other men, living and dead, from whose constant scrutiny of his performance he will never be free. "The tradition of all the dead generations weighs like a nightmare on the brain of the living," is how Karl Marx put it over a century ago (1848/1964:11). "The birthright of every American male is a chronic sense of personal inadequacy" is how two psychologists describe it today (Woolfolk and Richardson 1978:57).

That nightmare from which we never seem to awaken is that those other men will see that sense of inadequacy, they will see that in our own eyes we are not who we are pretending to be. What we call masculinity is often a hedge against being revealed as a fraud, an exaggerated set of activities that keep others from seeing through us, and a frenzied effort to keep at bay those fears within ourselves. Our real fear "is not fear of women but of being ashamed or humiliated in front of other men, or being dominated by stronger men" (Leverenz 1986:451).

This, then, is the great secret of American manhood: *We are afraid of other men.* Homophobia is a central organizing principle of our cultural definition of manhood. Homophobia is more than the irrational fear of gay men, more than the fear that we might be perceived as gay. "The word 'faggot' has nothing to do with homosexual experience or even with fears of homosexuals," writes David Leverenz. "It comes out of the depths of manhood: a label of ultimate contempt for anyone who seems sissy, untough, uncool" (1986:455). Homophobia is the fear that other men will unmask us, emasculate us, reveal to us and the world that we do not measure up, that we are not real men. We are afraid to let other men see that fear. Fear makes us ashamed, because the recognition of fear in ourselves is proof to ourselves that we are not as manly as we pretend, that we are, like the young man in a poem by Yeats, "one that ruffles in a manly pose for all his timid heart." Our fear is the fear of humiliation. We are ashamed to be afraid.

Shame leads to silence—the silences that keep other people believing that we actually approve of the things that are done to women, to minorities and gays and lesbians in our culture. The frightened silence as we scurry past a woman being hassled by men on the street. That furtive silence when men make sexist or racist jokes in a bar. That clammy-handed silence when guys in the office make gay-bashing jokes. Our fears are the sources of our silences, and men's silence is what keeps the system running. This might help to explain why women often complain that their male friends or partners are often so understanding when they are alone and yet laugh at sexist jokes or even make those jokes themselves when they are out with a group.

The fear of being seen as a sissy dominates the cultural definitions of manhood. It starts so early. "Boys among boys are ashamed to be unmanly," wrote one educator in 1871 (cited in Rotundo 1993:264). I have a standing bet with a friend that I can walk onto any playground in America where six-year-old boys are happily playing and by asking one question, I can provoke a fight. That question is simple: "Who's a sissy around here?" Once posed, the challenge is made. One of two things is likely to happen. One boy will accuse another of being a sissy, to which that boy will respond that he is not a sissy, that the first boy is. They may have to fight it out to see who's lying. Or a whole group of boys will surround one boy and all shout "He is! He is!" That boy will either burst into tears and run home crying, disgraced, or he will have to take on several boys at once, to prove that he is not a sissy. (And what will his father or older brothers tell him if he chooses to run home crying?) It will be some time before he regains any sense of self-respect.

Violence is often the single most evident marker of manhood. Rather it is the willingness to fight, the desire to fight. The origin of our expression that one has a chip on one's shoulder lies in the practice of an adolescent boy in the country or a small town at the turn of the century, who would literally walk around with a chip of wood balanced on his shoulder—a signal of his readiness to fight with anyone who would take the initiative of knocking the chip off (Gorer 1964:38; Mead 1965).

As adolescents, we learn that our peers are a kind of gender police, constantly threatening to unmask us as feminine, as sissies. One of the favourite tricks when I was an adolescent was to ask a boy to look at his fingernails. If he held his palm toward his face and curled his fingers back to see them, he passed the test. He had looked at his nails "like a man." But if he held the back of his hand away from his face, and looked at his fingernails with arm outstretched, he was immediately ridiculed as a sissy.

As young men we are constantly riding those gender boundaries, checking the fences we have constructed on the perimeter, making sure that nothing even remotely feminine might show through. The possibilities of being unmasked are everywhere. Even the most seemingly insignificant things can pose a threat or activate that haunting terror. On the day the students in my course "Sociology of Men and Masculinities" were scheduled to discuss homophobia and male–male friendships, one student provided a touching illustration. Noting that it was a beautiful day, the first day of spring after a brutal northeast winter, he decided to wear shorts to class. "I had this really nice pair of new Madras shorts," he commented. "But then I thought to myself, these shorts have lavender and pink in them. Today's class topic is homophobia. Maybe today is not the best day to wear these shorts."

Our efforts to maintain a manly front cover everything we do: What we wear. How we talk. How we walk. What we eat. Every mannerism, every movement contains a coded gender language. Think, for example, of how you would answer the question: How do you "know" if a man is homosexual? When I ask this question in classes or workshops, respondents invariably provide a pretty standard list of stereotypically effeminate behaviours. He walks a certain way, talks a certain way, acts a certain way. He is very emotional, he shows his feelings. One woman commented that she "knows" a man is gay if he really cares about her; another said she knows he is gay if he shows no interest in her, if he leaves her alone.

Now alter the question and imagine what heterosexual men do to make sure no one could possibly get the "wrong idea" about them. Responses typically refer to the original stereotypes, this time as a set of negative rules about behaviour. Never dress that way. Never talk or walk that way. Never show your feelings or get emotional. Always be prepared to demonstrate sexual interest in women that you meet, so it is impossible for any woman to get the wrong idea about you. In this sense, homophobia, the fear of being perceived as gay, as not a real man, keeps men exaggerating all the traditional rules of masculinity, including sexual predation with women. Homophobia and sexism go hand in hand.

The stakes of perceived sissydom are enormous—sometimes matters of life and death. We take enormous risks to prove our manhood, exposing ourselves disproportionately to health risks, workplace hazards and stress-related illnesses. Men commit suicide three times as often as women. Psychiatrist Willard Gaylin explains that it is "invariably because of perceived social humiliation," most often tied to failure in business:

> Men become depressed because of loss of status and power in the world of men. It is not the loss of money, or the material advantages that money could buy, which produces the despair that leads to self-destruction. It is the "shame," the "humiliation," the sense of personal "failure." . . . A man despairs when he has ceased being a man among men. (1992:32)

In one survey, women and men were asked what they were most afraid of. Women responded that they were most afraid of being raped and murdered. Men responded that they were most afraid of being laughed at (Noble 1992:105–6).

HOMOPHOBIA AS A CAUSE OF SEXISM, HETEROSEXISM AND RACISM

Homophobia is intimately interwoven with both sexism and racism. The fear—sometimes conscious, sometimes not—that others might perceive us as homosexual propels men to enact all manner of exaggerated masculine behaviours and attitudes to make sure that no one could possible get the wrong idea about us. One of the centre-pieces of that exaggerated masculinity is putting women down, both by excluding them from the public sphere and by the quotidian put-downs in speech and behaviours that organize the daily life of the American man. Women and gay men become the "other" against which heterosexual men project their identities, against whom they stack the decks so as to compete in a situation in which they will always win, so that by suppressing them, men can stake a claim for their own manhood. Women threaten emasculation by representing the home, workplace and familial responsibility, the negation of fun. Gay men have historically played the role of the consummate sissy in the American popular mind because homosexuality is seen as an inversion of normal gender development. There have been other "others." Through American history, various groups have represented the sissy, the non-men against whom American men played out their definitions of manhood, often with vicious results. In fact, these changing groups provide an interesting lesson in American historical development.

At the turn of the nineteenth century, it was Europeans and children who provided the contrast for American men. The "true American was vigorous, manly, and direct, not effete and corrupt like the supposed Europeans," writes Rupert Wilkinson. "He was plain rather than ornamented, rugged rather than luxury seeking, a liberty loving common man or natural gentleman rather than an aristocratic oppressor or servile minion" (1986:96). The "real man" of the early nineteenth century was neither noble nor serf. By the middle of the century, black slaves had replaced the effete nobleman. Slaves were seen as dependent, helpless men, incapable of defending their women and children, and therefore less than manly. Native Americans were cast as foolish and naive children, so they could be infantalized as the "Red Children of the Great White Father" and therefore excluded from full manhood.

By the end of the century, new European immigrants were also added to the list of the unreal men, especially the Irish and Italians who were seen as too passionate and emotionally volatile to remain controlled sturdy oaks, and Jews, who were seen as too bookishly effete and too physically puny to truly measure up. In the mid-twentieth century, it was also Asians—first the Japanese during the Second World War and, more recently, the Vietnamese during the Vietnam War—who have served as unmanly templates against which American men have hurled their gendered rage. Asian men were seen as small, soft and effeminate—hardly men at all.

Such a list of "hyphenated" Americans—Italian-, Jewish-, Irish-, African-, Native-, Asian-, gay- composes the majority of American men. So manhood is only possible for a distinct minority, and the definition has been constructed to prevent the others from achieving it. Interestingly, this emasculation of one's enemies has a flip side—and one that is equally gendered. These very groups that have historically been cast as less than manly were also, often simultaneously, cast as hypermasculine, as sexually aggressive, violent rapacious beasts, against whom "civilized" men must take a decisive stand and thereby rescue civilization. Thus black men were depicted as rampaging sexual beasts, women as carnivorously carnal, gay men as sexually insatiable, southern European men as sexually predatory and voracious, and Asian men as vicious and cruel torturers who were immorally disinterested in life itself, willing to sacrifice their entire people for their whims. But whether one saw these groups as effeminate sissies or as brutal uncivilized savages, the terms with which they were perceived were gendered. These groups become the "others," the screens against which traditional conceptions of manhood were developed.

Being seen as unmanly is a fear that propels American men to deny manhood to others, as a way of proving the unprovable—that one is fully manly. Masculinity becomes a defense against the perceived threat of humiliation in the eyes of other men, enacted through a "sequence of postures"—things we might say, or do, or even think, that, if we thought carefully about them, would make us ashamed of ourselves (Savran 1992:16). After all, how many of us have made homophobic or sexist remarks, or told racist jokes, or made lewd comments to women on the street? How many of us have translated those ideas and those words into actions, by physically attacking gay men, or forcing or cajoling a woman to have sex even though she did not really want to because it was important to score?

POWER AND POWERLESSNESS IN THE LIVES OF MEN

I have argued that homophobia, men's fear of other men, is the animating condition of the dominant definition of masculinity in America, that the reigning definition of masculinity is a defensive effort to prevent being emasculated. In our efforts to suppress or overcome those fears, the dominant culture exacts a tremendous price from those deemed less than fully manly: women, gay men, non-native-born men, men of colour. This perspective may help clarify a paradox in men's lives, a paradox in which men have virtually all the power and yet do not feel powerful (Kaufman 1993).

Manhood is equated with power—over women, over other men. Everywhere we look, we see the institutional expression of that power—in state and national legislatures, on the boards of directors of every major U.S. corporation or law firm, and in every school and hospital administration. Women have long understood this, and feminist women have spent the past three decades challenging both the public and the private expressions of men's power and acknowledging their fear of men. Feminism as a set of theories both explains women's fear of men and empowers women to confront it both publicly and privately. Feminist women have theorized that masculinity is about the drive for domination, the drive for power, for conquest.

This feminist definition of masculinity as the drive for power is theorized from women's point of view. It is how women experience masculinity. But is assumes a symmetry between the public and the private that does not conform to men's experiences. Feminists observe that women, as a group, do not hold power in our society. They also observe that individually, they, as women, do not feel powerful. They feel afraid, vulnerable. Their observation of the social reality and their individual experiences are therefore symmetrical. Feminism also observes that men, as a group, *are* in power. Thus, with the same symmetry, feminism has tended to assume that individually men must feel powerful.

This is why the feminist critique of masculinity often falls on deaf ears with men. When confronted with the analysis that men have all the power, many men react incredulously. "What do you mean, men have all the power?" they ask. "What are you talking about? My wife bosses me around. My kids boss me around. My boss bosses me around. I have no power at all! I'm completely powerless!"

Men's feelings are not the feelings of the powerful, but of those who see themselves as powerless. These are the feelings that come inevitably from the discontinuity between the social and the psychological, between the aggregate analysis that reveals how men are in power as a group and the psychological fact that they do not feel powerful as individuals. They are the feelings of men who were raised to believe themselves entitled to feel that power, but do not feel it. No wonder many men are frustrated and angry.

This may explain the recent popularity of those workshops and retreats designed to help men to claim their "inner" power, their "deep manhood," or their "warrior within." Authors such as Bly (1990), Farrell (1986, 1993), Keen (1991) and Moore and Gillette (1991, 1992, 1993a, 1993b) honour and respect men's feelings of powerlessness and acknowledge those feelings to be both true and real. "They gave white men the semblance of power," notes John Lee, one of the leaders of these retreats. "We'll let you run the country, but in the meantime, stop feeling, stop talking, and continue swallowing your pain and your hurt" (quoted in *Newsweek* 1992:41). (We are not told who "they" are.)

Often the purveyors of the mytho-poetic men's movement, that broad umbrella that encompasses all the groups helping men to retrieve this mythic, deep manhood, use the image of the chauffeur to describe modern man's position. The chauffeur appears to have the power—he is wearing the uniform, he is in the driver's seat, and he knows where he is going. So, to the observer, the chauffeur looks as though he is in command. But to the chauffeur himself, they note, he is merely taking orders. He is not at all in charge.[8]

Despite the reality that everyone knows chauffeurs do not have the power, this image remains appealing to the men who hear it at these weekend workshops. But there is a missing piece to the image, a piece concealed by the framing of the image in terms of the individual man's experience. That missing piece is that the person who is giving the orders is also a man. Now we have a relationship *between* men— between men giving orders and other men taking those orders. The man who identifies with the chauffeur is entitled to be the man giving the orders, but he is not. ("They," it turns out, are other men.)

The dimension of power is now reinserted into men's experience not only as the product of individual experience but also as the product of relations with other men. In this sense, men's experience of power-lessness is *real*—the men actually feel it and certainly act on it—but it is not *true*, that is, it does not accurately describe their condition. In contrast to women's lives, men's lives are structured around relation-ships of power and men's differential access to power, as well as the differential access to that power of men as a group. Our imperfect analysis of our own situation leads us to believe that we men need *more* power, rather than leading us to support feminists' efforts to rearrange power relationships along more equitable lines.

Philosopher Hannah Arendt fully understood this contradictory experience of social and individual power:

> Power corresponds to the human ability not just to act but to act in concert. Power is never the property of an individual; it belongs to a group and remains in existence only so long as the group keeps together. When we say of somebody that he is "in power" we actu-ally refer to his being empowered by a certain number of people to act in their name. The moment the group, from which the power originated to begin with . . . disappears, "his power" also vanishes. (1970:44)

Why, then, do American men feel so powerless? Part of the answer is because we have constructed the rules of manhood so that only the tiniest fraction of men come to believe that they are the biggest of wheels, the sturdiest of oaks, the most virulent repudiators of femi-ninity, the most daring and aggressive. We have managed to disem-power the overwhelming majority of American men by other means—

such as discriminating on the basis of race, class, ethnicity, age or sexual preference.

Masculinist retreats to retrieve deep, wounded, masculinity are but one of the ways in which American men currently struggle with their fears and their shame. Unfortunately, at the very moment that they work to break down the isolation that governs men's lives, as they enable men to express those fears and that shame, they ignore the social power that men continue to exert over women and the privileges from which they (as the middle-aged, middle-class white men who largely make up these retreats,) continue to benefit—regardless of their experiences as wounded victims of oppressive male socialization.[9]

Others still rehearse the politics of exclusion, as if by clearing away the playing field of secure gender identity of any that we deem less than manly—women, gay men, non-native-born men, men of colour—middle-class, straight, white men can reground their sense of themselves without those haunting fears and that deep shame that they are unmanly and will be exposed by other men. This is the manhood of racism, of sexism and of homophobia. It is the manhood that is so chronically insecure that it trembles at the idea of lifting the ban on gays in the military, that is so threatened by women in the workplace that women become the targets of sexual harassment, that is so deeply frightened of equality that it must ensure that the playing field of male competition remains stacked against all newcomers to the game.

Exclusion and escape have been the dominant methods American men have used to keep their fears of humiliation at bay. The fear of emasculation by other men, of being humiliated, of being seen as a sissy, is the leitmotif in my reading of the history of American manhood. Masculinity has become a relentless test by which we prove to other men, to women and ultimately to ourselves, that we have successfully mastered the part. The restlessness that men feel today is nothing new in American history; we have been anxious and restless for almost two centuries. Neither exclusion nor escape has ever brought us the relief we have sought, and there is no reason to think that either will solve our problems now. Peace of mind, relief from gender struggle, will come only from a politics of inclusion, not exclusion, from standing up for equality and justice, and not by running away.

NOTES

1. Reprinted from M. Brod and M. Kaufman (eds.), 1994, *Theorizing Masculinities*, Thousand Oaks, CA: Sage.

2. Of course, the phrase "American manhood" contains several simultaneous fictions. There is no single manhood that defines all American men; "America" is meant to refer to the United States proper, and there are significant ways in which this "American manhood" is the outcome of forces that transcend both gender and nation, that is, the global economic development of industrial capitalism. I use it, therefore, to describe the specific hegemonic version of masculinity in the United States, that normative constellation of attitudes, traits and behaviours that became the standard against which all other masculinities are measured and against which individual men measure the success of their gender accomplishments.

3. Much of this work is elaborated in Kimmel, *Manhood: The American Quest* (in press).

4. Although I am here discussing only American masculinity, I am aware that others have located this chronic instability and efforts to prove manhood in the particular culture and economic arrangements of Western society. Calvin, after all, inveighed against the disgrace "for men to become effeminate," and countless other theorists have described the mechanics of manly proof (see, for example, Seidler 1994).

5. I do not mean to argue that women do not have anxieties about whether they are feminine enough. Ask any woman how she feels about being called aggressive; it sends a chill into her heart because her femininity is suspect. (I believe that the reason for the enormous recent popularity of sexy lingerie among women is that it enables women to remember they are still feminine underneath their corporate business suit—a suit that apes masculine styles.) But I think the stakes are not as great for women and that women have greater latitude in defining their identities around these questions than men do. Such are the ironies of sexism: The powerful have a narrower range of options than the powerless, because the powerless can *also* imitate the powerful and get away with it. It may even enhance status, if done with charm and grace—that is, is not threatening. For the powerful, any hint of behaving like the powerless is a fall from grace.

6. Such observations also led journalist Heywood Brown to argue that most of the attacks against feminism came from men who were shorter than 5 feet 7 inches. "The man who, whatever his physical size, feels secure in his own masculinity and in his own relation to life is rarely resentful of the opposite sex" (cited in Symes 1930:139).

7. Some of Freud's followers, such as Anna Freud and Alfred Adler, did

follow up on these suggestions (see especially, Adler 1980). I am grateful to Terry Kupers for his help in thinking through Adler's ideas.

8. The image is from Warren Farrell, who spoke at a workshop I attended at the First International Men's Conference, Austin, Texas, October 1991.

9. For a critique of these mytho-poetic retreats, see Kimmel and Kaufman 1994.

Section II

Extensions

6

Erogenous Zones and Ambiguity
Sexuality and the Bodies of
Women and Men[1]

Laurence Thomas

Is that a pickle in your pocket, or are you happy to see me?
—Mae West

Power comes in many forms, as does fragility. Indeed, we men are sometimes moved to exercise power over others, to control them, that is, precisely because we are fragile. In his very important book, *Refusing To Be a Man* (1990), John Stoltenberg has movingly and convincingly articulated some of the profound ways in which men are sexist and, in particular, some of the ways in which sexism expresses itself through heterosexuality. I believe that in order to better understand this form of sexism, we must look at one of the profound ways in which men are fragile socially. The idea here is not to offer an account of the fragility of men such that men may appear to be less sexist. Rather, I want to make very explicit a set of factors that contributes to sexism among men.

To my mind one of Stoltenberg's most searching insights is that in the sexism of heterosexuality the self-identity of men is inextricably tied to their penises. It would be very liberating if men were to change in this regard. The result would be a power of self among men instead of a fragility of self which is often expressed through hostility to women. Throughout this chapter I am guided by the premise that men do not just have strengths and weaknesses, but we have them due to a certain history, and our bodies are a part of that history.

One of the most prized moral and spiritual goods is that of affirming sensuality. While there is no denying the power of words, it is nonetheless true that there are many instances in life when a touch can be more affirming than the most eloquent concatenation of words. There are ineffable moments of sadness, joy or profound connectedness to which only an affirming touch will do justice. Affirming sensuality is indispensable to a fulfilling human life. In my view, this form of affirmation meets a basic psychological need.

The central thesis of my essay is that one reason why men have exerted power over women is that they mistakenly believe this is the only way they can secure the prized moral and spiritual good of affirming sensuality. In the section following, I develop an account of the differences between women and men with respect to their bodies; extend that account to the issue of sexual ambiguity; and test the soundness of the account. To achieve the latter I use it to offer at least a partial explanation for the interesting phenomenon of heterosexual men being attracted to lesbian pornographic scenes or, at any rate, not repulsed by lesbian scenes. On the one hand, I suggest that touching is sensual and that sensuality admits of degrees by providing a quite compelling example. On the other hand, I suggest that the differences between women's and men's anatomical responses to feelings of eroticism make it easier for women to be ambiguous about whether or not the emotional energy between them has considerable sexual overtones.

To set the stage, I begin with some commonplace observations of differences between women and men with respect to erotic behaviour, differences which are routinely manifested in the public realm and in film.

THE PUBLIC BEHAVIOUR
OF FEMALES AND MALES

If a man had sex with women only, but enjoyed watching homosexual films from time to time or merely admitted that he often dreamt about having sex with men or men having sex, a great many would insist that he had (latent) homosexual desires. And no "real man" wants to have even latent homosexual desires. Indeed, openly admiring the physical appearance of another man is about as much as most "real men" can abide. Even then, if this admiration is not to occasion any suspicion of homosexuality it had better be done with a certain bravado: "You look good/cool," versus "You look sexy." There are straight men and there are gay men, end of story. In terms of social import, bi-sexual men are but a version of gay men. Interestingly, one of the only instances in which men are allowed to display (nearly) unrestrained physical affection for one another—usually for a dying partner—seems to be in the context of war. Or, so the mainstream cinema would have us believe. But then eroticism drops out of the picture. I shall return to this observation at the very end of the following section.

Now, one naturally supposes that the categories of straight and gay apply in a like manner to women. Well, yes and no. Contemporary popular and pornographic cinema presents very good evidence that things are significantly more complicated. Such thematically different movies as *The Color Purple* and *Basic Instinct* portray considerable sexual energy between women without really bothering anyone, to say nothing of lesbian scenes in pornography. For popular films to portray as much sexual energy between men would surely be a problem. In straight pornography, any gay scene that occurs is apt to be a very, very brief scene or a very small background part of a large sexual scene. We have a display of sexual energy between two people when they interact in ways that either or both parties would understandably find erotic to some extent or that, in any case, the typical viewer would naturally regard as being erotic to some extent. So actors performing a love scene have to do enough, given the conventions of the culture in which the film is being viewed, to at least be convincing to the viewing audience.

Interview with a Vampire is probably one of the most homoerotic movies ever produced for the general public. It helps that all this homoeroticism involved vampires, thereby blocking the suggestion that "real men" might have such feelings. *Interview* displays far more sexual energy between men than the movie *Threesome*. This is so although *Threesome* is expressly about a ménage à trois between one woman and two men, with one man being sexually attracted to the other, and although the movie contains a sex scene at the end between the three where the two men are mildly animated by one another's sexual desire even as each is having sex with the woman who is between them. For an American audience, especially, this last scene is particularly bold; as pornography that is intended for straight audiences reveals, two men with one woman is just fine, so long as each man is all but invisible in the eyes of the other. Any sort of erotic touching between the two men is absolutely out of the question.

Not surprisingly, *Threesome* was not a commercial success in the United States, nor were any of the characters played by major Hollywood actors. After all, this is not the sort of movie that two straight guys might go out to see together or that a straight guy would take a man to see; for no man would want anyone to think that he might have as a fantasy a ménage à trois involving himself, another man and a woman. In *Interview* there is a scene where one almost expects the two vampires to erotically kiss, whereas this expectation is never generated in *Threesome*. And it is clear that *Interview* is just about the intense need that one male vampire has for male vampire companionship.

From the very first bite on the neck, followed by the ascent into the air as the two men are locked in a blood-kiss (excuse me, I mean blood-bite) on the neck, sexual energy between the two leading male characters abounds. They are vampires, though, and that is absolutely crucial to the explanation for how all this explicit sexual energy between men remains relatively unproblematic for the audience. Since all of this sexual energy occurs between vampires, the audience does not perceive the male–male sexual energy as either a recommendation or an endorsement. Vampires being perverse creatures to begin with can get away with (in the mind of the audience) doing perverse things. Notice, however, that in order to portray intense sexual energy between women, we do not need the guise of vampires. Had *Threesome* been about two women loving one man, it probably would have been a hit. In the hopes that their woman companion might take a liking to the idea, all sorts of men would want to see the film with her, again and again!

No doubt the foregoing points are obvious upon reflection. They are true, even as it is also true that men have made substantial strides in the arena of touching and displays of emotions. These days, men can cry, especially in the arms of a woman, and embrace one another rather tenderly. Recent commercials showing men affectionately embracing their children can be very, very moving. Nonetheless, the latitude that women have in the matter of expressing or flaunting sexual energy toward one another far exceeds that which men have. Had *Philadelphia* been about a lesbian lawyer with aids, it is very likely that there would have been a scene between the lead female character and another women displaying enormous sexual energy. This was not the case with the leading male character in this film who portrayed a gay man. It could not have been done if the film was to be a commercial success. During the dance scene between the lead character and his lover they both wore gloves while holding hands!

A question that certainly suggests itself is, how can it be that society officially condemns homosexuality, and rather harshly at that, but yet accepts far more intense displays of sexual energy between women than it does between men? This turns out to be a two-tiered question, as society consists of both women and men. Yet, it is not as if only men are accepting of displays of sexual energy between women while women utterly abhor them. After all, these displays are portrayed for the eyes of both women and men to see. I assume that if women found displays of sexual attraction between women utterly abhorrent there would be far less of this sort of thing shown, except between lesbians. So, there is the very specific point that women are more accepting of displays of sexual energy between themselves than men are accepting of sexual energy between themselves. One quite naturally asks why this is so. In the hopes of gaining some insight into heterosexist attitudes on the part of men, it is this latter question that I want to answer in this chapter.

In my view, although I shall not fully develop the point here, for all their bravado, men are less comfortable with the richness of their sexual sensuality than women are. It is a fact of life that people often want to exercise power over those who make them feel uncomfortable. Recall that many traditions dichotomize the woman as either perched upon the throne of moral pulchritude or the very seat of lasciviousness. The way in which her life has been socially circumscribed in many societies—from chastity belts to virtual imprisonment in the home— reveals that in the minds of many men a woman can easily fall from moral grace. Consider the view, still held by many men, that a woman who was raped was really "asking for it."

Lest there be any misunderstanding concerning my view of women and sexual orientation, I hardly mean to deny that there are women who find lesbianism repulsive, and that many straight women generally do not want to be mistaken for being a lesbian. All the same, none of this detracts from the blatant reality that women are more accepting of displays of sexual energy between themselves than men are accepting of such displays between themselves. Such displays between women abound throughout Western culture, and are often instantiated by women who would never think of themselves as lesbians and who have little or no concern for their image as straight women being tarnished. There are times when it is even fashionable among segments of "real" women to pass themselves off as lesbians or, at any rate, to invite the suspicion that they might be. By contrast, never in recent decades has it been fashionable for straight men actually to invite the suspicion that they are gay.

It is for these reasons that I said "yes and no" to the question of whether the labels straight and gay apply in a like manner to both women and men. There seems to be an erogenous loop between being straight and gay that women can travel, but men cannot. This asymmetry between women and men is what I wish to explain. I should like to think that the account I develop nicely supplements many of the ideas which Stoltenberg develops in *Refusing To Be a Man* (1990).

Two caveats are in order. First, in talking about human beings, it is always important to remember that a pattern is not defeated by a single example to the contrary. For instance, the claim that the life expectancy of males in England is such-and-such is hardly undermined by the truth that there are males who die younger and males who die older. The account which I develop of the asymmetry between women and men speaks to a difference in patterns in the lives of women and men, a pattern to which there are exceptions. Second, it is a most significant fact that men generally have a higher social status than women. Indeed, as Claudia Card (private communication) has observed, women (who were tomboys) look back with nostalgia at the days when they were tomboys, whereas men (who were sissies) never talk fondly of having been sissies. Although they draw upon independent considerations, the arguments of this essay are very much consistent with this differential between the social status of women and men.

A final comment. At one level all forms of touching are tied to social conventions. Still, one might usefully distinguish between ritualized touches of affirmation and spontaneous touches of affirmation. The conventional pat on the buttocks among American male sports players, after a player makes a winning move or as he goes to take a position for a crucial play, is an instance of the former. Men do no such thing outside of the context of sports—say, on Wall Street after a winning deal. The greeting in France, between friends, of a kiss on both cheeks is also an instance of a ritualized touch of affirmation. Notice that the circumstances under which such touching can occur are very well defined; moreover, its endurance is momentary. The pat on the buttock is not used as a form of greeting among players; nor can they keep their hands on the buttocks of the other player. The circumstances under which spontaneous touches of affirmation can occur are, on the other hand, wide-ranging (receiving their greatest expressions between romantic partners who in public may engage in a wealth of touches of sensual affirmation) and the touching is not momentary. In Western culture, spontaneous touching between women is generally much richer and greater than spontaneous touching between men.

BODIES: WOMEN AND MEN

In response to my question regarding the asymmetry between women and men, it might seem that a natural line to take would draw upon the work of both Carol Gilligan in *In a Different Voice* (1992) and Nancy Chodorow in *The Reproduction of Mothering* (1978). Their view (speaking in broad terms) is that in a world where parenting is primarily the role of women, the boundaries of the self are less sharply drawn between females than is the case between males. Girls are to be like their mothers, but boys are not, of course. There is something to this view. Yet, I suspect that these thinkers would not, for a moment, have thought that their views offered an explanation for why women are more accepting than men of displays of sexual energy between themselves. Besides, since the very permeable boundaries between mother and daughter do not seem especially fraught with sexual energy, we are still left without much insight into why women are so accepting of sexual attraction between themselves. This suggests that another approach might be more fruitful.

Without denying that sexism might be a factor, it does not seem plausible that a complete answer would lie in the existence of sexism. More precisely, it seems to me that a satisfactory explanation must add to rather than merely echo the important truth that in general many societies have always allowed women to be in touch with and expressive of their feelings, whereas these same societies have rigorously discouraged this sort of thing among men. Why? Because, if nothing else, simply appealing to this truth confuses the issue. The most intense feelings of affection can be displayed between individuals without those feelings being sexually charged in the least. It may be true that sexual energy is far more widespread among people who are very much in touch with and expressive of their feelings than among those who are not. Still, this does not mean that in recommending greater expression of feelings and so forth one is thereby calling for greater expression of sexual energy.

I begin with the observation that women have noted, that breast-feeding an infant can be quite sensual. Yet, the sensuality of infant breast-feeding does not usually result in anything close to full-scale sexual arousal on the mother's part. The reasons include everything from the infant being seen as an improper object of sexual attraction to the extremely strong social taboo against incest. In any case, what is of considerable interest given the concern of this chapter is that women are able to view an extremely erogenous part of their anatomy in two radically different ways. Most significantly, it means that women quite successfully distinguish between the sensuality of breast-feeding and the sensuality of sexual interactions. So, as a matter of logic, while good sexuality entails the sensual, the sensual does not entail the sexual. It might be useful to distinguish between affirming sensuality and erotic sensuality, with breast-feeding being a straightforward instance of affirming sensuality. (The adjective "good" is necessary since it is certainly possible for there to be sex with little or no sensuality. A man or a women could be too uncomfortable owing to, for example, inexperience or intimidation.)

Relatedly, there is the very important fact that the vaginal passage is also the birth passageway. Thus another extremely erogenous part of the woman's anatomy is inextricably tied to a most significant function—the giving of life—that is quite disconnected from sex. Let me hasten to add here that I have not claimed that giving birth is sensual in any way.

Taken together, these two considerations make it clear that as women conceive of their bodies, not only is sensuality a complicated

phenomenon, not always connected to sex, but that two central erogenous zones of the body serve a life-based purpose quite separate from
sex. This complex bipartite conception of sensuality, ranging over the
affirming and erotic, is generally and routinely transmitted by mothers
to their daughters, a point which I shall elaborate upon just before the
conclusion of this section.

Needless to say, things are quite different with men's bodies. While
men have nipples, their nipples do not supply nutrients. So for men this
erogenous zone serves no significant life-based function unrelated to
sex. In general, the penis is the central erogenous zone for men. And
while sperm, of course, pass through the penis, it must be acknowledged
that the penis serves no life-based function that comes even close to
matching the saliency of bearing a child and giving birth to it. So, phe-
nomenologically, the central erogenous zones of the male body serve no
life-based function: the emitting of sperm is generally more keenly associated with the pleasures of ejaculation than providing an ingredient that
makes human life possible. As men conceive of their bodies, the sensual
and the sexual are very nearly interchangeable. At any rate, the appreciation which men acquire of the difference between affirming and erotic
sensuality is not informed by their body parts serving a life-based purpose. The foregoing considerations are obviously consistent with, but
independent of, the observation which I made in the introduction,
namely that men have a higher social status than women.

While the distinction between affirming sensuality and erotic sensuality is certainly a real one, the claim here is not that biology is des-
tiny, at least not as that expression is usually understood. Nothing I
have said entails that, as a matter of biology, women and men are more
suited to some social roles than others. I have said that owing to life-
based functions women conceive of their bodies differently than men
and that, in particular, biology requires women to conceive of sensuality in a more complicated way than it requires of men. But perhaps
even this is too strong. It would probably be better to say that biology
favours women (over men) when it comes to seeing sensuality in a
more complicated way. I have not claimed, nor have I meant to claim,
that men cannot, owing to their biological make-up, conceive of sensuality between adults in such a way that it does not always involve
sexuality. At the end of the following section, I shall further explicate
this point concerning being favoured.

As no doubt one has surmised, I want to say that an important part of the explanation for the asymmetry between female–female touching and male–male touching is that, unlike men, women readily, even if unthinkingly, distinguish between affirming sensuality and erotic sensuality. Precisely because this distinction is so operative for women, the very idea that the options are sensuality and sex or no sensuality at all is, generally speaking, a non-starter for them.

Of course, the line between affirming sensuality and erotic sensuality is a rather thin one that can be easily crossed either spatially (the touch was a little too close to . . .), temporally (the touch was a little too long), or physically (the touch was just a little too firm or intense). Non-verbal behaviour in general is extremely subtle. A wink can be sexual or friendly, depending on the social setting and other facial features. The same is true for the difference between a look of sexual interest, a look that simply finds a feature of the face curious, and a look where one is merely in the line of vision. Yet, people manage remarkably well to make out the difference. Flirting from a distance would otherwise be impossible. All of this is so notwithstanding the obvious truth that what counts as flirting behaviour is culturally linked.

While women are perhaps favoured to notice the distinction between affirming sensuality and erotic sensuality because of their bodies, what makes discerning the difference come "naturally" in the course of social interaction is years of experience, starting during childhood with their mothers. And it is the absence of continual experience that renders men so awkward at discerning the difference between affirming sensuality and erotic sensuality. Observe that mothers and daughters routinely touch and embrace in a way that fathers and sons generally do not, at least not after the son is well into his pre-teen years. "Routinely" here distinguishes between a sustained embrace between father and son that is usually occasioned by some significant event, and a like embrace between mother and daughter that may simply be a part of a casual conversation that reaches a poignant or tender moment. Notice that in a like manner, it is often the case that women embrace one another, whereas this is rather rare among men. It is certainly the case that women are depicted on television and in cinema as embracing and touching to a far greater extent than men are. I have to assume that the very pervasiveness of the difference between how women and men are depicted is not just a function of what men like, but that it also reveals a level of comfort that women have with touch between one another.

SEXUAL AMBIGUITY AND AFFIRMING SENSUALITY

Not having to reveal one's true feelings can certainly be advantageous. In fact, given the right contexts, cultivated ambiguity can be quite enjoyable. Part of the joy of a certain kind of flirting, for instance, lies in its ambiguity. It allows people to get a sense of their powers of sexual attractiveness or simply to engage in mild exploration without either party having to pay in the coin of commitment or rejection. Flirting can get out of hand in a number of ways, one of which is when it is taken too seriously. But that is just the point. If flirting gets out of hand precisely when it is taken too seriously, then flirting itself does not constitute a serious proposal, although that is what the flirting party may be warming up to. Flirting can also get out of hand by going on too long or by being directed at the wrong kind of person (a nun or a priest for example). In any event, flirting can be a way of masking keen sexual interest, or it may be just a way of having fun. And if the person flirting is good at it, then only self-disclosure need let someone else know.

Along with the distinction between affirming and erotic sensuality drawn in the preceding section, there is another factor in the explanation for why women are more accepting than men of displays of sexual energy between themselves. In the context of physical interaction, women can generally be ambiguous about whether they are experiencing arousal in a way that men cannot. Let me explain.

In the context of physical interaction, there would be no ambiguity to speak of if sexual arousal in women were accompanied by a physical movement as blatantly revealing as the male erection. Mae West's quip (quoted at the beginning of this chapter) gives voice to what I mean by blatantly revealing. The idea is that anyone familiar with the difference between a flaccid and an erect penis could, with even a most casual glance from across the room, say, easily recognize the latter on just about any nude adult male and would, in the case of any clothed adult male, readily associate a (heretofore absent) bulge in the groin area with an erect penis. A parallel claim cannot be made regarding women. This is neither to deny that there are bodily movements, such as erect nipples and an extended clitoris, that occur as a result of female arousal; nor to glorify the male erection. Rather, it is merely to point to a difference where there is one. Blushing is more apparent among people with very light skin than it is among people with very dark skin, although everyone blushes.

Nor, again, do I mean to deny that there are forms of behaviour in which people can engage that are tell-tale signs of sexual interest. It should be noted, however, that many of these forms of behaviour are culturally-tied and engaged in voluntarily, although they can appear to be driven by the very engine of desire itself. Part of what it means to be acculturated is to be able to display quite naturally learned behaviour which, in that culture, is characteristically associated with having various feelings or beliefs. However, I am interested here in autonomic displays of sexual arousal, and my thesis is that in the course of physical interaction, women can be more ambiguous about whether they are experiencing sexual arousal than men can be.

In this regard, it might be useful to distinguish between shadow and substantive sexual arousal. I do not have a precise way of drawing this distinction, but I assume that sexual arousal admits of a continuum. I assume that, at one end, there are occasions when one is sexually aroused by some stimulus in the environment (something one sees or hears), but that the arousal is not born of a longing for sexual satisfaction. Once the stimulus is no longer present, the arousal dissipates. This is what I call shadow arousal. At the other end of the continuum, there are occasions when one is aroused and that arousal bespeaks or latches on to a longing for sexual satisfaction. This is what I call substantive arousal.

To be sure, the space between the two can be crossed. In particular, a shadow arousal can become a substantive one. Consider the following story. At one institution where I taught, the majority of males rejected outright the idea of co-ed showers on their dormitory floor, much to the surprise of the women. (In the dormitory in question, shower stalls do not exist. Rather, each floor has a large shower-room with a series of shower units.) The sentiment of these males was quite straightforward: In the infinitesimally small amount of time which they allotted for getting up and getting to class, they did not want to have to be dealing with the issue of having an erection in the throes of showering to get to class. These males were expressing their awareness that, although they might be preoccupied with going to class, and so not at that moment entertaining the idea of having sex, they were nonetheless susceptible to having an erection given the mere presence of nude women in the same room. The male students described above were concerned that shadow arousal, occasioned by the presence of nude women in the shower room, would result in an erection.

To take an example of a rather different sort, I imagine that just about every man has had the experience of having an erection and inferring from it that he was very much interested in obtaining sexual satisfaction, only to discover upon having sexual intercourse or masturbating that his sexual appetite was not nearly as pronounced as he had thought it was. In my view, this is to experience shadow sexual arousal. As this example reveals, it is possible to be mistaken about whether one is experiencing shadow or substantive sexual arousal. But is it not possible to be more or less hungry than one thought that one was? There is no reason to suppose that epistemic certainty is a feature of the sexual appetite. For the sake of completeness, I should mention, as Lawrence May (personal communication) has reminded me, that there is a third category of erections which have nothing at all to do with sexual desire, namely the morning erection stemming from a full bladder.

The further point to be made here is that with men shadow sexual arousal has the very same bodily manifestation as sustained arousal, namely an erection. With women the bodily responses associated with sustained arousal occur far less frequently with shadow arousal.

For the sake of argument, I will make three assumptions: (i) sustained arousals can be detected easily enough in whomever they might occur; whereas with shadow arousals it is generally men who exhibit a tell-tale sign, since shadow arousals in men take the same form as sustained arousals, namely an erection; (ii) the line between affirming sensuality and erotic sensuality is thin enough that it can be unwittingly crossed; and (iii) it is very difficult for two people to display sufficient sexual energy between them to convince a viewer without running the risk of shadow arousal. Given human psychology, if (ii) is true, then (iii) is very likely to be true. (By the way, the argument does not presuppose that with men shadow arousal always results in an erection, only that this happens frequently. Nor does the argument presuppose that shadow arousal among women never results in bodily movements, but only that this is infrequent or the movements are less salient. Finally, it is also not presupposed that deep feelings of arousal must always be accompanied by bodily movements on the part of either women or men. Recall my remarks about patterns at the end of the introductory section of this chapter.)

At this point, one can perhaps anticipate the line of argument that I am about to pursue. It is no accident that many women are relatively comfortable with the ambiguity between affirming sensuality and erotic sensuality; crossing of that line results in shadow arousal only and is unlikely to result in any tell-tale bodily manifestations. With men, however, the problem is that shadow arousal alone frequently yields the tell-tale bodily manifestation of an erection.

The female–female scenes in such movies as *The Color Purple* and *Basic Instinct* surely flaunt the ambiguity between affirming sensuality and erotic sensuality. And in my view what makes that flaunting possible is the absence of consequent tell-tale bodily manifestations of arousal. For those female–female scenes are generally convincing, and this requires the requisite frame of mind if only to produce shadow arousal. (Recall that typically a male can, absent extant feelings of sexual desire, bring himself to the point of ejaculation for entirely non-erotic purposes—to obtain a sperm count or to donate to a sperm-bank—by concentrating on erotic images.) Yet because tell-tale bodily movements do not readily occur in women experiencing only shadow arousal, these scenes do not force the issue of whether or not the actors are in the least bit aroused sexually.

In a female–female sexual scene, a woman could very well experience shadow arousal, but without self-disclosure no one else need ever know. With men, on the other hand, self-disclosure is seldom an option. Hence it is no accident that there are virtually no male–male erotic scenes in movies for the general public. An erection would force the issue that either or both male actors found the scene arousing. The fact that the issue would be forced in this way is, indeed, the problem. It is this possibility of shadow arousal, and its concomitant erection, which in general men are absolutely unwilling to risk. For instance, in a gymnasium shower room with other men, every male knows that the one thing that he absolutely must not do, whatever else he might do, is have an erection. No explanation, short of sheer uncontrollable spasms, would be a good one. Women do not seem to have a corresponding worry concerning erect breasts and clitoral extension. Among other things, surely this has to do with the comparative difference in saliency between these phenomena and an erect penis. By contrast, penis and breast size are often a concern respectively for both men and women.

As Claudia Card has reminded me (personal communication), heterosexual men's repulsion of another man's erect penis or admiring another man's body is socially induced; women generally have no trouble admiring one another's bodies. I have certainly not denied this. Fortunately, this important truth is compatible with all that I have said about social ambiguity. Men are unwilling to risk shadow erection with their clothes on. Two clothed men rubbing up against one another in a bar scene would know soon enough whether either or both were aroused. Not so with two women engaged in similar behaviour. Men are even more unwilling to risk the possibility of shadow arousal in the nude.

The second part of the two-tiered question which I posed earlier reads: How can it be that society officially condemns homosexuality, and rather harshly at that, but yet accepts far more intense displays of sexual energy between women than it does between men? In sum, my answer is that, first of all, women generally have a richer view of their sensuality than men have and, second, there is much more ambiguity in the arena of sexual interaction for women than for men. In both cases, this is due to the difference between the bodies of women and men. In practice, this difference has the effect of creating an erogenous loop, between being straight and gay, that women can travel upon. Not all women feel comfortable cruising this loop, but clearly a significant number do. Not only that, those who do not feel comfortable seem to understand, if only from afar, that there is this erogenous loop for women.

I have carefully avoided saying that, as a matter of nature, women view sensuality in a more complex way than men. I do not believe that is true. What I have said, in effect, is that women are favoured by nature to view sensuality in a more complex way than men. This leaves unsettled what the actual outcomes will be. Consider a child whose parents both have the Ph.Ds. From the standpoint of education, this child is favoured over the child whose parents have a fifth-grade education. All the same, the former child may perform abysmally in school and the latter brilliantly. When it comes to attitudes and beliefs, how nature manifests itself is inextricably tied to the reality of the social circumstances in which people find themselves. This is so even when some ways of seeing the world are favoured by biology, as is presumably the case with women and the complexity of sensuality. But if what one sees in the world of concrete objects can be very much a matter of one's expectations, surely this is so with such a complex and amorphous phenomenon as sensuality. Justly arranged social institutions can enable one to see more clearly that which one would see ever so dimly or not at all on one's own.

Can there be a like erogenous loop for men? Surely, but we men would have to take a very different stance toward our bodies, attaching far less sexual significance to an erect penis than we presently do. We would have to stop glorifying it. I shall say something about this possibility in my conclusion. However, I assume that a shift in male attitudes along this line is at the very heart of Stoltenberg's (1990) challenge to the traditional conception of heterosexual male sexual identity. My account of the difference between female and male bodies supplements Stoltenberg's views in two respects. One is that the account offered draws attention to the reality that attitudes among women and men regarding sensuality are not simply parallel. The other is that the account offers an explanation of this difference between women and men that is more satisfactory than merely postulating the existence of sexism. Indeed, the account provides some insight into why sexism has manifested itself in the form of the different attitudes which women and men have toward sexuality.

But how does the account offered shed a measure of light on sexism and the concern of men to control women? Let it be granted that affirming sensuality is in fact a deep psychological need on the part of women and men alike, and that this need exists in the normal course of life but is especially prevalent during times of crisis. In view of the account of the differences in the bodies of women and men which I have developed, let it also be granted that only women in society are thought to be able to provide affirming sensuality. Together, these two considerations constitute an important reason, though not an utterly decisive reason, for men to want to control women. What is more, it would be a reason born of a sense of fragility on the part of men. Control is the issue here, because affirming sensuality is indispensable to our psychological well-being. Without control men cannot guarantee themselves access to the good of sensual affirmation.

As I have already indicated, I take it to be obvious that considerable affirming sensuality occurs between women. This is not to say that women are never uncomfortable with the affirming sensuality that occurs between them. In Western cultures for instance, women can hold one another's hand at length while conversing about a crisis. Men cannot do this. Even if upon occasion such hand-holding makes a women feel uncomfortable, the fact remains that displaying emotional support in this way is widespread among women; a woman who feels uncomfortable holding hands in such instances would be mindful of this. To be sure, there could be sexual energy on the part of one of the women. In most instances, however, that would certainly not be obvious and the most that a single instance would normally warrant is a very mild suspicion.

The fragility of men arises from the self-identity of males as "real" men (that is, men who are not gay) being so easily called into question. This is certainly so in comparison to the self-identity of females as "real" women (that is, women who are straight). Women can dance with one another although there are men available, and they can share the same bed without automatically inviting the suspicion that they are lesbians. An analogous claim most certainly cannot be made for men. Although there are signs of change, the fact remains that men must studiously refrain from engaging in just about any form of behaviour which would invite the suspicion that they are seeking nurturance from another male or that they are even comfortable with things appearing that way. The socially acculturated straight man in Western culture is readily threatened by such appearances. This speaks to the very heart of the fragility of men. When they might turn to one another for the nurturance of affirming sensuality, they must either find a woman or do without lest they should appear to be other than "real" men. What is going on here is, quite simply, the fact that "real" men invariably associate nurturance (between adults) with sex and so with their penis.

Suffice it to say that the lives of women would be different, for the worse, if they could turn only to men for the nurturance of affirming sensuality. American slavery, I am sure, would have taken a far greater toll than it did upon the lives of Black women had they not been able to turn to one another for the nurturance of affirming sensuality. Men must go through whatever psychological contortions that it takes to sustain this false view of themselves in the face of a reality that makes it clear, at least upon honest reflection, that things have to be otherwise. The case of children makes this abundantly clear. Girl and boy infants do not differ in their need for affection. Moreover, displays of affection among very young children themselves have no boundaries of gender. The explanation for the change here simply cannot be hormonal, since that would leave rather unexplained the blatant asymmetry between women and men.

I remarked at the start of this chapter that in the context of war men are permitted (nearly) unrestrained physical affection for a dying partner. I take this to be a profound concession among men to the human reality that there are times when no concatenation of words, however elegant, can substitute for the affirmation of touch. It is most unfortunate that in Western culture this concession is wrought by the context of death and war.

PORNOGRAPHY AND LESBIAN SCENES

I believe that the account developed in the above sections, especially the preceding one, casts some light on one of the most interesting questions that can be posed regarding the attraction of pornography: How is it that perfectly straight heterosexual men take such a liking to lesbian scenes where the women are fully animated by one another's sexual passion, leaving no room for the interpretation that they are awaiting a man for complete sexual fulfillment? (Since pornographic films which cater to straight males almost invariably do not include a homosexual scene, certainly not one that is both explicit and enduring, the parallel question with respect to women does not arise.) Lesbian scenes are a common feature of most pornographic movies for straight men. In some instances lesbian sex is but a prelude to heterosexual sex, but passionate lesbian scenes representing complete sexual ecstasy between two women are frequent enough. Yet, as a rule straight men do not generally regard these scenes as an affront to their masculinity; nor are they repulsed by passionate lesbian scenes. The very same men who find male–male sexual passion unnatural, do not seem to find female–female sexual passion unnatural at all.

Whenever I put the above question to men, the most common answer essentially ignores what I asked. I am usually told that "men like pleasing women; hence, the more the better." Perhaps, but as an answer to my question this response widely misses the explanatory mark. I did not ask why do men like watching pornographic scenes where the man has two or more female sexual partners. Nor did I ask why do men like watching pornographic scenes where women engage in (solitary) acts of self-eroticism. In this latter instance one can see how scenes of this sort are supposed to represent a prelude to the real act of sex, which is supposedly male vaginal penetration. A masturbating women can be readily construed as wanting a man. Moreover, a straight man watching women masturbate can easily enough draw upon other straight sexual experiences to augment the moment of vicarious participation. I can only assume that some form of vicarious participation is going on, otherwise why are men just about always in pornographic scenes?

Passionate lesbian scenes, however, are a different story altogether. Indeed, precisely because the visual is so powerful, it is extremely difficult to see how these scenes could be inviting to men. Scenes of the sort would seem to thwart vicarious participation. So to the typical response to my question, my counter-reply is: Watching passionate lesbian scenes would seem to be a most indirect route to the fantasy of pleasing women, so indirect as to appear off-course. How is the pleasure that men take in watching these scenes to be squared with their supposedly inexorable heterosexual inclinations? For the ideological brush of heterosexuality entirely paints every aspect of one's sex life, including one's sexual fantasies. As I noted at the outset, even if a man never had sex with men but only with women, in admitting that he fantasized about having sex with men or enjoyed watching scenes involving men having sex with one another such a man would, in the same breath, be admitting that his sexual orientation is not one hundred percent heterosexual.

Why are men so indifferent to lesbian scenes of the sort that I have described? The explanation that I shall offer is hardly complete. However, it does, I think, constitute an important beginning. There are a couple of background assumptions to be mentioned. One is that male–male expressions of affirming sensuality generate considerable cognitive dissonance for most people and, in particular, for most men. The other is that, in their adult interactions, most men blur the distinction between affirming sensuality and erotic sensuality, with the latter overshadowing the former.

As an aside, it is rather interesting that even for women male–male expressions of affirming sensuality generate a significant level of cognitive dissonance. This is because women frequently bemoan the fact that for men erotic sensuality often overshadows affirming sensuality which they (women) delight in for its own sake. Well, let me just say that women cannot have it both ways. If men are only "allowed" to express affirming sensuality toward women, it should hardly come as any surprise that this form of sensuality is often overshadowed by erotic sensuality. Need anyone be reminded that women express affirming sensuality not only toward men but also toward other women, and often with great intensity in both cases. But this is another issue. I take it for granted that people have an interest in sex. So what I mean to be explaining is not so much why men are attracted to lesbian scenes, but why they are not repulsed by them.

Essentially, my explanation has to do with the account of ambiguity offered earlier and particularly with the fact that shadow arousal among women is not as physically blatant as it is among men. For men, the mark of sexual arousal is the blatant physically revealing movement embodied in the erection. An erection is the salient sign that a man is ready for sex. In a sexist society, whether a woman is ready for sex is deemed irrelevant to a man's having sex with her, as defined in terms of vaginal penetration. In the minds of some men, a woman need not even be conscious so long as they can engage in vaginal penetration with her. Within a sexist framework, female readiness for sex is never the real issue, only male readiness is.

In my view, then, the male fascination with lesbian pornographic scenes would not exist if female sexual readiness were accompanied by a physically blatant bodily movement. Suppose that whenever women were sufficiently aroused their chest expanded in such a way that their two breasts invariably seemed connected and took on the appearance of one breast with one nipple. Moreover, a fluid was produced upon orgasm. Then in the sex act whether or not a woman is aroused and whether or not she achieves orgasm would be settled matters in roughly the way that things now are with men. Then heterosexual men would have to take seriously whether women are or are not ready for heterosexual sex in a way that they (men) do not now. If, whenever women were ready for sex, there would be the one-breast appearance phenomenon, then men could not delude themselves into thinking that they had aroused a woman, as either a man succeeded in producing the appearance of the one breast or he did not. Women could also not deceive men about their success in arousing women. Most significantly, just how arousing lesbian scenes are would be clear to all—participants and viewers (if there are any). In particular, it would be rather clear whether a woman is aroused by women and not men, by men and not women, or by both.

I maintain that this saliency with respect to sexual readiness would be too much for perfectly straight heterosexual men, if only because it would often force the issue of whether a man preferred having sex with a lesbian or a non-lesbian. As things stand, men often labour under the delusion that a woman, even a self-confessed lesbian, really wants sex in the form of vaginal penetration even if she is unwilling to admit it to herself. Well, in many cases that would change with the salience of the one-breast appearance as a sign of sexual readiness. The "proof" would be physically manifest, as it presently is for men. Notice that absent an erection, no woman supposes that she has sufficiently aroused a man; nor does the man even try to pretend that he has been sufficiently aroused by the woman. Notice, too, what I have already said several times in various ways: Nothing in Western culture is taken as more decisive evidence of a man's homosexuality than his being moved to have an erection owing to the presence or thought of another man. By undercutting the possibility of certain illusions or forms of self-deception, the fiction of the one-breast appearance would make the enormous difference sketched above even as the idea of vaginal penetration remains unchanged.

(My aim in this fiction of the one-breast appearance has been to imagine a salient physical difference among women on the order of an erection, without losing the significant feature that an erogenous zone serves a life-based function. Even if in this scenario there would be some loss of ambiguity, because a one-breast appearance would be detectable enough, a bipartite conception of sensuality would still be very much informed by the breasts of the body. In this regard, the breasts would still be fundamentally different from the penis.)

As I indicated when I began, I have offered only a partial explanation—a fundamental consideration, if you will—for why perfectly straight heterosexual men are so attracted to lesbian scenes. Indeed, if lesbian scenes are but women entertaining themselves in the absence of "real men," suffice it to say that I have sought to draw attention to an important consideration that makes it possible for men to maintain that illusion: Owing to the absence of perceived saliency with respect to female sexual arousal, men are able to avoid taking the sexual preferences of women seriously. Men are not forced to see lesbian scenes as women who are really lesbians who have no sexual interest in men. Hence, men can entertain the fantasy that a man could always make the difference in terms of the sexual fulfillment of these women. This illusory bubble would clearly have difficulty forming, let alone being kept afloat if the one-breast appearance were not a fiction.

Let me conclude this section by pointing out that one of the most subtle and difficult to dislodge manifestations of power over others is the failure to take seriously the preferences of others. This particular manifestation of power is at its most sublime when the others, themselves, fail to take seriously their own preferences or must struggle to discern what their own preferences actually are.

CONCLUDING REMARKS: SEXUAL MALLEABILITY AND MORAL BETTERMENT

In China, great emphasis was once placed upon women having small feet—so much so that the bones of the feet of women were crushed to prevent their feet from growing. While people in Western culture are hardly oblivious to feet, it would seem, at least in North America and most European countries, that far greater significance is attached to women's breasts than to their feet. But the case of China shows that human beings have a great deal of latitude in terms of what they associate with the erotic. After all, it is not as if feet, the vagina and the penis are or ever have been all on a par with one another with respect to either reproduction or the achievement of sexual orgasm.

In a different direction, there are cultures in Africa in which the semen of older males is thought to possess male enhancing powers; accordingly, there are rites of fellatio and anal intercourse between older and younger men. Once again, this is a view of the body that is pretty foreign to Western culture. What is striking in this instance is that what is the central erogenous zone for men in Western culture is being viewed in a much more complex way. It is not my intention to recommend either of the above practices. I mention them only because they make it clear that biology is hardly decisive with respect to one's conception of the erotic. So, it is not ludicrous to ask the question: "Could there be an erogenous loop for men between being straight and gay, as there is with women?" Nor is it ludicrous to suppose that men could view erections in a much more complicated way.

But what benefits might there be? Would it be enough, if men were far less threatened by deep affection between one another? Would it be enough that, if men were far less threatened by deep affection between one another, female–male relationships would be less plagued by violence and assertions of power and control? Of course, as Andrea Dworkin implies in *Right-Wing Women* (1983), if straightforward expressions of depth of affection were common-place between men, then the relationships between women and men would be radically different. Specifically, women and in particular sex with women would not be the only routes available to men for meeting their emotional needs. Thus, as women and men endeavoured to meet their emotional needs, there would be gender pairings of all sorts, and there would be people pairings of all sorts. If these pairings took place with honesty, integrity and purity of heart, would that be benefit enough? This would truly be a very different world. Women would no longer be the sole purveyors of affirming sensuality which, in a heterosexist world, has been the essence of what leverage they have. Or so Andrea Dworkin has argued.

In this essay I have perhaps seemed fixated with the male erection. In truth, however, I am mindful of the pain and hostility that is so prevalent in this world because men are often in great need of expressions of physical warmth and affection, both from women and other men. And I am mindful of how much worse things have become, along one dimension, when progress for women has essentially meant that for some women that they should be more male-like in their behaviour. Thus, without supposing that all things are phallic, I do often entertain the thought that this would be a better world indeed if penis-identity were not such a central part of male-identity. Things need not be this way.

Every time I see a young boy holding his father's hand, indeed every time I reminisce upon my walking hand-in-hand through the streets of Jerusalem with my friend's six-year-old son, I know that male-identity could change for the better. It is not given by biology that sons and fathers stop holding hands when sons reach their pre-teen years. And without supposing that everyone should be bi-sexual or some such thing, for I see no reason to suppose that homogeneity of sexual desire is itself a virtue, I am of the mind that this world would be a much better place if, as with affection between women generally, affection between men were a rich and ongoing part of the lives of men generally.

Affirming sensuality is rightly regarded as a very prized moral and spiritual good. However, it is one which all human beings are capable of offering to one another, regardless of gender or sexual orientation. Not surprisingly, a world full of contortions results when people attempt to limit affection to specific groups or to specific kinds of pairings; affection in its purest form knows neither groups nor specific kinds of pairings, but only affection and non-affection. In particular, if affirming sensuality is the prized good that I take it to be, it can be hardly surprising that men should take such an interest in controlling women, given the mistaken view that only women are capable of providing others with this good. Inspired by Stoltenberg, I have tried to show how this mistaken view might have come about, without ever suggesting that it is an immutable part of the fabric of human life. Quite the contrary is true. Still, the elimination of some things requires that they be properly identified and that their origins be correctly characterized. Such has been the aim of this essay when it comes to understanding the differences between women and men with respect to sensual affirmation.

This essay has a moral lesson to it. One thing more loathsome than controlling others in order secure a basic need—affirming sensuality in this case—is having a distorted self-concept which prevents one from seeing that one can provide for themselves the very thing for which they are exercising power over others in order to obtain.

NOTE

1. In writing this essay, thanks are owed to many, my colleagues in France: Edward De Sapereira, Charlottte De Sapereira, Claire Zeppilli and Carol Heidseick; the students in my Philosophy 191 course (spring of 1995),

who were a most gracious and important sounding board for my initial attempt to put these ideas into essay form; and Michael Patrick Evans and Joseph Kuypers for instructive comments on the penultimate draft of this essay. In thinking about matters of heterosexism over the years, Tom Foster Digby has been a godsend. Last, but certainly not least, I wish to thank Claudia Card (Professor of Philosophy, University of Wisconsin) and Lawrence May (Professor of Philosophy, Washington University at St. Louis), both of whom offered a most instructive set of comments, not all of which I have been able to take into account.

7

Power and Equality in Intimate Relationships[1]

Clark Wolf

A s I sit down to write, my wife Rebecca is in the other room nursing our three-month-old daughter, Rachael. The presence of a child has changed our relationship forever—something tender and quiet has come between us. Sometimes we find ourselves standing beside the crib just looking at our daughter without speaking. We both wanted children from the beginning, and it was a possibility we discussed several years ago during a desert hike in a hot Tucson autumn when we were just getting to know one another. That day seems as distant as a dream now. New dreams come quickly with a new child, although sleep has been scarce during the past months.

A new child comes in a package with a huge range of new decisions to be made, new obligations and new chores, along with the benefits. Most of these are pleasant and enriching, but of course not all of them are. Contrary to the preconceptions of non-parents, dirty diapers are among the least significant of the unpleasant burdens that come along with the benefits of new parenthood. Because of these new burdens when children come, parents are often forced to re-evaluate the structure of their own relationships. It is impossible to avoid questions of how these new burdens and benefits will be distributed. I have heard some people say that the arrival of their children led them to "sort out their gender roles." What they meant, I believe, is that they decided to distribute these burdens and benefits according to traditional gender roles, placing most of the excess burden on the woman.

The possibility that children might do this to our relationship was not appealing to me or Rebecca. Both of us are pursuing careers, and we hope to share joys and burdens together, as much as possible. It might be that the easiest way to deal with new decisions is to fall back on traditions, but traditional mores have commonly run roughshod over the preferences and interests of women. Besides this, the social circumstances that made more traditional roles possible have passed. For many couples, it is no longer possible to get by with one wage-earner and one "homemaker." The two-career family may once have been defended in terms of women's right to work and her need for financial independence, and championed as a vehicle for women's social equality. But for many couples, economic circumstances have turned this vehicle into a necessity.

However, even among couples who are pursuing dual careers, women's careers are often taken less seriously, and two career families do not typically distribute household burdens and benefits equally even when careers are in other respects equal. This raises a serious question: how can family members find a way to distribute these burdens and benefits fairly and justly, and in a way that will respond appropriately to the needs of parents and children alike? Jean-Jacques Rousseau said many questionable things about families in his novel *Emile* (1762), but one insight that deserves to be preserved is his insistence that it is in families that children first learn virtues of justice and self-command. This idea has been resurrected in recent feminist writings on the family, although feminist writers are sometimes uncomfortable with the insistence on justice, which some see as a moral concept that has its home in a patriarchal conception of moral relationships. Some feminists regard justice as a peculiarly male virtue that might be eliminated entirely if people were more readily motivated by altruism, empathy and care for others. The point Rousseau makes, however, is hard to deny, whether one frames it in terms of justice or in terms of other normative concepts. By watching parents relate to one another and participating as a member of a family, children learn social and moral skills that they will later bring to their own relationships.

The challenges faced by families are serious. Adults in contemporary families often do not relate to one another in terms of justice and equality and, all too frequently, inequalities in relationships reflect stable patterns not momentary lapses. If families are themselves unjust, with benefits and burdens within the family distributed in ways that are arbitrary or unfair, the moral development of children may be seriously impeded. It is symbolically significant, in what is probably an unfortunate way, that Rebecca is in the other room nursing our child while I am in my study writing. In our culture, and most others as well, women bear most of the burdens involved in childcare and housework—the work necessary to keep a household together—while men carry a larger share of the authority and decision-making power within the family.[2]

The ideal of relationships reflecting equality and mutual respect stands in stark contrast to the structure of families which is radically inegalitarian. "Women's work" has traditionally been work within the home, while men have traditionally had far more freedom to indulge in cultural and intellectual pursuits. It is relatively rare even for avowed feminist couples to move to follow a woman's career, although it is quite common for women to move wherever their husband's career takes the family. It is well documented that women do most of the housework and childcare even in families in which both parents work full time and earn similar salaries. And men frequently exercise more authority and power in family decision-making, and exercise most of the control over the family finances. If the family is, as Rousseau insisted, a kind of school where children learn how to relate to others and where people learn the virtues of justice, respect and equality, what are children likely to learn in families that are marked by the injustice of traditional sexism and the arbitrary inequalities that still characterize most contemporary families?

There are many kinds of families. I do not mean to sidestep important questions by restricting my discussion here to heterosexual families with children. Often, especially in contemporary American political rhetoric, the term "family" is used in a way that excludes gay families and single parent families altogether. Calls to "reinforce the family" are usually smoke screens for proposals that systematically ignore the needs of families that do not fit the standard heterosexist definition. As I understand the term here, a family is simply a voluntary association of people who come together to enjoy the benefits of an intimate relationship. Ideally, family members love one another and are willing to share burdens and joys.

I focus on heterosexual families not because I believe that they represent any kind of moral ideal, but because such families raise special questions about the distribution of power between men and women. While gay relationships (for example) hold a different set of difficulties for partners and for children, such families may be less likely to incorporate the arbitrary inequalities that characterize straight families since many of the most important of these inequalities exist because of socially entrenched gender roles. I focus on families with children because I believe that the presence of children may exacerbate the inequalities that are implicit in these gender roles, and because as a new parent these problems are of central concern to me personally. Because women bear the brunt of childbearing and childcare responsibilities in our society, and because in general women already do most of the household labour, children are likely to increase the inequality of the burden sharing within a family, and to shift power in intimate family relationships away from women and toward men. Such a shift in power within a relationship raises serious questions of fairness and justice.

Many first-wave feminists insisted that the family is a political institution, and that as such families can and should be judged according to political standards. This means considering whether the family is a just institution, whether burdens and benefits are distributed fairly, whether the bonds that tie members together are (or could be) *freely chosen*, whether family members respect one another's rights, and whether members deal with one another as equals or unequals, whether the structure of families is *democratic*, *hierarchical* or *autocratic*. If there are circumstances in which some family members exercise authority or power over others, the nature of this authority must be examined, questioned and criticized.

But another recent feminist tradition holds that the family is not a political institution, and that familial bonds and relationships cannot or should not be evaluated using the same terms we use to examine political institutions. Families, from this perspective, are neither just nor unjust since "justice" is a category that simply does not apply in the context of intimate personal relationships. As citizens, from the political standpoint, we often deal with one another in terms of the rights we possess. But something has gone seriously wrong when members of a family deal with one another in terms of justice and rights. Family members' assertion of their rights against one another is a sure sign that the bonds of love and affection are broken or damaged. If family members love one another, their interests are supposed to coincide, making justice and rights irrelevant. This view sees justice as a remedial virtue since appeals to justice and demands for just treatment will not be made unless the relationship is already on the rocks.

How family members view this question of justice is important. If people think of their relationships predominantly in terms of justice and rights, this may change the nature of their interaction. If they think of their relationships in terms of care, compassion and altruism, this will also influence choices and behaviour. Special problems may arise when different participants view themselves and their relationships differently. In particular, if men and women systematically understand the terms of their relationships differently, this will lead to inequality in control and power. Obviously justice connects with power.

There are different kinds of power that can operate within relationships. At the most basic level people may exercise physical power over one another. In the context of intimate relationships such power is an indication that things have gone seriously wrong. But at a more subtle level, one can measure the operation of power in relationships in terms of whose interests are best served by the terms of interaction. For example, in American society, women traditionally have sacrificed or compromised their careers for the careers of their husbands. This may not reflect an overt exercise of power by men over women, and the choice to compromise one's career may be consensual and cooperatively made. But when social institutions systematically work to benefit some people over others, it is valuable to look into their structure and to come to a better understanding of the way different participants understand the terms of their relationships differently. Only by looking to such implicit self-understandings can we come to an accurate understanding of the subtle structure of power in such contexts.

This essay focuses on several questions of general concern in moral and political philosophy, and of personal concern to many family members, marriage partners and parents. First, I consider whether standards of fairness and justice are relevant to families and to close intimate relationships in general. I argue that they are. If it is in families that children learn to relate to others as equals, and learn attitudes of respect and justice, then families themselves must be just. But this answer raises a second question: What conception of fairness and justice is appropriate in evaluating families? Under what circumstances is a relationship fair or just, and what kinds of inequalities within a relationship are compatible with justice? This discussion focuses on the concept of exploitation. After considering a contractarian account of exploitation,[3] I argue that a minimal necessary condition for the justice of families is that they must not be exploitative in this sense. To say that a relationship is nonexploitive may be scant praise, just as saying that a relationship is nonabusive is not to say that it is healthy or just. But many family relationships are exploitative, making it important, therefore, to understand *intimate exploitation*, and to understand how personality traits and social stereotypes reinforce this exploitation.

Finally, I consider how families exist within a larger social context, and how their structure cannot be entirely separate from that context. I argue that it may be impossible for heterosexual families to be fully just in a society that is characterized by sexism and injustice. If this claim is justified, and if people would like their private relationships to be just, then it would seem to follow that sexism needs to be eliminated in the public sphere as well.[4]

FAIRNESS, CONSENT AND EQUALITY AS FAMILY VIRTUES

I cannot nurse my daughter; I lack the proper equipment and Rachael has stubbornly refused to take a bottle in spite of our efforts. Our decision to breast feed Rachael was one we made together, but it implies a heavy obligation for Rebecca—an obligation that we cannot really share. However, Rebecca was the one who really chose to breast feed, since no decision of mine could possibly have done it. Without Rebecca's choice to breast feed, my choice to do so would have been irrelevant. I am grateful to her for this choice and as supportive as I know how to be. But when supper time rolls around, I can only watch.

The decision to breast feed is a good context to consider the distribution of power and obligation within a family. For just as the choice to breast feed can be made only by a woman, the decision itself imposes a burden that cannot be fully shared. This decision meant that for many weeks Rebecca was up on nursing duty every two hours or so, whenever Rachael woke up hungry.

It is easy to *say* that such burdens can be shared or compensated. For example, couples can get up together to tend a midnight baby, or men can take over extra household chores to compensate for women's late-night nursing. Rebecca and I at first tried to share this burden outright: every time the baby woke up, I would go to her, comfort her, and bring her to Rebecca to be fed. But since then, we have agreed to distribute burdens temporally: in these early months, while Rebecca has time off from work, she has borne an extra share of the childcare burdens. When she goes back to work and my teaching term comes to an end, I will take over. We are hoping that Rachael will be able to take a bottle by then. We have not distributed burdens equally (in part because Rebecca was able to take time off from work, while I was not), but we have tried to do it in a way that was mutually agreeable and best for all three of us. Does this make it fair? Does our mutual agreement guarantee that it is just?

Fairness as free, consensual choice

One conception represents fairness in terms of free choice. If a person freely chooses to join an association, implicitly choosing the corresponding obligations, labours and benefits, then an arrangement is fair. This conception interprets fairness within a relationship as analogous to fairness in a market contract: if a person freely consents to a contract, then it is fair to hold her or him to whatever terms that contract stipulates. Applied to relationships, this conception would hold that as long as people freely enter into relationships, their continued free participation guarantees that the terms of interaction must be fair. A consequence of this view is that as long as the agreement to associate is a free choice, parties cannot complain if benefits and burdens are unequally distributed. So, for example, using this conception of fairness, the feeding arrangement we made might not be unfair, even though it distributes burdens and benefits unequally. Unfortunately, this conception of justice does not take into account the determinants of "free consent." If women "freely" accept an inequitable distribution of burdens only because they have implicitly accepted the social stereotypes that assign heavier burdens to women, this might well undermine the sense that the agreement is truly free and fair. If the society a couple lives in is sexist, how can they avoid or minimize the influence that such stereotypic associations may have on the structure of the relationship?

Consider this first from the perspective of a man who believes that his partner's preference to "stay at home and care for the kids" is informed by her identification with the stereotype that assigns women the predominant burdens of childcare. It might be advantageous for men if women identify with this stereotype, since it would leave men freer to pursue their own careers without having to make difficult choices between family and career. On the other hand, men who want the best for their children and for their spouses may worry that such stereotypes systematically disadvantage women, and may be unwilling to accept them. How should men respond in such cases? Surely it would be unacceptably paternalistic for men to override their partners' "free consent" on the grounds that this consent is socially informed and therefore not fully free. If men were to simply override women's *expressed* consent in favour of their own conception of women's *true interests* it would hardly be an improvement. Rather it would be just one more example of men failing to take women seriously.

The problem may be no less difficult from a woman's perspective. Women in sexist societies may discover that their own preferences derive, in part, from harmful stereotypes and traditional understandings of a "mother's role." Recognition of this fact might be disturbing, but this disturbance may not be sufficient to bring about a preference change. The problem is made more difficult by the fact that traditional stereotypes are not unmitigatedly bad: the association of motherhood with care and compassion, and with willingness to sacrifice for one's children makes the traditional conception of motherhood attractive in many respects.

When obligations and decision-making authority are distributed equally, there may still be residual problems. For women, such equality may leave residual feelings of guilt since many women have absorbed a stereotype that assigns them a weightier obligation than equality implies. In the same egalitarian circumstances, men are likely to feel that their behaviour is supererogatory, and that they are exceptionally good fathers. When obligations and authority are distributed equally, men will exceed social expectations while women will fail to meet these expectations. So this kind of equal distribution may still yield an unequal distribution of feelings of guilt and pride. When the sources of consent are so complex, it is difficult to accept a contractual account of "fairness as free consent" as fully adequate. But alternatives to this conception of fairness may fare even worse in comparison.

Fairness as equality

Another account of fairness represents fairness as simple equality: when people bear equal burdens in a relationship the relationship is fair. Whenever burdens and benefits are distributed unequally the relationship is unfair. According to such a simple egalitarian conception of fairness, the feeding arrangement on which Rebecca and I settled seems to be unjust. But such a rigid conception of justice may sometimes be impossible to put into practice: often there is no practical way to arrange a precisely equal distribution of burdens. I will stay at home to care for Rachael in the morning, after Rebecca goes back to work. But I cannot claim that this will equalize or compensate for the burdens of pregnancy, delivery and nursing. I am deep in debt, and if fairness requires precise equality, it seems unlikely that I can ever provide full compensation for the burdens that only women can bear. One may be deeply committed to the ideal of perfect equality, but unsure how to go about it. But it would be premature to conclude from the fact that pure equality is not always possible, even when family members are trying to be just, that justice is not relevant within family or other intimate relationships. It would be too easy, too self-serving to claim that "justice does not apply" in such circumstances. Such a conclusion might sometimes be tempting as it provides an easy way to get off the hook: if families were a context in which justice does not apply, then there would be no need even to try to make them just.

Perhaps both of these conceptions of justice miss the mark to some extent. The first contractarian conception presents a model of the family-as-marketplace in which people participate and cooperate, but only when they can be certain that it will be individually profitable for them to do so. Families should not be like that, should they? Family members share burdens for one another, and are supposed to act from love and to contribute to one another's interests even when this involves personal sacrifice. "Fairness as equality," at least in its simplest form, does not seem appropriate either. There are circumstances in which it seems appropriate to distribute burdens unequally as different family members have different abilities and different needs. Within a loving family it is sometimes appropriate for some to bear unequal burdens for the sake of others. Families can call on the allegiance and altruism of their members in a way that is not well captured by the market conception of fairness as free acceptance of burdens. Perhaps it is considerations like these that have led some people to conclude that it is simply inappropriate to apply standards of justice to families. Family members *care* about one another, and any adequate analysis of family structure must incorporate the relevance of mutual care and concern that family members will ideally have for one another.

But such a conclusion would be premature. The fact that family members ideally relate to one another on the basis of care and compassion does not imply that families and intimate caring relationships cannot sometimes be unjust, or that standards of justice and rights do not apply to such relationships. For while the care, love and altruism that are supposed to characterize the family are crucial moral virtues, they are virtues that render people vulnerable to certain kinds of exploitation and mistreatment unless they are accompanied by reciprocal attitudes in others. Some feminists have argued that women understand moral relations differently from men, and that while men typically understand such relations in terms rights and duties, women typically understand such relations in terms of care and empathy (Nodding 1984; Gilligan 1982). This type of argument carries with it serious risks, for if women's moral understandings are different from those of men, these differences may be a result of conditioning in a sexist society.

If women in sexist societies tend to be more compassionate, altruistic and caring than men, as some feminists have argued, these forms of caring must be critically examined before they can be incorporated into a self-reflective feminist ethic (Davion 1993). Such gender-linked compassion and care may cease to be virtues if they lead women to overlook their own interests. Altruism can be carried too far if altruists passively allow others to take advantage of their good will. An ethic of care may easily pass into a morality of weakness and passivity if care is not qualified by proper self-respect. It might serve the interests of men quite well for women to be altruistic, compassionate and caring, especially if it were true that men conceive of moral relations exclusively in terms of individual rights and the reciprocity of free exchange. But if the moral psychology of men and women is different in the way some feminist writers suggest, then there seems little hope that relationships between men and women will ever escape the inequities in power that still characterize most heterosexual relationships. Many feminists have recognized this and have forcefully argued that the moral universes of men and women are not so distant from one another.[5]

EXPLOITATION, ALTRUISM AND CHOICE

An appropriate understanding of the morality of intimate relationships must account for the significance that care, compassion and love have in such relationships, but must also explain the limits of such motives. If caring and a propensity to altruism make people susceptible to certain kinds of exploitation, then a full understanding of their operation in a healthy, egalitarian relationship will include an account of when caring relationships become exploitative and oppressive.

To this end, David Gauthier (1986) offers a contractarian account of exploitation. In general, contractarians evaluate human relationships by considering whether their participants could freely consent to participate in them. If not, then the terms of interaction cannot represent a fair contract. It follows from Gauthier's contractarian view that a relationship is exploitative if the terms of association do not offer expected benefits to those involved. But Gauthier excludes from consideration those benefits that people might enjoy as a result of their altruistic or caring attitudes toward others. According to Gauthier, relationships are non-exploitative only if participants would agree to their terms even if they were selfish egoists:

> the contractarian sees sociability as enriching human life; for him, it becomes a source of exploitation if it induces persons to acquiesce in institutions and practices that, but for their fellow-feelings would be costly to them. Feminist thought has surely made this, perhaps the

core form of human exploitation, clear to us. Thus the contractarian insists that a society could not command the willing allegiance of a rational person if, without appealing to her feelings for others, it afforded her no expectation of net benefit. (Gauthier 1986:11)

Gauthier does not explicitly apply this standard to relationships, and may not have intended that his model be so extended. But these remarks surely suggest a general account of exploitation. Exploitative institutions, in Gauthier's view, are institutions that people would reject if they were egoists, although they might actually accept them if they care for others, feel compassion for them, or love them. One might plausibly wonder why such a conception of exploitation should be relevant to persons like ourselves, since we are *not* egoists or sociopaths, and since we are often moved by love and care for others. Caring spouses who stay with their partners to nurse them through crippling terminal illnesses are often motivated simply by their love for their partner. If we applaud such behaviour and regard such relationships as non-exploitative, it cannot be because of the compensatory benefits such caretakers receive.

A model like Gauthier's may seem so distant and esoteric that it should not be used to evaluate actual relationships. But I would not dismiss Gauthier's account of exploitation so quickly. Gauthier would almost certainly acknowledge that there is far more to intimate caring relationships than can be captured by his simple models. The kernel of insight behind Gauthier's contractarian model is worth preserving nonetheless: People can manipulatively take advantage of one another's care and affection, and such manipulation constitutes an important kind of exploitation. If intimate relationships involve manipulation of the altruistic impulses of others, they are exploitative and oppressive. To understand why such relationships are exploitative, it will not do simply to consider whether participants' preferences are satisfied. When altruism leaves people open to exploitation by others, it is their unreciprocated preference for the welfare of others that renders them vulnerable. In such circumstances, as Gauthier suggests, it may be appropriate to consider the relationship in abstraction from the altruistic interests of the parties involved. Jean Hampton offers a sympathetic reading of Gauthier's argument:

As I understand Gauthier's remarks, he is not suggesting that one should never give gifts out of love or duty without insisting on being paid for them; rather he is suggesting that one's propensity to give gifts out of love or duty *should not become the lever that another party who is capable of reciprocating relies upon to get one to maintain a relationship to one's cost.* (Hampton 1993a:239)[6]

The problem of exploitation arises, according to Hampton, when one person freeloads on another's altruistic good will. It is arguable that the traditional "feminine virtues" are peculiarly well suited to render those who possess them especially susceptible to such exploitation. And while one may find altruism and care for others to be morally praiseworthy characteristics, in the extreme they may constitute a kind of vice. To care for others so completely that one is blind to one's own interests (allowing those one cares for to take advantage of one's good will) is to lack an important kind of self-respect. Similarly, to manipulate the affections of another person in order to gain that person's cooperation is to treat her or him with lack of respect. There is something repugnant about such a relationship even if the cooperation of the more altruistic party is freely given and motivated by love. The answer is not to eliminate altruism and care or to deny that they are virtues. It is possible to be altruistic and caring but to be unwilling to allow others to take advantage of one's good will. Proper self-respect requires that one be unwilling to exploit others in this way, but it also implies that one should be unwilling to allow oneself to be exploited.[7]

What explains the fact that women in our society bear a disproportionately large burden of household labour, and enjoy a disproportionately small amount of the power and authority in intimate relationships? One way to explain a phenomenon is to show that it should have been expected. If it is true that in North American society women are conditioned to be altruistic and to understand moral relations in terms of care and compassion, while men are conditioned to be less altruistic and to understand moral relations in terms of individualist rights and liberties, then it seems that one should expect to find just what one does find: one should *expect* to find that women bear a disproportionate burden of household responsibilities, and that men enjoy a disproportionate share of power and authority. In such circumstances, it is likely that these inequalities will reflect the kind of exploitation and injustice identified by Gauthier and Hampton. While this account of exploitation is contractarian, and focuses on the moral standards of choice and consent, it is a virtue of Gauthier's analysis that it explains how exploitation may take place in relationships even when all participants freely consent to the terms of interaction.

SEXUAL STEREOTYPES AND THE STABILITY OF THE TRADITIONAL FAMILY

Studies that purport to show that women are in fact "naturally" more altruistic and caring are inconclusive at best, and I do not mean to put too much weight on them here. Perhaps they reflect the influence of a sexist ideal of femininity-as-self-denial that is diminishing in importance as women overcome barriers that traditionally keep social power in the hands of men. Certainly it is in the interest of *men* for women to conform to an ideal of altruistic self-denial. This alone should be enough to lead us to question the ideal, and to consider whether or not it might be an artifact of an oppressive stereotype rather than a revelation of women's natural propensity for care and altruism. Marilyn Frye articulates this worry clearly:

> if one thinks there are biologically deep differences between women and men which cause and justify divisions of labour and responsibility such as we see in the modern patriarchal family and male-dominated workplace, one may not have arrived at this belief because of direct experience of unmolested physical evidence, but because our customs serve to construct that appearance; and I suggest that these customs are artifacts of culture which exist to support a morally and scientifically insupportable system of dominance and subordination. (1983:35)

We should not be too quick to regard altruism and care as biologically grounded features of women's psychology. But it is still worthwhile to consider how the images of masculinity and femininity that are implicit in the stereotypes influence the structure of intimate relationships. Perhaps even more importantly, we need to consider how these images and stereotypes influence our own preferences and psychologies. Stereotypes taught and socialized into us can find expression in reality, since we may succeed to some extent to embody them. In this way, stereotypes can represent a kind of self-fulfilling prophesy.

Imagine a society in which many or most heterosexual men, even if they are otherwise committed to gender equity, happen to be attracted to women they perceive to be slightly deferent to their own (men's) talent, intelligence and ambition. In this perhaps purely fictional place, men find women threatening when they are not modestly deferent. Men's passions, fantasies and patterns of sexual attraction are tied up with these attitudes and, as a result, men and women tend to form relationships and partnerships that incorporate this deference and the consequent inequalities that deference implies. In this place, heterosexual women, even women who are passionately committed to gender equity, are products of the same cultural background as men and, in keeping with cultural traditions, they tend to develop reciprocal patterns of deference to men. Their own expectations, preferences and fantasies are bound to the same cultural patterns as are men's, and their choices reflect this. In such a society, men and women might be passionately committed to each other and to values like equality and democracy, but it is unlikely that the relationships they form would be truly equal or democratic.

We must each ask whether or to what degree our own society fits this hypothetical description. Does this accurately describe the general pattern of heterosexual relationships we see around us and participate in? We are not simply products of our cultural traditions and stereotypes, but we cannot entirely escape their influence either. If the reciprocal attraction of men and women follows the pattern described above, we should expect to see inequalities in power and decision-making authority. We should expect to find that these inequalities characterize many facets of intimate relationships, and that the patterns that create these inequalities are passed on to the children raised in these families.

Social institutions are stable when the norms that sustain and reinforce them are passed on more or less intact from one generation to the next. The institution of the traditional male-dominated family has, unfortunately, been a fairly stable institution in American society and in many others. Clearly stability is not always socially desirable: in political contexts, dictatorial regimes are often more stable than democratic ones, but few people would regard this as a moral argument in favour of dictatorship. In the context of intimate relationships, democratization of the family may well imply a certain amount of instability, since a more democratic family structure requires that family decisions be equally responsive to the needs and valid claims of all members. The instability may have deep social costs. But the stability of unjust relationships may be nothing to celebrate and may cause much greater harm in the long run. The stable perpetuation of the traditional male-dominated family has deep social costs since such families are in an important sense unjust.

This perpetuation works at the deepest psychological level and is not typically the result of intentional or self-conscious sexism or bias. Men are not, for the most part, self-conscious oppressors, nor are women simply an innocent and oppressed group. Such simplistic models of oppression needlessly vilify men and imply that women lack responsibility for their lives and autonomy to initiate change. Sexist social institutions are passed on in patterns of thought common to both men and women, and both men and women must change before these institutions can be improved.

What are we to do if we find that our preferences are part of the problem in that they result in a family that mirrors the rejected old patriarchal ideals much more than we would like? We cannot simply deny our preferences without being false to ourselves. But if we recognize that these preferences are formed in compliance with sexist socialization and that they serve to reinforce and reproduce this sexism, then we cannot passively accept them either. If we regard the imbalance of social power within traditional families as unjust, then we have good reason to try to minimize the influence of the harmful and exploitative aspects of this traditional institution on our relationships, and to avoid socializing our children to conform to the ideals implicit in it. But how can this be achieved when our own patterns of thought and preference may reflect, to some extent, the patterns we would like to reject?

The problem for some of us may be a real conflict between the desire to be just and the desire to be true to ourselves. In the context of the democratic family, failure to express our care and our willingness to sacrifice for our partner might be a way of being false to ourselves. But to allow others to take advantage of our altruistic tendencies would show lack of self-respect. People who find that their relationships incorporate deep inequalities but who are committed to ideals of equal respect and who are unwilling to allow themselves to be exploited must find themselves faced with a serious dilemma: the distinction between behaviour that constitutes "praiseworthy altruism and care" and other behaviour that constitutes "excessive altruism and willingness to be exploited" may be difficult to draw.

What this dilemma shows, I believe, is that even couples who are seriously committed to one another, who respect each other and who are committed to the democratization of their own families may not always clearly see how to enact their ideals. Without simply denying our preferences and attitudes, how do we reject the inegalitarian structure of the families that these attitudes imply. This problem may be just as difficult for women as for men, since the perpetuation of the traditional family depends on the complicity of both women and men. Only by bringing the inegalitarian features of the institution to critical consciousness can we hope to change it and avoid socializing our children to conform to the patterns it recommends. But there is no guarantee that critical self-examination will be sufficient.

Since our attitudes and patterns of thought are first formed in the context of our families, it follows that if we want to eliminate sexism, we need to democratize the family, to make the family a more just institution. Such democratization may not be sufficient, but it is surely a necessary condition of sexual justice. More to the point, we need to democratize our own families to avoid, as much as this is possible, passing on to our children the traditional gender biased ideals of family life and family relationships. This is not an easy thing to do as it requires a re-examination of ourselves and of our own preferences and attitudes which are implicated in the institution we would like to change.

SOCIAL INEQUALITY AND INEQUALITIES IN THE FAMILY

Many features of contemporary relationships exemplify the inequalities in power between men and women. However, as already mentioned, one feature is especially poignant: it is still rare, even among avowed feminist heterosexual couples, for families to move to follow a woman's career. Couples might take some obvious steps to insure that the decision to move is mutually agreed to be appropriate and best for the family, all things considered. But even if the decision-making process *within* the family is non-sexist and democratic, it does not follow that the decision made is non-sexist. One reason for this has already been discussed: if women are more likely to be altruistic and willing to bear costs for the sake of their spouses, then a democratic agreement may reflect the interests of men more than those of women. Willingness to move for the sake of a partner's career might reflect one's care for one's partner, and one's concern that he or she be happy and successful. When such decisions are made cooperatively and are mutually agreed upon, are they not democratic and fair?

Unequal care and altruism may undermine democratic decision-making. In the starkest example, if A's judgment about what the family should do is based only on his own self-regarding interests, while B takes into account both her own interests and those of A as well, then there is a sense in which A's interests have been counted twice: once in his own vote, and again in the consideration for his interests granted by B's care for him. In more realistic cases, both parties may care deeply for one another. Relationships, we may hope, are rarely as starkly unequal as the case described. But milder inequalities may exist, and this may partly explain the fact that couples so frequently make collective choices that imply disproportionate sacrifices for women.

There are additional reasons for thinking that democratic decision-making *within* the family may not be sufficient to guarantee justice within the family. In spite of some efforts to eliminate sexism in the workplace, women still earn far less than comparably skilled men (Folbre 1995). Since family welfare depends to a significant degree on total family earnings and since, in a society that undervalues women's labour, women are likely to earn less than men even if they have approximately equivalent qualifications, it follows that if families tend to move when total family earnings will increase as a result, families will more often move to follow men's careers. Unfair disadvantages in the workplace will thus yield further unfairness within the family. There are two principal mechanisms by which the unequal social power of men and women produces inequalities within intimate heterosexual relationships. One consequence of the fact that women earn less is that women are unable to maintain their standard of living when relationships fail. While men's standard of living typically increases after divorce, women's standard of living typically plummets (Wishik 1986; Okin 1989). Because of this women are disproportionately dependent on their relationships for the maintenance of their and their children's well-being. Divorce is simply less costly for men than it is for women in general, and consequently men may be less hesitant to use the threat of divorce as a bargaining tool. Even if couples do not divorce and never consider divorce, this unequal reliance on the relationship creates inequalities in bargaining power that can yield deeper power inequalities.

A second way that social inequalities can lead to the inequalities in traditional heterosexual relationships is closely connected to the above: even when family decision-making is democratic and based on mutual love and concern, decisions may systematically benefit men more than women. For example, if family decisions about where to live and when to move are determined on the basis of overall family income, it is more likely that families will move to accommodate men's careers at the expense of women's careers. Putatively neutral grounds for group decision-making may not be truly neutral as they may smuggle in social sources of arbitrary inequality and bias. If families wish to avoid such arbitrary inequalities in power within their relationships, perhaps they must be willing to accept that justice itself may come at a price. Families may find that it is better to strive to make their relationships just, even when this means moving to follow women's careers, and even when this will reduce overall family income. Such considerations also provide an additional reason to promote social and economic equality for women (formal equality of opportunity). Formal equality may not be sufficient for substantive equality, but it is surely necessary. Until women achieve formal equality of economic and social opportunities, couples will be unable to achieve substantive equality or true democracy within their relationships.

CONCLUSION

There are limits to self-understanding that make it difficult to overcome the barriers implicit in traditional conceptions of men's and women's roles. There are traditional social constructs that are so deeply embedded that we are unable to bring them to critical consciousness and analyze them. Even when we are able to analyze and better understand our thoughts and behaviours, it is often easier to come to an intellectual understanding than to alter our behaviour. Because of these limits, it is appropriate for us to approach our lives and relationships with a degree of humility, and with a ready willingness to question and revise our understanding of fairness and justice in intimate relationships. The conclusions of moral arguments are always tentative and uncertain, since we are fallible and are typically unable to see our own biases and blind spots.

This partly explains why self-righteous moralizing is so repugnant: it betrays a false certainty and implies a condemnation of others who might earnestly disagree with our views. Perhaps one generation sees earlier relationships from a perspective that was not available to those who formed them, and this provides a critical insight that was not possible before. My children may well look at the current institutions with new insight, freed from some of the biases and blindspots of my generation. It is likely that they will find grounds for criticizing the structure of contemporary families and relationships. Parents cannot guarantee that their children will agree with them, or approve of parental choices, but parents can at least hope that their children will respect their effort to make their families both loving and just. By bringing the problems of traditional families to critical consciousness, parents can hope to make choices in a way that is reflective and informed. Perhaps this is the best anyone can do.

In this paper I have argued that standards of justice do indeed apply to intimate relationships, even where participants' interaction with one another is regulated by their care and love for one another. I have stressed Rousseau's insight that it is in families that children learn virtues of justice and care. However, traditional conceptions of justice are inadequate to capture the sense of justice that applies in intimate family contexts. Neither simple egalitarianism nor crude contractualism can be applied directly to family interactions: some family inequalities are not unjust, and sometimes free and consensual interactions can be exploitative. Even when family participation is free and consensual and governed by altruism and care, there remains a possibility that a subtle form of exploitation may still exist, such as when one family member manipulatively uses the care and altruism of another. If families are to be just, such exploitation must be recognized and eliminated. In sexist societies, conceptual associations between traditional ideals of "womanhood and motherhood" and virtues of "care and altruism" render women especially susceptible to this subtle form of exploitation. Consequently, it is women who are most frequently harmed and exploited in this sense. Other factors contribute to this subtle, intimate exploitation of women: I have argued that systematically diminished economic opportunities leave women disadvantaged when family decision-making is based on considerations of overall family income. Consequently families are unlikely to be fully just until women have achieved formal equality of economic and social opportunities. Such equality of opportunity is not sufficient, but it is a necessary condition for justice in intimate relationships.

The image with which this chapter opened is one that draws on sources of emotion and understanding that are deeply embedded in Western culture. For many people, the image of a mother nursing a child is tinted with warm associations and with a conception of motherhood that celebrates altruism, care and self-sacrifice. I have argued that these associations are not entirely benign, and that they are implicated in a conception of a women's role that is partly responsible for the inegalitarian structure of heterosexual relationships in the United States and elsewhere. There are related, but importantly different associations between this understanding of motherhood and the traditional conception of fatherhood and of the social role of men. Some of these associations are also positive: they include ideals of altruism and care that are crucial elements of a healthy moral psychology, as are the ideals of responsibility and strength that are partly constitutive of our traditional conception of fatherhood. But this traditional conception of fatherhood also includes more pernicious ideals which have allowed men to be single-minded in the pursuit of career goals, and have allowed unequal burden sharing in intimate family contexts. Is it possible to preserve what is valuable in each of these traditional social ideals, and to incorporate those valuable features into a new conception of parenthood that is not gender-associated in an unfortunate and arbitrary way? Those who hope for justice in their personal relationships should hope that this objective can be achieved. I am convinced that it is possible for men and women to form relationships that are truly equal, and that this need not involve relinquishing all of the virtues that have traditionally been associated with women's (or men's) roles. Through thoughtful analysis, we can come to better understand our concepts and our attitudes. There is hope that we can transform and improve our relationships when we bring this understanding to bear on our interactions with those we love. Such analysis may lead to new self-understandings, and may help us find ways to move away from being "women and men," and "fathers and mothers," bound to the traditional roles and associations that these categories still typically imply. Only then can we move toward a critically revised understanding of ourselves as *"persons"* and as *"parents."*

NOTES

1. Thanks to the University of Georgia Humanities Centre, and the University of Georgia Research Foundation for providing support for my work on this paper, and to Pam Sailors whose comments and insights were especially helpful. Errors and fallacious inferences are my own responsibility.

2. See Nussbaum and Glover (Nussbaum 1995) for discussion of the degree to which such gender inequalities exist in traditional cultures worldwide. Such inequalities are not limited to Europe and its cultural children.

3. In general, a moral theory is *contractarian* if it regards moral principles as principles that can be freely consented to as the object of a collective choice. Contractarian theories place special emphasis on the moral status of free consensual agreement.

4. Many feminists have argued that the "private/public" distinction is itself implicated in sexist oppression. For example, the view that domestic abuse is a *private matter* has often been used as an excuse to ignore it. While I cannot make the case for this claim here, I believe that there is a useful and non-sexist way to reintroduce such a distinction. It is worth emphasizing, however, that I do not intend to use this distinction in the traditional sexist sense.

5. See Davion (1993) and Hampton (1993a and 1993b), Nussbaum and Glover (1995) and Nussbaum (1995) for arguments against the claim that psychological or cultural differences imply differences in obligation.

6. Perhaps Hampton's reading of Gauthier is excessively sympathetic: a relationship might be "exploitative" in Gauthier's sense even if there were not the self-conscious manipulation of care and altruism Hampton describes. For

example, in Gauthier's account, the sacrifices parents make for their children, or the sacrifices partners make for their spouses might be "exploitative" even if these sacrifices take place in a context of mutual love and in the absence of manipulation. This suggests that Hampton's account of exploitation as manipulation is somewhat different from Gauthier's and may represent an improvement on it.

7. Richard McKenzie and Gordon Tullock (1989) offer a similar, although more formalized account of emotional exploitation.

8

Men's Movement Politics and Feminism[1]

Bert Young

In the dynamics of power, the relations between men and women are not necessarily more fundamental because they are more universal; but they necessarily are more universal because they intersect with *all* forms of oppression. (Noel 1994)

This chapter examines men's responses to feminism and the question of men's power. Feminists have consistently argued that men in general have neither understood nor actively supported the women's liberation movement. Their analysis even extends to the so-called "pro-feminist" men's movement (Noel 1994; Richer 1995; Wajcman 1993; Bishop 1994).

Meg Luxton, in her analysis of men's reaction to feminism, argues that although there is now popular acceptance of the goal of gender equality, men still have serious difficulties with feminist critiques of their power and privilege. She adds that many men do not actively support the fight against sexism. Luxton suggests that men need to work toward being capable of forming a strong coalition with women.

One of the things feminists most consistently ask of men is that they take responsibility for educating themselves and other men, pushing to differentiate those who unintentionally perpetuate ordinary sexism

from active sexists and woman haters. The more effectively men can
isolate the latter, the stronger the anti-sexist political movement will
be. (Luxton 1993:370; see also Frank 1993)

Feminism does require men to fundamentally question much of
what they were taught about being male and how they were supposed
to respond to women. Feminists have been asking men to radically
alter their perceptions and behaviour concerning male dominance. It is
hard to believe that most men have not had problems with this or that
they have resolved all the contradictions simply. Luxton (1993) notes
that there is a need for a history of the men who have been involved in
and responded to this anti-sexist political movement. Her conclusion is
that feminism has enjoyed few positive responses and that pro-feminist
men in particular could be much more effective in their endeavour.

A workshop at the 1987 Kingston, Ontario, Men's Conference was
one of the first opportunities in Canada for men to discuss their
responses to feminists and the women's liberation movement. Not surprisingly, the men present had various responses to the challenge of
feminism and the women involved in the struggle. Few of the
responses were what anyone would have defined as serious. Many
assumed that it would be politically correct to remain silent at the conference. Those who did respond were non-committal to the movement.
A small minority expressed concerns about how best to respond as men
to this radical demand for change.

Because questions of power were not confronted by most at the
conference, many men assumed that their attempts to become more
sensitive to gender issues comprised enough of an effort toward ending
sexism. They were trying, but their attempts may have been more self-
serving than they were ready to acknowledge. An opportunity was
missed. As a participant I felt what better way to announce to feminists
that we men were serious about the challenge. What better way to also
protect ourselves from criticism since we were not the common variety
of sexist men. Nevertheless, our response did relieve some of our guilt,
and we did work on our homophobia, our competitive spirit and our
insensitivity to others. We were to some degree changed by our
involvement in the conference and our desire to challenge other men.
But, in my opinion, we were a long way from becoming active anti-
sexist men.

SOCIALIST STUDIES AND PRO-FEMINISM

Another example of not meeting the challenge came when the Society for Socialist Studies held a gender studies session at the Learned Societies Conference in Manitoba in 1987. The two men and two women who had organized this session on Power and Sexual Relations had been involved in promoting a feminist critique of and discourse on socialist studies over the previous five years. This was the first time that academic professionals of both genders met initially in joint session, then separately, and then together again to compare and draw conclusions.

The men's group had much to say concerning sexual/social relations and ran over the allotted time. The women also had a lot to say, with one crucial difference. While the men were discussing their perspectives on sexual and gender problems, the women were discussing the chilly climate of academia and the considerable difficulty they face in getting a foot in the male academic world.

At the coffee break, the four organizers met to compare notes. The women reported that their group was so angry and distraught that they had considered not meeting with the men as planned. When the two groups did get together the chilly climate had not dissipated. While the men's group had concluded that there were a number of gender issues men had raised which were worthy of discussion, the women were stating that the past and present power/sexual relations within universities and the world around them continued to keep many qualified women out of the classrooms. They also noted examples of male colleagues who, although Society for Socialist Studies members, had done little or nothing to promote gender-fair hiring.

Many pro-feminists, at the end of the session, were very dissatisfied with socialist men's "demonstrated" lack of potential as partners in the struggle for gender equality. However, this dissatisfaction did not result in socialist feminists giving up the fight; they continued to work collectively, to publish material on theory and practice of socialist feminism and to demand a fairer share of university positions.

THE MEN'S NETWORK FOR CHANGE (MNC)

In an earlier article I wrote about the establishment of the Canadian MNC and some of its shortcomings, including men's lack of account-ability to the feminist struggle (Young 1993). Since then, the network has lost many of its active participants and its desire to continue. In August 1996 twenty-five members of the network met to decide whether the organization could survive in its present state. A strength of the meeting was the presence of pro-feminist men from across Canada. Although there was a commitment to continue and to plan a national conference the following year, it appeared doubtful whether the network would survive.

There seem to be some attempts by more liberal men to respond more effectively to feminist challenges. For example, the edited ver-sion of the recommendations coming from the 1991 National Men's Conference, Ending Violence Towards Women, Children and Our-selves, sets the agenda for pro-feminist men's action, in concert with women, for the next century. Unfortunately, since the conference there has been more emphasis on symbols and myths than on growth and action. In fact, a critical assessment of the "accomplishments" of the men's movement in Canada would likely find that the White Ribbon Campaign is its only success.

In reality, most middle-class men in Canada seem to be having a convoluted discussion with themselves. They are saying, wait a minute here, let us think about this and we will get back to you. We want time to establish a social organization to deal with this; we will call it the men's movement. While this may appear to be a defensive mode of action, it is an approach we can use to our advantage. We can start developing a new male culture, one in which men will get together with other men and find ways to tell women: we are working on it, give us some space to develop a better model of masculinity. Support us in this endeavour because we do accept your request to be "better men" and be more sensitive and understanding.

Chart 1. Summary of Five Conference Themes

IT BEGINS WITH ME	TOWARDS EMOTIONAL LITERACY & NON-VIOLENT LEARNING	CREATE A SECURE WORLD FOR WOMEN & CHILDREN	ZERO TOLERANCE FOR VIOLENCE	MEN'S CHALLENGE & RENEWAL
Daily life action commitment	Child's education & socialization to prevent abuse	Women's rights free of male abuse/exploitation	Lobby mass media: Men's violence is wrong	Not giving credence to hierarchy
Responding to sexual remarks & visuals	Lobby school boards on: Sexual stereotyping Sexist violence	Address men's violence programs Re-politicize not De-politicize Homophobia	End violence & discrimination against gay men, lesbians & bisexuals	Work to challenge & end patriarchy
Challenge media Challenge colleagues Challenge employees	Develop service plans to intervene early to: counter male violence Outreach to all populations Retrain trainers to deal with violence	End men's domination over women & children	Raise issue of men & environment next conference	Personal intervention challenge the culture of acquiesence
Start & sustain men's groups	Alter all school curriculum to reflect issues of violence	Re-instate rape shield legislation Combat workplace harassment Legislate protection	Start men's education & action groups	Men's Network for Change Dec. 1–6 White Ribbon Week

This is an edited version of the chart summary produced at the first National Men's Conference: Ending Violence Towards Women, Children and Ourselves. Ottawa, Ont., Oct. 18–20, 1991.

POWER AND THE POLITICS OF MASCULINITY

One of the most important observations to make here is that most men supposedly concerned about gender issues have opted for a masculinist position. In my view, a masculinist position seeks to reclaim and redefine powers assumed to be exclusive to men. The rise and success of the mytho-poetic movement and the more recent Christian men's movement indicate a retreat from struggling for gender equality and a growing backlash to the feminist movement.

Proof of this backlash in the mytho-poetic movement is revealed by
Bly (1990) and his followers' search for their lost boyhood as a way to
recover their authentic masculinity. Kimmel and Kaufman suggest this
helps to explain the paradoxes that result from these men's retreats:

> Men's movement leaders speak to men not as fathers but as sons
> searching for their fathers. But curiously, the attendees at the workshops
> are middle-aged men, many of whom are, themselves, fathers. How-
> ever, at the retreats, they are also asked to honour the elders, the older
> men at the weekend retreats, who are seen to embody a certain deeply
> male wisdom. But wait, are these not the same elder men (fathers) who
> abandoned their sons? (Kimmel and Kaufman 1994:282)

Kimmel and Kaufman point out that these men want to have it both ways,
they are "the victim of what others (fathers or sons) have done to them"
(Kimmel and Kaufman 1994:282). This of course provides these men with
a convenient smoke screen which ignores both their relationship with their
own children and the power imbalance between men and women.

Similarly, McBride notes that most of the rituals adopted at hese
retreats and workshops enact a wish "to graft the modernist impulse to
the supposed vitalism of aboriginal cultures."

> Reflecting the colonialist mentality of progressives from a previous
> era, theorists of the movement selectively appropriate "the primi-
> tive"—It is clear, however, that these "rediscovered," yet decontex-
> tualized, rituals are not for the benefit of indigenous cultures but the
> renewed virility of a Western (mainly white) patriarchal society in
> crisis. (1995:197–98)

The Christian men's movement embodies another search for the ideal
masculinity. Recent feminist' challenges to inequality in the power structure of the church and the liberation of sexual orientation have profoundly
disturbed the centre stone of masculine Christian theology. It should be
no surprise that there is a desire for a "real men" version of the devoted.
This consists of the call for the traditional family to be restored; divorce
is now seen as failing to be a "real man," and homosexuality is a sin.

The mission statement of the Promise Keepers, an American evan-
gelical men's ministry, asserts the belief that God will use Promise
Keepers, "as a spark in His hand to ignite a nationwide movement

calling men from all denominations, ethnic and cultural backgrounds to reconciliation, discipleship and godliness" (Ellis 1995:84). The ministry claims that it drew over 50,000 men to its revival in Anaheim, California, over 60,000 to Hoosier Dome in Indianapolis, and a capacity crowd of 52,000 to Folsom Field in Boulder, Colorado.

Thus the men's movement has mostly focused on maintaining male privilege. Despite twenty years of engaged feminism, men have not woken up to the reality of the genuine political struggle for gender equality (see Luxton 1993). In contrast to most (white middle-class) men, women have been excluded from power. Men, as the power brokers, have not experienced this exclusion and therefore their prime motivation for getting together is mutual protection from women's demands for equality. For most men this amounts to spending a lot of time trying to explain and comprehend the men's movement. There is not much to explain, other than the reality of power. Men's studies may be a justifiable pursuit, but as a movement there is little talk of joining women in the struggle to overthrow paternalistic power relations. Most men do not want a transformation of gender relations, so instead they have created a mythic and self-gratifying response to women's liberation.

Thus the lines between liberal, mytho-poetic and Christian masculinists have become blurred. In fact, most men's movement men have found a way to restore their lost manhood by attempting to become de-feminized. Of course this route to manhood is much easier than through gender equality since the former requires no dialogue, no confrontation and no second guesses as to what is at stake for both genders. The masculinist response to gender equality is a far cry from Luxton's challenge.

The latest example of this masculinist response comes from Andrew Kimbrell's recent book on the politics of masculinity, *The Masculine Mystique* (1995). His understanding of the new "men's movement" is that

> these men are joining together to recover the lost elements of masculinity, mourn the lost fathers and sons of the last decades, and reestablish their relation to one another and to the earth. Together they are searching for ways to fundamentally challenge the social structures responsible for the problems of so many men. (xv)

Kimbrell's central argument is that the feminist struggle for liberation has deliberately ignored the hidden and public cost to men of men's oppression. Kimbrell's solution is the same as most men's movement thinking: feminism has not helped, on the contrary it has made things worse and we men should now take over again and solve the problems. This is his set of solutions:

- Men must fight for reduced work hours and a shorter work week.
- Men must struggle inside the business world to develop pro-father policies.
- Men need to fight the discrimination they face in family courts.
- Men need to fight for custody legislation that "demilitarizes" divorce and allows both parents maximum contact with children after divorce.
- Laws must also be enacted that encourage unwed fathers to play a central role in their children's lives.
- Federal, state and local governments, and the private sector should be encouraged to support expanded counselling and job training programs for unwed fathers.
- Welfare reforms must include changes that eliminate the current anti-father bias.
- Federal programs should encourage establishment of paternity.
- The men's movement must be at the forefront in educating parents on the potential risks faced by children of single-parent families.
- Federal tax policies should be changed to encourage the maintenance of two-parent families.
- Each father and son should take action within their own family to become better fathers.
- Men must launch a national effort to recruit men as teachers for elementary school grades.
- Each man should do mentoring.
- There should be counselling for unemployed men.
- Men must work to increase job safety and there should be more emphasis on protecting male health.
- Men should be at the forefront of struggles to protect the natural world.
- Men should promote appropriate human-scale technologies.

(Adapted from Kimbrell 1995:314–27)

Kimbrell's conclusion is that men should stand up, take over and destroy forever the masculine mystique!

If these "solutions" were attained they would constitute the largest and most dangerous backlash against women's advances over the last two and a half decades. The assumption inherent in this manifesto is that, given legislative changes, most men/fathers would come flocking to the nest ready to greatly increase their parental participation. It assumes that without giving up much of their present status and privilege, men would do whatever is necessary to rid themselves of sexist and homophobic attitudes and behaviours. It also assumes men would become non-violent, sensitive and caring lovers and respect their partners' sexual autonomy without being ready to compromise their own.

Since women have struggled for many years, and have been at the forefront of the ecology and appropriate technology movement, men will resist by taking over and demanding their *rights* to participate. Kimbrell's manifesto assumes that while structural changes may contribute to greater male participation, they will be at the expense of the established safety nets for women and children. The dire effects his solutions would have demonstrate nothing but social conservatism. One needs only look at the "dangers" of one-parent families to realize that the threat comes from under-funding, not lack of a father.

Moreover, there is no indication that these solutions are to be co-ordinated by a coalition of men and women. This suggests that Kimbrell's arguments are anti-feminist and sexist; men want their power restored and intact. He assumes that the neglect of men has occurred because women were too busy liberating themselves. It would seem that men were so busy reacting to the demands of feminism that they ignored their own health and happiness. Kimbrell does admit that a small powerful group of men have held the majority of political and financial power over most other men and women. What he does not address is that much of this power is institutionalized and as such, is more beneficial to most men, regardless of their social status.

Kimbrell does not suggest that men and women working together constitutes a solution. In fact, he is much more adamant that a group of men must rise to reassert their new found masculinity, free of guilt and blame, to build a spirit of community. He has little or no desire to trust women and feminism. In his words, feminists have been the traitors of liberation. He sees them as selfish and misguided, and supported by academic dreamers and others who have ignored the plight of most men. Instead Kimbrell offers men a new family dynamic and community where they can once again be healthy, wealthy and wise.

GENDER AND POWER POLITICS

Ironically, Kimbrell ends his treatise on the politics of masculinity where he should have begun. Much like the 1991 National Men's Conference and its growth and action chart, the dialogue must begin and end with women. This is the only solution. A true dialogue between men and women about gender equality cannot begin with a catalogue of the horrible things happening to men and why everyone should care!

The masculinist approach also ignores the socially constructed reality of global restructuring and neo-feudal politics. The dismantling of the social security network, the rise of social conservatism and a fear-infested employment future all point to the precarious future agenda for men and women.

Kimbrell and others can demonstrate that many dead-beat fathers are penniless, that Black and white single-parent families do not do as well as intact families and that most men need to rid themselves of the masculine mystique. But it is naive and wrong to think that these social conditions can be changed by presenting a manifesto for men. The much more difficult alternative is for both genders to set their priorities together in view of building respect and equality. Once agreed upon, a common priority promoting the greatest general level of economic well-being for all would have a far better chance of success.

Can men respond to Meg Luxton's challenge? I hope so. After all, like most challenges, achieving equality must have its own rewards that are worth the risk of sharing power and privilege. To think otherwise is to ignore men's fear and anxiety and to project it onto women. Reversing the blame for the problem and remaining divided leaves the male power brokers relatively safe.

Hope for a positive male response to the feminist challenge has to start with an understanding of the false-victim psychology prevalent in much of the masculinist discourse. Michael Kimmel provides insight into a group he calls "marketplace men." He argues that the constant fear of not living up to the demands imposed by the cult of masculinity produces a paradox in which men have virtually all the power and yet feel powerless as individuals. Much frustration and anger stems from the feelings of men who were raised to believe themselves entitled to feel power, but do not (Kimmel 1994).

This paradox, however, will not be resolved by segregated male events. According to McBride, it only reinforces hostility against mothers and women in general.

> The intellectuals of the men's movement claim that the solution to the violent potential of "warrior energy" lies in the separation from women and the renewal of male identity in segregated men's groups. Yet this proposal does little to address the issue of the origin of male hostility. (1995:207)

The following examples are proof positive that many men want to defend their *masculine* right to power; they do not want to take the risk of losing it or sharing it. Troy Rampey, a cohort of Robert Bly, reflects these feelings:

> Anti-feminism is not what the men's movement is about that I can see. It's about men saying "I'm doing everything I'm supposed to, and it feels awful." There are three options for women. They can be full-time mothers, full-time careerists or half-time each. And men have three options too: make money to support the family, make money to support the family, make money to support the family. The women's movement is political: they want equal rights and pay. The men's movement is not focused at all, beyond men saying, "Our lives suck. We're white middle-class men, supposedly the envy of the world—so why doesn't it feel good." (cited in Brown 1991:D4)

The same cry is heard from one of Bly's co-leaders, Robert Moore:

> It is time for men . . . to stop accepting the blame for everything that is wrong in the world. There has been a veritable blitzkrieg on the male gender, what amounts to an outright demonization of men and a slander against masculinity. (cited in Johnston 1992:29)

Another example comes from a Vancouver Island men's newsletter, *Island Men*, in a comment on the issue of violence against women:

Men's physical violence is reported daily in the media. Against women, such violence is more than likely an act of cowardice. But how often does it derive from a sense of powerlessness in the face of other more subtle and less visible acts of violence? We cannot begin to solve it by blaming each other. (Doyle 1992:9; see also Kimmel 1994)

CONCLUSION:
THE POWER OF COALITION POLITICS

While the head butters and the pledge takers have reached out to those men who feel dispossessed at the same time as they exercise real social power over women, progressive men have yet to come up with an agenda which connects their feelings of alienation to the futility of the marketplace approach. Ironically, while these feelings remain unresolved they block out the gender equality debate and divert men's focus away from supporting feminists' efforts to reorganize power relationships.

As pro-feminist men our difficulty is having to shed our traditional safety nets and take the risk of declaring ourselves political activists. David Gutterman argues that there exists a subversive potential for pro-feminist men:

> Profeminists are often most effective when they use their culturally privileged status as men as a platform from which to disrupt categories of sexual and gender identity. . . . Thus whereas women and gay men often are forced to seek to dismantle the categories of gender and sexuality from culturally ordained positions of the "other," profeminist men can work to dismantle the system from positions of power by challenging the very standards of identity that afford them normative status in the culture. (1994:229)

While this may work on the individual identity level, Gutterman also recommends a politics of coalition. He argues that coalition politics works best when the players accept the contingency and fluidity of masculinity rather than trying to figure out a new cultural script for masculinity. McBride agrees that men cannot work through these conflicts by talking to each other; men need a coalition with women, not a movement of their own.

Gender equality is thus a good and a necessary goal for all but a chosen few. Let us not write a history of the "men's movement," but rather let us help make and write the history of the gender equality movement.

NOTE

1. I would like to thank Eileen Young, artist and partner, for reading an early draft of this chapter, and Carl Witchel, humanities instructor at John Abbott College and long time friend, for his editing and constructive criticism.

Gay Male Pornography/ Gay Male Community
Power Without Consent, Mimicry Without Subversion
Christopher N. Kendall

ON POWER AND THE NEED FOR COMPASSION

I came to New York to find a community. Well, I found one—one in which *who* I am is irrelevant and *what* I am is everything. And what I am, I am now told, is "a bottom," a role defined for me by men who don't give a damn about me as a person—men who care only about using me to make sure they are "on top." Men who would rather fuck than talk and for whom sexual gratification is one-sided. (Ken, aged 21, 1995)

I realized a couple of months ago that I was gay. So I bought some porn magazines because I thought that would be a good way to learn about what it all means. What I learned was that I am too ugly to be gay. I can't look like that. I'm too skinny and not butch enough. I don't have a lot of money for nice clothes and, frankly, the sex part is all a bit scary. How can I enjoy something which looks so painful? I have always been told that I was a sissy. I had hoped other gay men might not care. I couldn't have been more wrong. (Thomas, aged 16, 1995)

Something has gone terribly wrong with gay male liberation. The notion of empowerment, of encouraging a self-confidence that ultimately leads to the public expression of dissent and the rejection of those values that daily result in all that is anti-gay, has been replaced with a selfish, misguided commitment to male dominance and the right to overpower. Equality, in the form of compassion, mutual trust and respect, has been abandoned for a community ethic and identity politic that encourages and promotes the very essence of inequality: hyper-masculinity and a polarization of gender such that "male" equals top, equals power.

For gay men who have always been ridiculed and abused for their perceived failure to achieve the hyper-masculine ideal, the power offered from conformity to it, while initially appealing, is both a facade and politically myopic. Nonetheless, many gay men have adopted this ideal as their preferred form of identity. The result is a gay male liberation committed to hierarchy and the inequality, including gay male inequality, that results from heterosexual male dominance and the power that sustains it—a movement committed more to the idea of being "men," as socially defined, than to challenging those character traits and enforced gender stereotypes that have always been the source of gay men's inequality and which will continue to result in the suppression of any discourse which strives to validate our right to be gay.

Gay men need to re-evaluate what being gay means, why being gay is deemed socially unacceptable and how we, as a community, respond to systemic stigmatization and hate. More importantly, however, we need to re-examine what we are saying to each other about appropriate gay male behaviour. We need to determine if the model of behaviour we are advocating is a positive and effective challenge to homophobia and systemic inequality or simply another medium through which to sustain male gender privilege and the harms that result from gender hierarchies.

In this chapter, I argue that the gay male community is presently obsessed with physical and psychological masculinity, with obtaining and benefiting from male power and privilege—a commitment which only supports those who seek to render gay men socially and politically invisible. Commencing with an analysis of gay male pornography,[1] I argue that the message conveyed in it—a message now readily defended by many gay male activists and academics alike as liberationary and progressive—pervades all aspects of gay male culture such that we now find ourselves promoting a model of behaviour more concerned with self-gratification and the right to dominate and control than with self-respect and respect for others. This adherence to power in the form of hyper-masculinity simply reinforces those models of behaviour that are the source of heterosexual male privilege and the homophobic rejection of any public expression which challenges it.

What is needed is a definition of gay male sexuality and identity that is radically subversive—one in which erotic empowerment is linked to companionship, trust and partnership. What is needed is an identity that rejects assimilation, masculine mimicry and the notion that power over someone is sexy—one which instead finds strength in compassion, self-respect and respect for others. What is needed is the gay male rejection of a community and culture that has bought into the myth of male entitlement and that continues to valorize and eroticize sexist and homophobic power relations. What is needed is a community and identity which encourages justice-doing and which is based on mutual trust and the type of pleasure which can only be found in relationships built on equality. In other words, we need a community which embraces sex equality and which turns its back on the homophobia and sexism that presently permeates gay men's sexual and social practices.

Why sex equality?

One might have hoped, given the amount of political effort expended by feminist women on behalf of gay men, before and after the onslaught of AIDS (Ross 1995), that the gay male community might join in and participate in the feminist struggle for sex equality. Unfortunately, quite the opposite has occurred. Confident that gay male liberation is just that—gay male and gay male alone—many gay men have severed ties with early and present feminist commitments to social justice and have instead embraced a "men only" ideology far removed from the fight for sex equality (Frye 1983; Edwards 1994). They have developed and now promote a movement which they believe promotes social justice but which actually goes a long way toward ensuring that sexual and systemic equality will never be achieved.

I suppose the question for many gay men is: so what? Why worry about sex equality if the real issue is homophobia? An answer to this question is vital for I remain convinced that until gay men fully understand that sexism and homophobia are inextricably linked, they will not understand that their present drive toward manhood is also of necessity anti-woman and, as such, very much the source of all that is anti-gay. Admittedly, the fact that our present obsession with being "male" typifies all that is sexist, discriminatory and selfish should be reason enough for rejecting it. Unfortunately, given the incredible reluctance on the part of many gay men to look outside their own community, I am skeptical that the reality of *other* disenfranchised persons and our role in creating their reality will prove sufficient as a means of convincing these men that they need to radically rethink *their* attitudes and behaviours. What is needed instead is a rather blunt analysis of the meaning of homophobia for gay men and society at large—what it does, who it benefits and why. More importantly, however, what is needed is a timely reminder about the relationship between homophobia and sex discrimination and the need to attack both simultaneously.

To reap the benefits awarded those who are "male" means to accept, indeed worship, masculinity—i.e., a socially constructed set of behaviours, ideas and values which ultimately define who belongs to that gender class and which dictates who gets and maintains the power commensurate with male gender privilege.[2] To benefit from male privilege also requires that one support compulsory heterosexuality—an ideology and a political institution which embodies those socially defined sets of behaviours and characteristics that ensure heterosexual male dominance generally and the resultant gender inequality (Rich 1980; Goss 1993).[3] The hostility directed at gay men finds its source in a male power structure directed at preserving compulsory heterosexuality. The notion that relationships, monogamous or otherwise, can function without gender inequality, without male power expressed over and in control of a female subordinate, sends a rather disturbing message to those for whom male power and the gender inequality that results from it is so very important.

Gay men, to the extent that they choose to build same-sex relationships based on mutuality and respect, relationships which reject hierarchical gender roles and the power relationships that result from gender polarization, are seen as a threat to male supremacy because they challenge the social constructions assigned to the definitions "male" and "female." In a world built on sexual hierarchy, nothing is more threatening to those who benefit from it than the notion that there can be love and justice between equals, that inequality need not be. Homophobia—which is a reaction to the actual or perceived violation of gender norms—is aimed at silencing gay men because the public expression of their sexuality is seen as undermining male dominance, for which gender inequality is necessary. Its effect is to ensure that men do not violate those gender roles central to maintaining male power and that gay men are stereotyped and ultimately suppressed to the extent that they do violate them. For gay men, this results socially in silence, for fear of being identified, and results in invisibility. And this is exactly what homophobia is about: ensuring that gay men, to the extent that they do not conform, to the extent that they do not partake in a system of sex inequality, are brutally suppressed and ultimately rendered invisible (Pharr 1988).

It is this last point upon which the remainder of this chapter focuses, for this is exactly what gay male pornography and the community built around its value system is about—promoting/ensuring conformity through masculine mimicry, a system that upon examination can be seen to promote all that is pro-male dominance, hence anti-woman and of necessity anti-gay. It is my belief that gay male pornography is at a very basic level homophobic (Stoltenberg 1990a; Kendall 1993). At its core is the idea that power can only be found via hyper-masculinity and that those who fail to adopt that power are disempowered and ultimately stripped of male privilege. Homophobia works to maintain gender roles because it silences those whose sexual identity and behaviour, it is believed, will bring down the entire system of male dominance. Gay male pornography works to maintain gender roles by encouraging gay men to adopt an identity that valorizes male dominance and by stating unequivocally that those who do not adopt this identity have no value, no power. It is thus homophobic and, as such, is also a form of sex discrimination (Koppelman 1988; Fajer 1992). It ensures that those models of sexual behaviour which might undermine sex inequality are suppressed and that women and those men who *do* fail to conform remain unequal.

In supporting a medium which is homophobic, gay men maintain their own oppression by guaranteeing that sex inequality remains intact, for without sex discrimination, without the need for a compulsory heterosexuality through which sex inequality is maintained, society would not need homophobia—one of the means through which sex discrimination is preserved.[4] By rejecting pornography as identity, by rejecting a model of identity replete with homophobic deployments of gendered and genderizing power relations, gay men would reject that means of maintaining sex inequality. In so doing, they would further erode homophobia as an oppressive system of sexual regulation. By failing to do so, gay men commit to a male, heterosexist power structure that is central to their own oppression and the oppression of all women—a commitment which, in addition to being all too typically sexist, is politically short-sighted given the extent to which sexism and homophobia are intimately connected. This becomes even more apparent once we examine what gay male pornography is and what it says about the meaning of "gay male" and the community through which gay men aim to find support, confidence and empowerment.

PORN'S MUSCLE, GAY MANHOOD

Available Now From Champions Video Releases

MARINES ($39.95): Marines are the macho men with the most of everything important. Watch with eager anticipation as they stroke their weapons into a shooting frenzy. Are you man enough for the marines?

DON'T KISS ME ($42.95): Body builders, gymnasiums, sweat, muscle, showers, sex. The bodies and meat are hard. Give my muscle a good work out. Can you remember the first time? I can, but don't kiss me. I'm straight. (*Champions Video of Australia*, November 1994)

No where is the definition and meaning of gay manhood more evident than in the now widely produced, distributed and consumed gay male pornography. Defended as free speech (Strossen 1995),[5] promoted as the source of all that is liberation (Stychin 1992) and justified as self-affirming (Sherman 1995), gay male pornography has been effectively marketed as radical and anti-establishment.

As a gay male too often silenced for challenging the idea that heterosexuality must be compulsory, I am acutely aware of the need for free speech. As a gay male raised in a society in which same-sex sexuality, my sexuality, remains taboo and is not discussed, I am also aware of the need for positive images of that/my sexuality. As a gay male now educating students about gay rights and the need for gay liberation, I am also aware of the need for effective education and communities of support. To me as a gay male, free speech, liberation and self-affirmation mean a great deal. What I would like to know, however, is what exactly pornography has to do with my right to be free from homophobic attack, my right to express dissent and my right to develop a gay male identity free from socially encouraged self-loathing and self-hate.

Gay male pornography offers those who use it two choices. It tells them they can either be the straight/dominant "men" society has told them they have never been or they can be the feminized/subordinate "others" used by those "men." In so doing, it invites them to participate in a sexual dynamic premised on hierarchy, the polar opposite of all that is equality. With titles like *Fuck Me Like a Bitch*, *I Was a Substitute Vagina*, *Beat Me Till I Come*, *Muscle Beach*, *Slaves to the SS* and *Stud Daddy*, gay male pornography sends a very clear message about what the gay male is or should be today: young, muscular, "good looking," preferably white, definitely able-bodied. In all of these materials, it is the physically more powerful, more dominant, ostensibly straight male who is idealized (Kendall 1993:31). Racial difference is a factor but only to the extent that racial stereotypes are sexualized and perpetuated (Mercer 1988; Fung 1991; Forna 1992; Browning 1993) and this too contributes to a sexuality that is rarely, if ever, mutual and based on compassion or equality.

What one gets from gay porn then is a sexuality that epitomizes inequality: exploitation and degradation of others, assertiveness linked with aggression, physical power linked with intimidation and non-consensual behaviour advanced and sexually promoted as liberating—in sum, an identity politics which encourages/is all that is "top" and masculine and which rejects all that is non-masculine, gender "female." The result is a sexualized identity politic which relies on the inequality found between those with power and those without it, between those who are dominant and those who are submissive, between those who are top and those who are bottom, between straight men and gay men, between men and women—a politic which is the very essence of homophobia and sexism.

It has been argued that any perceived inequality evident in gay male pornography is immediately rendered non-harmful, indeed subversive, because in it, unlike in heterosexual pornography, women are not sexually exploited. Men assume the submissive role normally afforded women and the whole idea of male dominance is thus questioned because it becomes evident that men too can be dominated (Stychin 1992:878). This argument is not sustainable.

Power is not dependent upon the biological capabilities of those who exert it. Straight pornography is harmful not simply because it presents a biological male violating a biological female, but because of the model of behaviour offered the biological male and presented/sexualized as normal, male gendered behaviour. The mere absence of biological "opposites" does very little to undermine the very real harms resulting from materials in which "male" equals masculine, equals dominant, equals preferable.[6] The fact that a biological male can also be bottom is in many ways irrelevant if, in order to be that bottom, he is required to assume those characteristics which ensure that those who are "men," socially defined, remain on top and are worshipped as such. The coupling of two biological males does nothing to undermine sexual and social power hierarchies divided along gender lines if those behaviours central to the preservation of gender hierarchy (cruelty, violence, aggression, homophobia, sexism, racism and ultimately compulsory heterosexuality through which heterosexual male dominance is preserved) are not themselves removed from the presentation of sexuality as power-based. Because gay male pornography reinforces gender stereotypes and the inequalities inherent in them, it reinforces those characteristics and behaviours which ensure that heterosexuality remains the norm and is compulsory because it does little to advance a model of gay identity that *subverts* those socially prescribed gender roles through which heterosexual male privilege is maintained.

The argument has also been made that the harms of gendered power inequalities evident in straight porn are undermined in gay porn because the men in gay porn and gay men generally have the "option" of participating in a role reversal not normally afforded women. That is, they can "take turns" being top and bottom, thus further challenging the idea that gender roles are fixed or immutable and thereby questioning the assumption that men must always be on top.

What arguments of this sort overlook is the fact that although roles can be reversed, there are still clearly defined roles which support a "which of you does what to whom" mentality. There is always a top and there is always a bottom, carefully articulated so as to differentiate between those with and those without power. What proponents of gay porn are really advocating is that gay men participate in a rather bizarre form of mutuality based on reciprocal abuse. In other words, I am expected to find strength in and be empowered by a model of "equality" which liberates by stressing that while I might at one level be expected to assume the status of a weak, submissive, subservient "bottom" at the hands of a descriptively more masculine "top," any resulting disempowerment is rendered non-harmful because I also have the option of becoming that top if I so desire. Frankly, I desire neither. I neither want to control or be controlled. I neither want to dehumanize or be dehumanized. I neither want to overpower or be overpowered. What I want is *real* equality, something not offered in gay male pornography. For what this focus on role reversal as a means of undermining gender inequality overlooks is the fact that the pleasure to be found in gay porn remains very much the pleasure derived from being controlling and dominant. Hierarchy remains central to the act and while there is "mutuality," it is only to be found in the form of shared degradation and sexualized inequality.

Admittedly, some will argue that they find validation in the pornographic representation of dominance and submission because it reaffirms that they can be sexually penetrated and should not feel ashamed of the pleasure found in anal intercourse (Bronski 1984). In other words, while there is strength to be found in power-over (Fox 1979), there is also affirmation in power-under. I would probably be more willing to accept this argument if the pleasure promised did not require that the person penetrated (in the context of all pornography, dominated) assume the status of someone being punished for their failure or inability to be a gendered equal. I want to ask those men who find validation in the pornographic sexualization of submission what it says about being gay generally that our chosen identity must be realized at the hands of a masculine, ostensibly straight male. Why, specifically, must sexual pleasure and the empowerment allegedly promised by it be found only in the form of submission presented as atonement for perceived gendered inadequacy? Why must sexual pleasure for some of us be found only in the form of punishment and abuse? And for those who choose instead to abuse, I have another question. What does it mean for their liberation and mine that power is found only in the ability to emulate those sexual/social behaviours that, once accepted, ensure that sexual power is afforded only those who reject equality and who, in so doing, reinforce the very foundations of compulsory heterosexuality and the harm, including homophobic harm, that results from it.

The "pleasure" which pro-porn advocates argue is found in role reversal is a pleasure which relies on sexualized hierarchy. It is a pleasure defined by power and by those who already have power. While some might gain pleasure from being dominated, from being verbally and physically abused and ridiculed (and again one must ask why), it is worth noting that not all of us are eager to participate in any process of shared dehumanization. By promoting its distribution, by defending/justifying its message, however, and by masking the abuse presented as an issue of consent or free will, gay men do little to offer protection to those of us for whom this deemed consent is anything but consensual.

I also question whether the pleasure allegedly found in being the bottom to a masculine top and the ability/willingness to take turns being that bottom (the pornographers' corrupted version of reciprocity) is in fact as readily promoted in gay porn as advocates would have us believe. For while we acknowledge that there is always a bottom in gay porn, it is I think probably also widely accepted that the real power promised by gay porn, the real focus of all that is deemed to be sexually stimulating, is found in the hands of those who are presented on top[7] and who, as such, assume the status of real men. And while this top might assume the role of a submissive bottom, the fact remains that when he does so he becomes descriptively less relevant, less powerful. He is stripped of the male power derived from eroticized masculinity and instead assumes the role of someone whose manhood is lessened.

Hence, while gay men have the option of being both top and bottom, the fact remains that there is always a top and *he* is very much the focus and idealized masculine norm. As that top, he alone is given liberty to refer to those beneath him as "girlie," "whores," "bitches," "sluts"—read "female" socially defined. In essence, because he is overtly masculinized, he ensures that those beneath him are in turn feminized. The gay male pornographic focus on the party who ultimately penetrates, and valorization of the more aggressive, more masculine, more male penetrator, thus offers much support to the argument that in order to "fuck" you need to be superior and that in order to be "fucked" you need to be sexually accessible and socially inferior.

Some have argued that, gender inequality (that "feminist issue") aside, gay male pornography is necessary as a mechanism for the dissemination of safe-sex education. Again, I remain unconvinced. To begin with, most gay pornography today fails to deliver a safe-sex message. The condom is neither seen nor discussed. In addition, in discussing safe sex it is very difficult to put the issue of gender inequality aside. Safe sex within the context of sex between unequals is also very much a feminist issue. What one sees in gay porn is a sexual model that copies the power inequalities present in straight sex—wherein (male) power is gained by controlling/dominating those one fucks—power which "is predetermined by gender, by being male" (Dworkin 1987:126).[8]

Gay sex today attempts to look (and does so quite successfully) a lot like the sex that straight men have. Socially, the act of penetration, of fucking, determines who controls whom and who, as a result, gets male power. All pornography focuses on the right of the masculine top to penetrate the disempowered bottom, be it a woman or a less aggressive male who as such is socially feminized and rendered socially less significant. It is not surprising, therefore, that gay porn continues to present unprotected penetrative sex, that is, penetration in which the condom is either not used or, for the purposes of pornographic sale, is carefully concealed (Patton 1991). Because AIDS is still viewed as a gay disease, safe sex has come to be regarded by society at large as gay sex.[9] For gay men desperate to be real men, rejecting safe sex thus allows them (or so they believe) to become less gay, more masculine, more like the straight men they are told they should be—the real identity sold in gay male porn and one which, once accepted, has particularly horrific results.

Given what the sex in gay porn has come to represent, it is clear that in many ways safe sex stands to emasculate the pornographic symbol. For safe sex to work, one needs to accept that both parties have rights—the right to protection and, more importantly, the right to a recognized human existence. In a sense, safe sex represents a form of negotiation imposing limits on sexual conduct. It represents a negotiation between relatively equal parties. It also recognizes that there are limits on what one can do without the consent of the other. Given then that gay porn presents a sexuality in which men do not need consent and safe sex undermines the apparent right of men to do as they please, it is not surprising that any "appliance" which imposes a limit on this right is not promoted. In straight sex, women are generally made responsible for protecting themselves physically with contraceptive techniques and devices which can cause irreparable harm and sometimes cause death. In straight sex men are deemed to have no responsibility whatsoever for the safety and comfort of their partners. Similarly, in gay porn, real men do as they please while fags simply hope for the best—an arrangement which is troubling given that queers in gay porn are offered no voice with which to insist on safe sex and are instead told that they should simply find gratification underneath the weight of a real man who wants to use them.

Like heterosexual pornography, gay male pornography thus glorifies those who have always had power and who have always benefited from dominance and social inequality—white, able-bodied, straight men. It tells gay men that they can choose between an identity which requires that they remain that which society has told them they already are (i.e., weak, feminized) and one which requires that they become that which society has told them they are not (i.e., masculinity linked with aggression)—"options" which do nothing to undermine the very power dynamics which result in the often violent rejection of any gay male expression not supportive of heterosexual male power.

PORNOGRAPHY AS COMMUNITY AND THE MEANING OF INVISIBILITY

Sydney: Slave looking for businessman/lawyer with speedos. I will obey your every command.

Me: 32 (look much younger), average looks, solid. Bottom only, into hot oral and big equipment, receiving dildos and into fist-fucking. Ready to meet heavy, strict, cruel, use anyway you want master. Punish, torture if it pleases. I'm yours for the taking. (Classified advertisement 1993:83)

It's like a fraternity and the initiation is working out. ("Dom," self-described muscle boy as quoted by Dickson 1994)

Pornography does not end on the page or on the screen. In addition to the very real harms caused to the young men used to produce it,[10] gay male pornography has a much larger systemic effect and one which is now more apparent than ever before—i.e., a gay male culture and community obsessed with manliness and a sexuality defined by power and the right to overpower. Whether it be within the confines of the gay bar, the gym, the bathhouses or cruising parks, or even on the street, gay male identity today is an identity concerned less with compassion and any commitment to others than with self-gratification and the satisfaction of knowing that gay men can also reap the benefits afforded "real" men as long as they are willing and able to become real men. Gay men argue that they have redefined manhood by cloning their oppressors such that it is now difficult to distinguish between straight and gay. This is not a redefinition. It is merely mimicry and assimilation leading to gay male invisibility. Gay men have excelled at becoming the men society has told them they should be. But this has not come without a price.

The gay male entering a gay bar or seeking physical, sexual contact in gay zones like the bathhouses, is confronted with a community quick to define his status, his role in that sexual "game" we call cruising. Given the power and influence of gay male pornography in our community, it is not surprising that cruising—objectifying others or waiting to be objectified—relies heavily on the role play and models of behaviour offered in gay pornography. Gays in bars cease to be people. They are denied a human identity and are instead offered a pre-determined sexual identity void of humanity. They (attempt to) become the chests, buttocks and bulging biceps meant to turn others on and if they fail to meet the sexual standard, they simply cease to exist. The result for many is a concerted effort to become the embodiment of physical perfection. They follow a recipe for success in which masculinity is the main ingredient and soon define and are defined according to what they think they are going to do *to* others or *for* others.

This need to "blend," to be all that a community obsessed with manliness says a man should be, results in incredible self-loathing, low self-esteem and self-hate. The standard set is one that is not easily met and cannot easily be maintained. As Dr. Richard Quinn, a Sydney-based gay physician explains:

> People can develop serious psychological problems from images presented to them, and images in porn videos contribute to this. So many gays feel they haven't got anything to offer because they can't live up to the expectations that are thrown at them on how they should look. They feel that because they don't have that certain look that nobody wants them. (Harris 1993:46)

For many gay men who have long been denied participation in a society quick to suppress their self-expression and individual development, the imagery the gay male community offers as identity also results in overwhelming despair and a sense of non-belonging. Should it surprise us then that this too, combined with the effects of homophobic rejection generally, has already taken its toll on our community and the community at large? The spectre of AIDS has shown the gay community that we can care and we must care. We have not, however, carried this over into our sexual relationships and, perhaps ironically, this has only worsened the reality of AIDS in our community. Gay men assert that we are not to blame for AIDS. I agree. We cannot, however, state with the same certainty that we offer our youth any incentive to care about themselves, to look to the future and to recognize that their lives are worth preserving. We tell our youth that to be gay is to live for the moment: use your pumped up body while you have it and make sure that if you do not have it you work hard to get it.

Because we are encouraged to participate in a sexual game devoid of caring and compassion, either for ourselves or others, a game which focuses only on controlling or being controlled, we define our personal integrity through our sexual encounters—by how often we get sex and with whom. For many, the power of sex, of finding approval and validation in the sexual act, of being told that you still have what it takes, far outweighs any need for self-preservation. When desperate for approval and believing that you have no right to question, that you should simply be happy that a real man wants you, self-respect and personal safety take a back seat, often with catastrophic results.[11]

Blade Thompson, American porn "star" is quoted as stating that "people who have problems about their appearance or weight shouldn't blame porn videos or magazines for their problems" (Harris 1993:50). Really? If, as advocates assert, gay porn is for gay men a sole sexual outlet, then why should it surprise us that for many, gay porn videos and magazines—with their presentation of "pumped up blondes and smooth dark men with large penises" (Harris 1993:49)— only compound already socially enforced feelings of poor self-image? Of course, the argument is made that gay men do not have to use gay porn. They can instead find validation elsewhere. Like in the bars perhaps? The bars which promote the same imagery and where they can again be reminded that they fail to meet the expectations of an image-conscious scene obsessed with muscle and beauty? If not in bars, then where? Should they avoid being judged and sneered at by others and instead resort to that "sole outlet" of positive imagery where the only ones sneering and judging are themselves? The choices offered are far from appealing. Criticism, from others or self-inflicted, takes its toll. For many it results in the silence found in disempowerment whereas empowerment is what is most needed by a minority community in search of justice. Aware that they cannot participate, many gay men simply refuse to do so, thus limiting the public strength found in numbers and thus ensuring that the mass visibility needed to effect change never emerges.

And what of those who do "fit in," who find the validation promised in assimilation through masculine mimicry, and become what our community and its models of masculine behaviour say they should be? Will they alone ensure gay male liberation? I think not. Mimicry only ensures that those who cannot or who choose not to conform—and who, as a result, continue to threaten heterosexual male privilege—become the victims of greater physical and emotional abuse and discrimination. Because they continue to challenge the normality of gender polarity and in the process undermine male supremacy, these "non-conformists" will remain the objects of brutal suppression. This in turn reinforces the idea that gay men can either fail to conform to male standards and be the feminized "other" society has always told them they are (and thus be further abused) or they can copy straight male standards. Copying them, however, will not make their effect less harmful. Gay men who choose concealment through assimilation do little more than eroticize their own oppression—

making a fetish of that which ultimately muzzles them (Kleinberg 1987:123). The result is a politic which ensures that masculinity remains the only gender construct allowed expression—a politic that straight male culture has supported all along, resulting in gay male silence and heterosexual male superiority.

The desire to mimic manhood is, in a homophobic society, socially appealing. While no one should underestimate the power of homophobia and the extent to which it literally terrorizes gay men into wanting to pass as "real" men, this construct must nonetheless be rejected. Becoming a "real" man ensures only that the elimination of male gender dominance, necessary for gay male liberation, will be more difficult. For some, it will result in self-hate. For others, it will result in assimilation and the invisibility that results from it. In either case, the only "victors" are those most served by homophobia and sex discrimination—those straight men for whom gay male invisibility and female subordination are a must.

CONCLUSION

To those who are gay and who defend gay male pornography, I say only the following. Swept up in the rhetoric of those anxious to promote *their* right to speak as the ultimate and only right worth protecting, you have promoted "speech" at the expense of real equality—*your* equality and the equality of those persons most in need of it. To defend gay pornography as free speech and as a source of liberation is to forget that not all speech is equal and to deny that some speech is in fact the very source of that inequality. Gay porn is about speech but it is the speech of those who already have it—white, heterosexual men for whom being "real" men and all that that entails ensures male supremacy, female inferiority and gay male invisibility.

Andrea Dworkin accurately notes that homosexuality is generally perceived as a failure to learn (1989:105). Gay men today are "learning" but continue to read from the wrong book. They mimic but do not subvert. Gay rights has come to mean male dominant rights, the very essence of all that is anti-gay. Defined solely by the pornographic sexual exploitation of others, from whose presentation we are told to define our identity and community, we have now accepted and promote a model of identity which is more concerned with the use and abuse of others found in the form of sexual hierarchy than with liberation from that hierarchy. What I long for is a gay male sexuality which includes and is compassion, sensuality, tenderness, intimacy, inclusive love-making and the equality found only in a life-affirming reciprocity that does not depend on reciprocal harm. What has happened in the name of gay liberation is quite the opposite. Ultimately, gay men may find that they have at last achieved manhood and the power that comes with it. But at what price? Becoming a man, learning to be one, does nothing for gay male liberation. It ensures only that some of us become more heterosexually acceptable—a liberation tactic which is devoid of strategy and neither radical nor empowering.

NOTES

1. This paper focuses on gay male pornography only. It does not analyze what is referred to as lesbian pornography. Although I remain unconvinced that many of the gendered power structures inherent in gay male pornography are not also evident in lesbian pornography, this paper does not address this issue (see Reti 1993). The issue of how best to deal with the legal regulation of gay male pornographic harm has received considerable attention in both Canada and the United States during the last couple of years. Recently, the British Columbia Supreme Court addressed this issue in the case of Little Sisters Book and Art Emporium. This paper does not address this recent legal decision. Nonetheless, some of the arguments and ideas in this paper appear and are further developed specifically within the context of the Little Sisters case in Kendall (1997).

2. On gender difference as a social construct defined by specific behaviours which ultimately result in the categories "male" and "female," rather than something which is biologically determined, see Catharine A. MacKinnon's *Feminism Unmodified* (1987) and *Towards a Feminist Theory of the State* (1989). As MacKinnon explains, "gender is an inequality, a social and political concept, a social status based on who is permitted to do what to whom" (MacKinnon 1987:8). "Male is a social and political concept, not a biological attribute, having nothing whatever to do with inherency, pre-existence, nature, essence, inevitability, or body as such" (MacKinnon 1989:114). It is this social definition of male and female, with defining and rigidly enforced characteristics for each, which ultimately results in gender inequality.

3. Robert Goss notes that:

Gay and lesbian sexual identities form a counterpractice that decon-
structs the rigid definition of masculinity and femininity and social
constructions based on these definitions. They transgress many dual-
istic strategies that support heterosexist sexual identities. Gay and
lesbian power arrangements (thus) challenge the unequal production
and distribution of heterosocial power in our society. (1993:26)

To this I would only add/clarify that gay male power relations have the
potential to challenge the patriarchal definitions of "male" and "female"
through which those who subscribe to compulsory heterosexuality find privilege, *not* that present gay male power relations do indeed do so. To do so
effectively, gay men must, as Frye explains "be the traitor to masculinity that
the straight man has always thought he was" (1983:146). This is a course of
action upon which most have not embarked and which many apparently
oppose.

    4. As Pharr explains, homophobia is central to preserving sexism and
ultimately patriarchy:

Patriarchy—an enforced belief in male dominance and control—is
the ideology and sexism the system that holds it in place. The cate-
chism goes like this: who do gender roles serve? Men and the women
that seek power from them. Who suffers from gender roles? Women
mostly and men in part. How are gender roles maintained? By the
weapons of sexism: economics, violence and homophobia." (1988:8;
see also Lerner 1986)

    5. For an excellent review/critique of Strossen's defense of pornog-
raphy as free speech see Russel (1995) and Hussey (1995).
    6. On masculinity as a set of cultural codes which define who and what
is gendered male identity see Buchbinder (1994).
    7. As Mark Simpson explains within the context of gay male porn
"star" Jeff Stryker:

the portrayal of anal sex seems to have become even more constructed as "the desire to achieve the goal of visual climax"—the
desire, that is, of the fucker, who in the person of Jeff Stryker is one
who never experiences the pleasure of anal sex in any other position
except that of the fucker. In other words, Stryker's screen persona in
gay videoporn seems to deny his own anality and just endorses the
pleasure any "stud" can get in plugging any hole. (1994:134)

    8. As Andrea Dworkin explains:

Intercourse occurs in a context of power relation that is pervasive and incontrovertible. The context in which the act takes place . . . is one in which men have social, economic, political and physical power over women. Some men do not have all those kinds of power over all women: but all men have some kinds of power over all women: and most men have controlling power over what they call their women—the women they fuck. (Dworkin 1987:125)

9. A point brilliantly made by Mark Simpson who notes that condoms "remind the viewer not just of AIDS—the gay plague—but also safer sex, something invented by gay men and now something of a credo, a sign of belonging, in the gay community" (Simpson 1994:136).

10. Gay male pornography frequently places its "models" in scenarios which promote and hence are violent, cruel, degrading, dehumanizing and exploitive. While deemed merely representational, hence "fictional," the "fantasy" offered in gay male pornography uses real people—a factor most pro-porn advocates overlook. The men used in gay male pornography are frequently involved in it precisely because they are psychologically and financially at their most vulnerable. As such, they are easily exploited by an industry driven by its ability to manipulate those least likely to possess real life choices (Kendall 1993).

11. A 1993 report by the San Francisco Health Commission found that "almost 12 percent of 20 to 22 year old gay men surveyed were HIV positive, as were 4 percent of 17 to 19 year olds. If those figures are not quickly reversed, health officials say, the current generation of young urban gay men will have as high an infection rate by the time they reach their mid 30s as middle age gay men are thought to have today—close to 50 percent" (Bull 1994).

10

Growing Up Male
Everyday-Everynight Masculinities
Blye Frank

Evan, age nineteen: Men act in ways that produce masculinity. That's what sports is about. That's what fighting's about. That's what having a girlfriend or having a good body is about. Those are things that gain you authority, power over other men and women. Men's relationships are about competition. You compete through women. You compete through sports. You compete through fighting. You compete through body size, through various things.

Some weeks ago I went to a grade six classroom to observe a student teacher. This is part of my work as a faculty member in a university department of education. As I took off my coat and proceeded to hang it in the student cloak area, a young girl leaned over to me and said: "That's the girls' side." I hung my coat just the same. At the end of the observation time, I asked the classroom teacher: "The girls and boys hang their coats in different places?" "Oh yes", she replied. "The boys say that their clothing would be 'contaminated' if they hung it with the girls." I inquired if "contaminated" was their word. She assured me that it was. She said the notion of "girl germs" was prevalent among her students. And she chose to do nothing about it.

As I drove back to my office at the university that morning, I thought: How is it that teachers do not make the *connections*? How is

it that murder of fourteen young women by a man at the École Poly-
technique in Montreal on December 6, 1989, and the boys claiming
"contamination by girl germs" in a grade six classroom are not seen to
be connected? How is it that so many educators seem to choose to do
nothing about the overt sexism and misogyny found in our Canadian
schools?

This is not to suggest that what teachers do in schools regarding
gender and sexuality has a direct causal relation to the massacre in
Montreal, nor is it to blame the teacher in this particular grade six
classroom. I am not arguing that schools alone establish the social relations that are played out daily in society regarding gender, race, sexuality, ability, class and so on; however, I am arguing that schools, like
the family, religion and other social institutions in Canadian society,
develop and reinforce patterns of relations between people that privilege some and marginalize and oppress others. This is not a new argument in any way. Yet, when it comes to understanding masculinity,
there continues to be inadequate research and political analysis of, and
minimal attention given to, the everyday/everynight activities of boys
and men in these social institutions, particularly in schools.

By teasing apart the most ordinary of our practice, both as individuals and as a collective, we men might begin this process of understanding our masculinity. In doing this, teachers, for example, might
see that "incidents" such as the separation of coats by sex so as to
avoid contamination by girls are not incidental moments in time, disconnected from the larger society. I want to suggest in this chapter that
it is the humdrum, the usual, that which seems just ordinary that we
men need to investigate and change if we are to begin to put the world
together in a more equitable and less violent way. As feminists have
said for years: the personal is, indeed, political.

These "incidental moments" weave together to create a blanket of
sexism, racism, heterosexism, classism and all the various relations
that privilege heterosexual, abled, white men and marginalize and
oppress others. By unravelling this blanket we can begin to illuminate
how we men, in particular, can assist in weaving the threads in a different pattern. Once we begin to "see," sexism, racism and heterosexism become apparent in the ordinary features of our lives: in classes
when someone says, "all right you guys settle down," when half the
class is young women; at the dinner table when dad's chair is the only

one with arms; in the media when we hear that the seventh woman this year has been murdered by her male partner; on the playing field where young men who are not winning are referred to as "pansies"; in the corridor where "faggot" and "queer" are common everyday language; on the public address system in a high school when the announcement says that coming to the dance will cost you $10 as a (heterosexual) couple but $6 on your own; in the school budget where the money spent on boys' sports is ten to twelve times that spent on girls' sports. Once we begin to see these ordinary features of life as problematic, it may be as Polanyi wrote in 1958, "Having made a discovery I shall never see the world again as before. My eyes become different; I have made myself into a person seeing and thinking differently" (143).

POSTMODERNISM AND MASCULINITIES

My present thinking about masculinity and my own practice as a man are influenced by the writings of contemporary postmodern philosophers (Nicholson and Fraser 1990; Sands and Nuccio 1992; Alcoff and Potter 1993). They speak of "aerial" views. These are "grand narratives," historically produced by men, based on foundational "truths" that rule out or restrict understanding the complexities, contradictions and discrepancies in the routine of the day (Lyotard 1984). Through these narratives, the uncertainty and messiness of the everyday practice of masculinity are reduced to binaries, e.g., self/social, heterosexual/homosexual, privilege/oppression, gender/sexuality. In the absence of "situated knowledge" (Haraway 1988) that arises from specific narratives of men's and boys' lives, society has received a "manmade" theory-world of men that is linear, bounded, dichotomized and disconnected from the everyday relations in which men exist and practice their masculinity.[1]

These grand narratives of men's lives—"the worlding of the world" as Patti Lather (1991) calls it—have produced a theoretical discourse about men that reinforces a masculine hegemony that pervades many arenas: medical, legal, religious and educational, to name a few (Kinsman 1996). This textual hegemony, with its power to both name and invent men's lives, should never be underestimated for it is most often how men come to "know" the world. This hegemony influences

teacher–education programs, curriculum change and hiring procedures; indeed, it affects the very way teachers think about men and
boys. As a result of the textual hegemony, partial and fragmented
accounts of men's lives elevate certain ways of seeing and understanding men and boys over others, in part by allowing some voices to
go unheard or to be misrepresented by others (hooks 1984). The
"silent" or "distorted" voices may be physically present in a variety of
forms, including in the lived text of our classrooms, but are often in
psychic exile due to a profound sense of alienation or fear. It is no
secret that cultural representations by oppressed men (gay and bisexual
men, men of colour, physically and mentally challenged men, men
who "cross-dress"), within the category of men, often form the least
funded, least seen cultural layer in our society, perhaps especially in
schools.

The failure of much of the "new" men as victims scholarship on
men and boys which tend to reinvent these "grand narratives," do not
give voice to the men and boys who have been screened out. Many
men and boys find themselves "on the outside looking in" (hooks
1990:25), both in the case of theory of masculinity and all the ways in
which many researchers represent "the" culture of men's lives,
including men's representation of self.

The young men whom I interviewed are the experts I consulted for
descriptions of their own lives. Their talk demonstrates clearly that
much past psychological research which claims that masculinity is a
character trait that can be assessed, "fitted" somewhat nicely to a curve
and, if not adequate, "restored" through a variety of methods, such as
shock treatment, re-socialization or cognitive therapy, is inadequate in
explaining masculinity. Such research assumes that each man has a
more or less fixed amount of "maleness," usually called "masculinity."
A few men are seen to be very masculine, many are in the middle, and
a few are considered "subnormal," including homosexuals, transves-
tites, transsexuals, sissies, effeminates and so on (Connell 1987). The
conversations of the young men interviewed for this research demonstrate that there is nothing "fixed" about their masculinity. Rather, their
masculinity is constituted and reconstituted over negotiated circumstances and time, and it consumes a great deal of thought and energy.

THE PROJECT: EVERYDAY MASCULINITIES

This chapter is part of a much larger project called "Everyday Masculinities" (Frank 1987, 1990, 1991, 1992, 1993, 1995). As a whole, the project explores the ordinary, routine, everyday/everynight activities of boys and men. It recognizes the messiness of life, including all the ambiguities, tensions and contradictions, as well as the privileges and pain that men experience (Kaufman 1993). The approach taken in this project, as in much of the more recent work on men and masculinity (Brod 1987; Connell 1987; Kaufman 1987; Kimmel 1987; Brittan 1989; Clatterbaugh 1990; Messner and Sabo 1990; Kimmel and Messner 1992) assumes that reductionistic notions of how "boys become men" (e.g., socialization theory), do not adequately explain the complexities and struggles of getting gendered and sexed. The "Everyday Masculinities" project attempts to reveal the individual and collective practice of masculinity in the lives of young men and male teachers. For those of us interested in the complexities and pluralities of gender and sexuality at school, for example, it tells us that in the everyday/night lived terrain of the classrooms, the corridors, the playing fields, the staff rooms and the most ordinary activities, masculinity does not happen smoothly or easily. My interest in doing this work arose out of my awareness and experiences as both a boy and then a teacher, of the social terrorism experienced and perpetuated by boys and men in schools. Increasingly upset by the sexism, homophobia, heterosexism, racism and violence against property, self and others in the greater society, I wanted to talk to men and boys about what it means to be men and boys.

The data referred to in this chapter were gathered primarily from interviews with young men in Nova Scotia. Two different, in-depth one-on-one interviews were conducted in 1987 and 1988 with fourteen young men between the ages of sixteen and twenty years. A second set of interviews was conducted with twenty-four young men from three high schools during 1992 and 1993; a third set was conducted in 1996 with twenty-three young men from various high schools. These are data, therefore, from a total of sixty-one young men, one of whom identified himself as gay. In addition, recent interviews were completed with thirty-one male teachers in Nova Scotia, thirteen of whom identify themselves as gay.

In the first group of interviewees, the fourteen boys were all from one school, all were in the academic stream, all were white and anglophone, and most were from economically secure households. None was physically or mentally disabled. The second group of interviewees comprised boys from three schools in very different areas and reflected more diversity. And the more recent interviews with students were carried out in eight urban and rural schools throughout the province of Nova Scotia. The interview questions focused on family, school and probing feelings about masculinity.

Voices of the boys speaking on "what it takes to be masculine"

Trent: Well, it isn't like it just happens. It takes a lot of time to be sure that you're always doing it right.

Mike: Sports, looks, and a woman. I think that's what every guy needs to be masculine.

Jim: Well, I think you have to keep trying. It's not just sports that count. Things like having a driver's license and having access to a car are very important. You need a car to transport females from point A to point B. But that's not enough. Then you need to have sex with females so you prove that you're not a homosexual. And if that means beating a homosexual up, then that's what you do. You should be a good size.

John: Sports is probably the biggest thing to prove you're a real man, besides not being a fag.

Trent: Some guys use cars, some guys use weights, some guys do it through what they eat, how they stand, the deep voice, some guys see how much alcohol they can drink, and some use girls. There are a lot of different ways to keep at the top.

Thomas: Yes, if you can't be male enough in one area of your life, you can always make it up in another. If you don't have a lot of knowledge, then you can have a girlfriend. You're always working on it so if you fall down in one area, you try to make up for it in another. But you got to work at it.

Bill: I think there is a three-way tie for the top male behaviour: there's girls, weights and sports, and violence.

Sean: In the end, that's all men have is their masculinity. Money really doesn't do it. Women can leave you. If you are gay with lots of money, it might help, but you could still lose your job or get put out of your apartment. All you've got left is yourself, your masculinity, and so that's all you can count on and the best way to demonstrate it is through your body.

BODIES, SPORTS AND SEXUALITY

The boys interviewed had a lot to say about their lives as boys and the topics of conversation ranged widely, from family to the future. However, within their talk, three sites of practice of masculinity stand out as important: the body, sports and sexuality. As Jim suggests: "Sports, looks, and a woman, that's what every guy needs to be masculine." However, while one might "locate" masculinity in three social sites, one must be careful not to oversimplify the issue of practice. It is not necessary, for example, that each boy engage in sport, produce and maintain what is considered an appropriate masculine body, or engage in heterosexual sexual activity (Pronger 1990). The actual activity is not the critical feature; rather, it is the ideological support and advancement of these three pillars that are central to the maintenance of masculinity for each individual boy, as well as in the broader social structure (Bunch 1975; Connell 1989a). Power in and through the body has always been an important part of the production of masculinity (Messner 1989). For the boys interviewed, power takes the form of violence, sexism and heterosexism expressed and practiced in and through the body (Kidd 1987). For some of them, their bodies become their suits of armour that carry them into the social world and offer security, protection and freedom from harassment and harm (Messner 1990).

Luke: Well, you're nothing if you don't play boys sports.

Thomas: You're expected to support them even if you're not involved directly. So whether you participate or watch, it influences you in the same way. It makes you part of the male group.

Derrick: Sports is an aspect of being manly. It shows that you are a real man. And the rules are that you're not allowed to fight, right? But you have to learn not to care about those rules. You learn to compete and you learn to be tough. Sometimes it really bothers me. I don't like hurting people, but you have to do it that way if you expect to win, and that's what it's all about. What you have to do is learn not to care about anyone when you're out there in the game. Sometimes I'm told to injure another human being. You just go for him. But when you trip someone on purpose, and they break bones, which is often great because it puts them out for the season, you really feel for the guy. Once one of the guys on the hockey team got sticked and lost most of his front teeth. Now that's not cheap to repair.

Danny: More companies are supplying the money for travelling and for the time clocks and stuff. Look at McDonald's and Pepsi and the beer companies, they spend a lot of money on high school and college sports. They don't want to sponsor a losing team. They want their team to win. No pain, no gain. If you're going to win, there's pain involved. Sometimes you hurt yourself. Those are the chances you take if you're gonna play. I've had a lot of injuries. There's almost always some level of violence. Always. You gotta get hit, that's automatic. A guy will hit you with an elbow, you'll get him back. He'll get you back, things like that. And then you'll have an exchange. You exchange words, and then a fight will happen. As long as it doesn't affect your game, the coaches let it go. Coaches don't really say anything about it. You've got to be physical. And there's certain players they'll put in to "be the goon," as they say.

Eric: It's brutal. Some of the things that people were asked to do, like, "Knock him over," "Kick him in the head" are pretty bad. I found soccer to be the worst. They always call it a gentleman's sport, but it is just insane. On the bottom of your shoes you have a three-quarter inch aluminum stud. If I step my feet on pavement it will take chunks of pavement out. I have scars from my knees down of where people have jumped on my leg. There's a way you can do it, if you sink your two front studs in the back of a guy's ankle, you can screw his ankle up for the rest of his life. I don't know how many times I've seen people lose teeth. It's just totally brutal because you're dealing with no gear protecting. Just shin guards, and you have basically four or five little knives on the bottom of your feet that could easily hurt someone.

Mark: Look at the new gym that was just built. There are two great big sets of double doors so the ambulances can back up easily. They were built because people are going to get hurt.

Many of the young men said they are willing to put vast amounts of time, money and energy into producing a body that helps them gain power and offers them protection, often at the expense of other things such as their health or academic success in school.

Mike: The ultimate for a man is to be big. Big men are it. The big body-builder body is the pinnacle; it's the gladiator, it's the warrior. Underneath it's what most men would like to be because it's so safe.

For others, their bodies offer them little protection or security against an often hostile social environment.

Trent: I've been made fun of a lot by people who think that I'm not appropriately male. I've been harassed because of the way I choose to decorate my body. I can't even tell my father that I want to go to drama school next year and eventually be a dancer. He wouldn't be happy his only son a dancer! I cope through violence, and sometimes when it becomes too much I just stay at home.

But for all of the boys interviewed, the ongoing process of negotiating—both psychically and socially—the complex reactions to the body is full of tension. Each boy finds himself with multiple contradictions in relation to his body and struggles to both fit into and challenge the dominant codes of masculinity. Several boys reported that they purposely hide many things from other male friends, and sometimes from their fathers, including their caring for houseplants, their

interest in cooking, sewing or cleaning the house, their desire to care
for children and their dream of becoming a nurse. Certain choices of
activity and occupation are not available to them. Their lives often
demonstrate blocked paths, and school does little to open up their possibilities and allow them to break out of socially prescribed and regulated gender and sexual roles (Connell 1989b).

Their relations with other men in sport come with a history and
reveal the broader ideological, psychological, social and economic
relations of gender and sexuality (Sabo 1986). And here again, the relation of many of the boys to sport is never simple or easy. Their sport
activities and endeavours preserve inequality between and among
them along divisions of physical size and strength, class and sexual
orientation (Messner and Sabo 1990). The accompanying violence,
often accepted and celebrated by many staff and coaches, creates anxiety, fear, low self- esteem and self-loathing for some of the boys. They
never seem to be able to measure up.

Thomas: It's a training. It's a mental training for people to get the
right mentality for competition and all that in later life. Not
just physically, but it's the idea of competition and success
and domination. Sport, more than anything else, separates
the men from the boys.

These boys' comments inform us that the problem is not simply
schools and those who work in them. The values that sport embodies
are tied to a much larger set of practices that are admired and rewarded
in the broader society: competition, violence, winning and profit
(Messner and Sabo 1990). For some of the boys, sport gives them a
sense of masculine self-worth and power. But the contradictions and
the tensions always poke through, and some boys are clear that they do
not value the very practices in which they frequently engage.

In addition to the attention given to bodies and sports, their statements illuminate how sexuality is not simply individually formed, but
is instead a set of practices saturated with meanings that are often con-
fusing and difficult (Steedman 1987).

Derrick: Well, if you're labelled a fruit or a fag or so on socially, you
might as well forget about it because you won't get a girl-

friend, you won't get invited to any parties, you won't play any sports, you won't get invited to come over and jam on the drums. You have to sit at home or work at a department store. Being a heterosexual is definitely at the top. But at the same time, you're not allowed to hang out with girls or be too nice to them. That's a real no-no.

The boys describe how sexuality is organized around activities saturated with different amounts of power

Luke: Sex is all about image. I think that a lot of guys when they go out they put it on. It's like this hard shell. It's like a jacket. They put it on before they step out the door and they strut their stuff and then they take it off when they come home, or if they come home with the guys they leave it on. And a big part of that is making sure that others know you're not a queer.

Jim: There are guys that everyone considers losers. To be a loser is to not have asserted your heterosexuality in society yet. You're a wimp or a fag. If you don't participate in sports, then you're at the bottom and at the same time that you got a girlfriend, you can't be too nice to her. The guys, including my father, would say that she wears the pants if you let her make the decisions.

Their lives, often fragmented and filled with doubt, demonstrate how the practice of masculinity is always under construction for any one individual boy, as it is for all men.

Eric: I find it's easy getting along if you play your cards right. You have to make strategies. First of all, I got on a sports team to get accepted by the administration. If you're on a sports team, you're rewarded. You're let off things. I did that at the first of the year so I wouldn't be hassled as much throughout the year by both other students and the administration. I hang around with the bigger guys who also play sports, the more popular people. I have a girlfriend. Those things make life pretty safe.

In short, the boys' practices show how their masculinity is historically specific, socially constructed, imposed and personally embodied,
but at the very same time sometimes resisted and refused (Connell
1987). Just because the school reinforces and supports many of the
strategies used to maintain dominant hegemonic masculinity does not
mean that the boys are simply determined by it. As the dialogue
demonstrates, there are cracks and crevices in the dominant definitions
of masculinity. Some boys develop strategies to protect themselves as
they also develop outside the definitions and practices of hegemonic
masculinity. For example, a young gay man may develop his sexual
relationships in secret while, at the same time, he works out at the gym
two hours a day to give a particular shape to his body, thereby out-
wardly reflect the dominant heterosexual masculinity.[2]

POSSIBILITIES

As Kinsman (1996) points out, heterosexist or homophobic assertions
about the "naturalness" of heterosexuality and the "abnormality" of
other forms of sexuality are not simply backward ideas, they are organized through the social relations of masculine heterosexual hegemony. This heterosexism relates the practices of heterosexual hegemony to the institutional and social settings of the boys (families,
church, sports, bodies, schools) and to their sex and gender relations
(misogyny, sexism, violence). Things that are seen as a personal
response by boys—the "faggot" jokes, the portrayal of gay men as perverse and sick, the name-calling, the physical and psychological abuse
of gay or effeminate men on a daily basis—are really *organized heterosexist discourse*. These responses are not merely attitudes.
"Reality" for the boys with whom I spoke is interpreted through the
schema of what are considered to be "expert sources" (teachers,
coaches, police, policy booklets, government and legal policies), all of
which confirm the dominant interpretation of male gender relations
and sexuality. Schools perpetuate these relations through, for example,
support of violence in sports, failure to recognize and support diverse
gender and sexual practices, and total exclusion from the curriculum of
material on gay men.

It is clear that most school teachers, both male and female, encourage this obedience to hegemonic heterosexual masculinity. They uphold the hegemonic model. However, this dominance does not turn boys into "social dupes" who simply are acted upon by the culture and defined in and through the discourse of the hegemony. Even in schools, there was a hierarchy always struggling to establish and maintain its position, and boys can clearly articulate what it is (heterosexuality, physical size, misogyny, violence). But the hierarchy shifts and moves, twists and turns. Heterosexuality does not remain dominant without effort or without resistance. Idealized body size is not established without great effort. Misogyny and violence do not exist without attention and practice.

Masculinity, as reflected in the interviews, is not simply a two-layered structure of power, creating a tension between two practices, such as heterosexuality and homosexuality, from which any boy can make a choice. Nor is it a multilayered structure in which all boys head along an unidirectional path to the imagined pinnacle: heterosexuality, patriarchy and physical strength. Rather, boys' and men's practice is in a constant state of flux, even with the same boy.

Trent: I find that you have to be constantly letting everyone know that you're not going to take any shit from anyone; that you're not going to be stepped on. You have to work at it all the time or else someone will be there to take your place.

Some of the boys interviewed revealed that their public and private practices of masculinity differ radically. Some find their actual practice is at odds with their "internal" practice (Messner 1989). Their internal dialogue addresses the conflicts and difficulties that they face, yet this "voice inside" is shared with very few friends, family members or teachers. Analogously, just as the boys develop socially visible strategies that appear hegemonic to assert their masculinity and deal with the world around them (a heterosexual public but a homosexual private practice), they also develop private strategies (often a fantasy life at odds with their actual practice) to mediate the disjunction between the public and the private. Any given boy or man can engage a combination of many diverse and wide-ranging practices: heterosexuality with heterosexual fantasies; heterosexuality with heterosexual external practice; a practicing heterosexual with homosexual fantasies;

assumed heterosexual practice practicing homosexual sex; or all of the above.

The boys create their masculinity, sometimes successfully and sometimes not. But because there is no culmination to the process of masculinity, there is no end to the process of negotiation. Success is not about "getting there," but rather is itself a process. The boys give meaning to and practice their masculinity in inner and in interactional contexts.

It is also true that the "fixity" of hegemonic masculinity, for some teachers, is not always so fixed. Interviews show that a few administrators and teachers resist and reject the codes and scripts of this hegemony: a teacher may provide an analysis from a feminist standpoint and change his curriculum and pedagogy to demonstrate a different approach; a coach may decide that winning at all costs is not the point of sport. For the boys the task is complex. While they strategize around the differing hegemonic and non-hegemonic institutional notions, they must figure out the relation of these options to the dominant hegemonic masculinity that most teachers model and reward.

NEEDS

For the young men interviewed, it is clear that their lives are full of tensions and struggles around measuring up to their own and others' expectations of hegemonic masculinity. Many of the boys spoke often of the fear that they experience daily: Fear of being excluded, of harassment, ridicule, humiliation and rejection. As they struggle to fulfill their needs, they measure their struggle against the larger structures of masculine authority. And, given the advantage and privilege accorded by schools—as well as other institutions such as the family—to boys who meet the standards of heterosexual masculine hegemony, it should come as no surprise that most boys put forth a great deal of energy to develop successful strategies to meet these standards (Connell 1987). The fear of the repercussions of not abiding by the rules can keep many young men captive to the hegemonic notions of masculinity.

Jim: Some guys are usually looking to exterminate anything that doesn't fit their idea of the norm. Jocks mainly use jokes, and with some guys it's mainly kicking and beating up people. The main way I can cope is by appearing in public with a girl. If people know you have a girlfriend, then they say "Well, he must not be a homosexual." If you dress alternatively and you're not seen with a girl, then you're automatically seen as a homosexual. There are guys in this school who have alternative ideas or dress and they are left alone because they have girlfriends. There are other guys who do the same but don't have girlfriends, and they really get hassled.

ORGANIZING FOR CHANGE

Much of the political organizing around masculinity, in schools and elsewhere, focuses on such issues as the violence in young men's sports, sex education, date rape, high school dropouts, AIDS, the apparently increasing rate of youth crime, and antihomophobic education. These types of analysis and organizing leave much of the daily/nightly support of hegemonic masculinity intact. Until men refuse to support the pillars of hegemonic masculinity, both individually and collectively, we will not change much in the gendered and sexed relations of schooling with respect to men and boys. This is difficult work. Understanding how boys' needs are woven into social structures demands a careful rethinking of how teachers and educators do their work (Connell 1989b). Changing gendered language, the pictures in textbooks, or the hiring practices of school boards are necessary steps, but in the end these tinkerings will not address the foundations of the practice of masculinity.

CONCLUSION

Optimistically, the interview process revealed that the possibility of change is a reality for these boys. There is no lack of interest in questions of masculinity, gender and sexuality among the boys. During the interviews we had been *making our masculinity* as we talked about it: our masculinity had not been made "behind our backs." Through our talk the possibility emerged that we could begin to live our lives a bit differently. Our talk always carried over to family, friends and teachers; many people asked the boys interviewed about our discussions, and we told them that we were talking about what it means to be a man.

The process and the content of the interviews, however, also affirm that these young men, like the collective of men, create, mediate and transform their practice, most often in what they see as their own best interest. Misogyny, sexism, heterosexism, violence and competition all became part of their strategic practice. However, contradictory feelings and practices often surface: sensitivity, caring, nonexploitive relationships with women and other men, nonviolent sports, acceptance of the diversity of sexuality, nonabuse of power. These very contradictions and tensions of masculinity allow insight into how some men and boys manage, even under adverse conditions, to do masculinity differently. Perhaps it is also in these spaces that one can see how people both stand against the prevailing definitions of the masculine hegemony and how they develop and fulfill needs that are in opposition to the hegemony. This is no easy task; the forces of resistance to counter-hegemonic masculinity can be overwhelming. It has been my experience that even politically experienced men who are involved in the politics of resistance (antiracist education, antimilitarism and so on) often fail to see how masculinity operates in and through their own daily lives and their own ordinary routine practices as men. Or, if they do see this, they still have difficulty standing against or outside of it. But every step toward change can represent a "new man" struggling out of a history. That struggle has real consequences that may involve loss (Brod 1987). For many men this might be the loss of a certain profession; it may mean an end to teaching young children, for example, for a gay man. It might mean the loss of the known safety and security that hegemonic heterosexual practice brings.

I often think that what men need to do is provide "pauses," regardless of how brief, in the hegemonic masculinity experienced by men and boys. Pauses could allow boys and men to re-evaluate, reflect upon and find practical ways to deal with issues of gender and sexual politics. Teachers could be more proactive, as well, by developing courses where issues of gender and sexual politics are central, and by encouraging research that gives voice to the lives boys and men actually live. For the young men interviewed, indeed for most boys and men, such a course would be an exception. It needs to become a given.

In teasing apart the complexities of the postmodern world, we need to be careful that we not offer up, once again, some of the reductionistic understandings—such as all men are strong, all men are heterosexual—of gender and sexed relations (Yeatman 1993). An analysis of the lives of boys and men needs to account for how power operates in and among men, as well as over us (Connell 1983). Change is not simply a matter of changing attitudes, nor is it located within an individual act of will, even though this too is part of the necessary change if men are to live differently. As long as men and women value oppression, competition and thus the violence that is necessary to achieve those relations, we are trapped in the very processes that support the authorial voice of the hegemony (Stoltenberg 1977). And, as long as we willingly support and reward these processes in our classrooms and other institutions, hegemonic masculinity will continue to operate because it gets rewarded.

Schools, like most social institutions, fuse together race, class, ability, gender and sexual politics (Brittan 1989). Disentangling the complex and intertwined ways that social processes help maintain hegemonies is a necessary part of the analysis. For example, far too often researchers continue to conduct a class analysis without attending to how hegemonic masculinity weaves itself in and through class practices (Frank 1987). Or we conduct an antiracist analysis giving little attention to how particular practices of masculinity are interwoven with race. Within all these analyses, surely we need some focus on hope, on possibilities and on celebration, not in a way that produces a romantic vision of the future, but in a way that leads us away from victimization and toward seeing alternatives and ways of living them out. Within the stories of the boys' confusion, anger, hurt and frustration, there is hope of finding better ways. Young men spoke about their lives, and in the speaking came reflection, insight and possibilities for real change.

NOTES

1. The recognition that men's and boys' practice of masculinity is always local, temporal (Connell 1987), ever shifting and intermeshed rather than sequential, and with boundaries that materialize only in social interaction,

should not persuade men and women to abandon an exploration and investi-gation of men or to despair in men's efforts to bring about change in men's lives. Rather, this recognition strengthens the argument for the "situatedness" of this research. It also should give men and women some hope for it points to the possibilities rather than just to the limitations. By locating my work in the everyday lives of boys and men, the seams and the ruptures of the *not*-so-rational self and of men's *not*-so-unified daily/nightly practice are exposed; the diversity, multiplicity and pluralism of both the self and the practice become illuminated and clarified, but perhaps not classified. Once one begins to take apart the foundational blocks of masculinity (heterosexuality, ratio-nality, privilege and so on), with all their cracks, crevices and cross-overs, one can no longer offer up explanations of a concrete stability which one thought existed (Bernstein 1983; Smith 1987; Haraway 1988; Harding 1990, 1993). Dismantling the theoretical assumptions of masculinity to which many of us as researchers still cling "allows us to demystify the resulting foundational realities that we have created" (Lather 1992:96). As a result the pillars of both the rational subject and the unified structure begin to crumble. Seeing how masculinity "works" allows for different insights about how one might pro-ceed to bring about change in schools, as well as in other institutional settings.

2. For example, some same-sex practice means self-devaluation, extreme guilt, and even attempted suicide; the gay man often practices his own homophobia and heterosexism. Many teachers fail to realize that the values of the hegemony are woven into the personality structure of the boy who carries out the non-hegemonic practice. This, in itself, is immensely complicated, and becomes increasingly complex if we are to deal with these issues in schooling and change not only the violence between girls and boys and among boys themselves, but also the violence that some men and boys inflict on themselves, including suicide. This type of analysis would suggest that changing curricula, language practices or hiring procedures would not suffice.

References

CHAPTER 1

Bly, R. 1990. *Iron John: A Book About Men.* NY: Vintage.

Brod, H., and M. Kaufman (eds.). 1994. *Theorizing Masculinities.* Newbury Park, CA: Sage.

Farrell, W. 1993. *The Myth of Male Power.* NY: Simon and Schuster.

Haddad, T. (ed.). 1993. *Men and Masculinities: A Critical Anthology.* Toronto: Canadian Scholar's Press.

Kaufman, M. 1993. *Cracking the Armour: Power, Pain and the Lives of Men.* Toronto: Viking.

Kuypers, J. 1992. *Man's Will to Hurt.* Halifax: Fernwood.

Poundstone, W. 1992. *The Prisoner's Dilemma.* NY: Doubleday.

The Backlash. Bellevue, Washington: Shameless Men Press.

CHAPTER 2

Bresnan, Joan. 1995. "Levels of Representation in Locative Inversion: A Comparison of English and Chichewa." Cited in S. Pinker, *The Language Instinct.* NY: Harper Perennial.

Brod, Harry. 1993. "Toward Men's Studies: A Case for Men's

Studies." In M. Kimmel (ed.), *Changing Men: New Directions in Research on Men and Masculinity*. Newbury Park, CA: Sage.

Buber, Martin. 1970. *I and Thou*. Translated by Walter Kaufmann. NY: Scribner.

Gray, John. 1992. *Men Are from Mars, Women Are from Venus*. NY: Harper Collins.

Kimmel, M. 1993. "Letters." *Changing Men* 26 (Summer/fall):66.

Pinker, Steven. 1995. *The Language Instinct*. NY: Harper Perennial.

Stoltenberg, John. 1990. *Refusing to Be a Man: Essays on Sex and Justice*. NY: Penguin.

———. 1994a. *The End of Manhood: A Book for Men of Conscience*. NY: Penguin.

———. 1994b. *What Makes Pornography "Sexy"?* Minneapolis, MN: Milkweed Editions.

CHAPTER 3

Dinnerstein, D. 1977. *The Mermaid and The Minotaur: Sexual Arrangements and The Human Malaise*. NY: Harper Colophone.

CHAPTER 4

Barrett, M., and M. MacIntosh. 1982. *The Anti-Social Family*. London: Verso.

Beneke, T. 1982. *Men on Rape*. NY: St. Martin's.

Benjamin, J. 1988. *The Bonds of Love*. NY: Random House.

Bly, R. 1990. *Iron John: A Book About Men*. NY: Vintage.

Brod, H., and M. Kaufman (eds.). 1994. *Theorizing Masculinities*. Newbury Park, CA: Sage.

Bronstein, P., and C. Cowan. 1988. *Fatherhood Today*. NY: John Wiley and Sons.

Burstyn, V. Forthcoming. *The Rites of Men: Manhood, Politics, and the Cultured Sport*. Toronto: University of Toronto Press.

Carrigan, T., R. Connell and J. Lee. 1987. "Hard and Heavy." In M. Kaufman, *Beyond Patriarchy: Essays by Men on Pleasure, Power and Change*. Toronto: Oxford University Press.

Cath, S., S. Gurwitt and J. Ross. 1982. *Father and Child*. Boston: Little Brown.

Chodorow, N. 1978. *The Reproduction of Mothering*. Berkeley: University of California Press.

Connell, R. 1987. *Gender and Power*. Stanford: Stanford University Press.

Dinnerstein, D. 1977. *The Mermaid and the Minotaur: Sexual Arrangements and the Human Malaise*. NY: Harper Colophon.

Farrell, W. 1993. *The Myth of Male Power: Why Men are the Disposable Sex*. NY: Simon and Schuster.

Goldberg, H. 1976. *The Hazards of Being Male: Surviving the Myth of Masculine Privilege*. NY: Signet.

Hearn, J. 1987. *The Gender of Oppression*. Brighton: Wheatsheaf.

Horowitz, G. 1977. *Repression: Basic and Surplus Repression in Psychoanalytic Theory*. Toronto: University of Toronto Press.

Kaufman, M. 1987. *Beyond Patriarchy: Essays by Men on Pleasure, Power and Change*. Toronto: Oxford University Press.

———. 1993. *Cracking the Armour: Power, Pain, and the Lives of Men*. Toronto: Viking.

Kimmel, M. (ed.). 1990. *Men Confront Pornography*. NY: Crown.

———. (ed.). 1995. *The Politics of Manhood*. Philadelphia: Temple University Press.

———. 1994. "Masculinity as Homophobia." In H. Brod and M. Kaufman (eds.), *Theorizing Masculinities*. Newbury Park, CA: Sage.

Kimmel, M., and M. Kaufman. 1993. "The New Men's Movement: Retreat and Aggression with America's Weekend Warriors." *Feminist Issues*, 13(2).

———. 1994. "Weekend Warriors: The New Men's Movement." In H. Brod and M. Kaufman (eds.), *Theorizing Masculinities*. Newbury Park, CA: Sage.

Kimmel, M., and T. Mosmiller (eds.). 1992. *Against the Tide: Profeminist Men in the United States 1776–1990: A Documentary History*. Boston: Beacon.

Lamb, M. (ed.). 1981. *The Role of the Father in Child Development*. NY: John Wiley and Sons.

Levine, S., and J. Koenig (eds.). 1980. *Why Men Rape*. Toronto: Macmillan.

Macpherson, C. 1973. *Democratic Theory*. London: Oxford University Press.

Mahfouz, N. [1956] 1990. *Palace Walk*. NY: Anchor.

Money, J., and N. Enrhardt. 1972. *Man & Woman, Boy & Girl*. Baltimore: John Hopkins University Press.

Nardi, P. (ed.). 1992. *Men's Friendships*. Newbury Park, CA: Sage.

Osherson, S. 1986. *Finding our Fathers*. Newbury Park, CA: Sage.

Pharr, S. 1988. *Homophobia: A Weapon of Sexism*. Little Rock, AR: Chardon.

Rubin, L. 1984. *Intimate Strangers*. NY: Harper Colophon.

Yogman, M., J. Cooley and D. Kindlon. 1988. "Fathers, Infants, Toddlers: Developing Relationship." In P. Bronstein and C. Cowan. *Fatherhood Today*. NY: John Wiley and Sons.

CHAPTER 5

Adler, A. 1980. *Cooperation Between the Sexes: Writings on Women, Love and Marriage, Sexuality and its Disorders*. In H. Ansbacker and R. Ansbacker (eds. and trans.) NY: Jason Aronson.

Arendt, H. 1970. *On Revolution*. NY: Viking.

Bly, R. 1990. *Iron John: A Book About Men*. NY: Vintage.

Brannon, R. 1976. "The Male Sex Role—and What it's Done for us Lately." In R. Brannon and D. David (eds.), *The Forty-Nine Percent Majority*. Reading, MA: Addison-Wesley.

Connell, R.W. 1987. *Gender and Power*. Stanford, CA: Stanford University Press.

Farrell, W. 1986. *Why Men Are the Way they Are?* NY: McGraw-Hill.

———. 1993. *The Myth of Male Power: Why Men are the Disposable Sex*. NY: Simon and Schuster.

Freud, S. [1933]1966. *New Introductory Lectures on Psychoanalysis*. L. Strachey (ed.). NY: Norton.

Gaylin, W. 1992. *The Male Ego*. NY: Viking.

Goffman, E. 1963. *Stigma*. Englewood Cliffs, NJ: Prentice Hall.

Gorer, G. 1964. *The American People: A Study in National Character*. NY: Norton.

Kaufman, M. 1993. *Cracking the Armour: Power and Pain in the Lives of Men*. Toronto: Viking.

Keen, S. 1991. *Fire in the Belly*. NY: Bantam.

Kimmel, M. 1996. *Manhood in America: A Cultural History*. NY: Free Press.

———. (forthcoming). *Manhood: The American Quest*. NY: Harper Collins.

Kimmel, M., and M. Kaufman. 1994. *Theorizing Masculinity*. Thousand Oaks, CA: Sage.

Leverenz, D. 1986. "Manhood, Humiliation and Public Life: Some Stories." *Southwest Review* 71 (Fall).

———. 1991. "The Last Real Man in America: From Natty Bumppo to Batman." *American Literary Review* 3.

Marx, K., and F. Engels. [1848]1964. "The Communist Manifesto." In Tucker (ed.), *The Marx-Engels Reader*. NY: Norton.

Mead, M. 1965. *And Keep Your Powder Dry*. NY: William Morrow.

Moore, R., and D. Gillette. 1991. *King, Warrior, Magician, Lover*. NY: Harper Collins.

———. 1992. *The King Within: Accessing the King in the Male Psyche*. NY: William Morrow.

———. 1993a. *The Warrior Within: Accessing the Warrior in the Male Psyche*. NY: William Morrow.

———. 1993b. *The Magician Within: Accessing the Magician in the Male Psyche*. NY: William Morrow.

New York Times. 1993. "What Men Need is Men's Approval." January 3, C-11.

Newsweek. 1992. "Have We Got a Husband for You!" November 5:41.

Noble, V. 1992. "A Helping Hand From the Guys." In K.L. Hagen (ed.), *Women Respond to the Men's Movement*. San Francisco: Harper Collins.

Osherson, S. 1992. *Wrestling with Love: How Men Struggle with Intimacy, with Women, Children, Parents, and Each Other*. NY: Fawcett.

Rotundo, E. 1993. *American Manhood: Transformations in Masculinity from the Revolution of the Modern Era*. NY: Basic Books.

Savran, D. 1992. *Communists, Cowboys and Queers: The Politics of Masculinity in the Work of Arthur Miller and Tennessee Williams*. Minneapolis: University of Minnesota Press.

Seidler, V. 1994. *Unreasonable Men: Masculinity and Social Theory*. NY: Routledge.

Symes, L. 1930. "The New Masculinism." *Harper's Monthly* 161 (January).

Tocqueville, A. de [1835]1967. *Democracy in America*. NY: Anchor.

Wayne, K. 1912. *Building the Young Man*. Chicago: A.C. McClurg.

Weber, M. [1905]1966. *The Protestant Ethic and the Spirit of Capitalism*. NY: Scribner.

Wilkinson, R. 1986. *American Tough: The Tough-guy Tradition and American Character*. NY: Harper and Row.

Woolfolk, R., and F. Richardson. 1978. *Sanity, Stress and Survival*. NY: Signet.

CHAPTER 6

Gilligan, C. 1992. *In a Different Voice: Psychoanalytic Theory and Women's Development*. Cambridge, MA: Harvard University Press.

Chodorow, N. 1978. *The Reproduction of Mothering: Psychoanalysis and the Sociology of Gender*. Berkeley, CA: University of California Press.

Dworkin, A. 1983. *Right Wing Women*. NY: Perigee.

Stoltenberg, J. 1990. *Refusing To Be A Man: Essays on Sex and Justice*. NY: Penguin.

CHAPTER 7

Davion, V. 1993. "Autonomy, Integrity, and Care." *Social Theory and Practice* 19(2): 161–82.

Folbre, N. 1995. *The New Field Guide to the U.S. Economy*. NY: New Press.

Frye, M. 1983. *The Politics of Reality: Essays in Feminist Theory*. Freedom, CA: The Crossing Press.

Gauthier, D. 1986. *Morals By Agreement*. Oxford: Clarendon.

Gilligan, C. 1982. *In A Different Voice*. Cambridge, MA: Harvard University Press.

Hampton, J. 1993a. "Feminist Contractarianism." In L. Anthony and C. Witt (eds.), *A Mind of One's Own: Feminist Essays on Reason and Objectivity*. Boulder, CO: Westview.

————. 1993b. "Selflessness and the Loss of Self." In W. Paul, F. Miller and J. Paul (eds.), *Altruism*. NY: Cambridge University Press.

McKenzie, R., and G. Tullock. 1989. *The Best of the New World of Economics*. Homewood, IL: Irwin Publications in Economics.

Nodding, N. 1984. *Caring: A Feminine Approach to Moral Education*. Berkeley, CA: University of California Press.

Nussbaum, M. 1995. "Human Capabilities, Female Human Beings." In M. Nussbaum and J. Glover (eds.), *Women, Culture, and Development*. NY: Oxford University Press.

Nussbaum, M. and J. Glover (eds.). 1995. *Women, Culture, and Development*. NY: Oxford University Press.

Okin, S. 1989. *Justice, Gender, and the Family*. NY: Basic.

Plumwood, V. 1993. *Feminism and the Mastery of Nature*. London: Routledge.

Rousseau, J. [1762]1974. *Emile*. London: J.M. Dent and Sons.

Warren, K. 1990. "The Power and Promise of Ecological Feminism." *Environmental Ethics* 12(2):121–46.

Wishik, H. 1986. "Economics of Divorce: An Exploratory Study." *Family Law Quarterly* 20(1):79–107.

CHAPTER 8

Bishop, A. 1994. *Becoming an Ally: Breaking the Cycle of Oppression*. Halifax: Fernwood.

Bly, R. 1990. *Iron John: A Book about Men*. NY: Vintage.

Brod, H., and M. Kaufman (eds.). 1994. *Theorizing Masculinities*. Newbury Park, CA: Sage.

Brown, I. 1991. "New Men." *The Globe and Mail*, November 30: D3.

Doyle, M. 1992. "Taking the (M)en Out of Violent—and Coming up Smelling Like Violets." *Island Men's Network* 7:6–7.

Ellis, C. 1995. *A Men's World*. NY: Harper Collins.

Frank, B. 1993. "The 'Men's Studies' and Feminism: Promise or Danger?" In T. Haddad (ed.), *Men and Masculinities: A Critical Anthology*. Toronto: Canadian Scholar's.

Gutterman, D. 1994. "Postmodernism and the Interrogation of Masculinity." In H. Brod and M. Kaufman (eds.), *Theorizing Masculinities*. Newbury Park, CA: Sage.

Haddad, T. 1993. *Men and Masculinities: A Critical Anthology.* Toronto: Canadian Scholar's.

Johnston, J. 1992. "Something For The Boys." *New York Times Book Review* February 23.

Kimbrell, A. 1995. *The Masculine Mystique: The Politics of Masculinity.* NY: Ballantine.

Kimmel, M. 1994. "Masculinity as Homophobia: Fear, Shame, and Silence in the Construction of Gender Identity." In H. Brod and M. Kaufman (eds.), *Theorizing Masculinities.* Newbury Park, CA: Sage.

Kimmel, M., and M. Kaufman. 1994. "Weekend Warriors: The New Men's Movement." In H. Brod and M. Kaufman (eds.), *Theorizing Masculinities.* Newbury Park, CA: Sage.

Luxton, M. 1993. "Dreams and Dilemmas: Feminist Musings on 'The Man Question.'" In T. Haddad (ed.), *Men and Masculinities: A Critical Anthology.* Toronto: Canadian Scholar's.

McBride, J. 1995. *War, Battering, and Other Sports: The Gulf Between American Men and Women.* New Jersey: Humanities.

Noel, L. 1994. *Intolerance: A General Survey.* Montreal: McGill-Queen's University Press.

Richer, S. 1995. "Reaching the Man: Inclusion and Exclusion in Feminist Teaching." In S. Richer and L. Weir (eds.), *Beyond Political Correctness: Towards the Inclusive University.* Toronto: University of Toronto Press.

Wajcman, J. 1993. "The Masculine Mystique: A Feminist Analysis of Science and Technology." In B. Probert and B. Wilson (eds.), *Pink Collar Blues.* Melbourne: Melbourne University Press.

Young, B. 1993. "Feminism and Masculinism: A Backlash Response." In T. Haddad (ed.), *Men and Masculinities: A Critical Anthology.* Toronto: Canadian Scholar's.

CHAPTER 9

Bronski, M. 1984. "Gay Publishing: Pornography." In *Culture Clash: The Making of a Gay Sensibility.* Boston: South End.

Browning, F. 1993. *The Culture of Desire: Paradox and Perversity in Gay Lives Today.* NY: Crown.

Buchbinder, D. 1994. *Masculinities and Identities*. Carlton, VIC: Melbourne University Press.

Bull, C. 1994. "The Lost Generation: The Second Wave of HIV Infections Among Young Gay Men." *The Advocate* 68 (May):36–40.

Classified Advertisement. 1993. *Campaign*. 208 (July):83.

Dickson, K. 1994. "Gay Tribes: Skinheads, Punks, Leather Men and Muscle Boys—The Many Faces of the Gay Male of the '90s." *Campaign* 215 (February):35–38.

Dworkin, A. 1987. *Intercourse*. NY: The Free Press.

———. 1989. *Pornography: Men Possessing Women*. NY: Plume.

Dyer, R. 1985. "Coming to Terms." *Jump Cut* 30:31.

Edwards, T. 1994. *Erotics and Politics: Gay Male Sexuality, Masculinity and Feminism*. London: Routledge.

Fajer, M. 1992. "Can Two Men Eat Quiche Together? Storytelling, Gender Role Stereotypes and Legal Protection for Lesbians and Gay Men." *University of Miami Law Review* 46:511–651.

Forna, A. 1992. "Pornography and Racism: Sexualizing Oppression and Inciting Hatred." In C. Itzin (ed.), *Pornography: Women, Violence and Civil Liberties*. Oxford: Oxford University Press.

Fox, M. 1979. *A Spirituality Named Compassion*. Minneapolis: Winston.

Frye, M. 1983. *The Politics of Reality: Essays in Feminist Theory*. Freedom, CA: The Crossing Press.

Fung, R. 1991. "Looking For My Penis: The Eroticized Asian in Gay Video Porn." In Bad Object Choices (eds.), *How Do I Look? Queer Film and Video*. Seattle: Bay Press.

Goss, R. 1993. *Jesus Acted Up: A Gay and Lesbian Manifesto*. San Francisco: HarperCollins.

Gough, K. 1975. "The Origin of the Family." In R. Reiter (ed.), *Toward an Anthropology of Women*. NY: Monthly Review.

Harris, W. 1993. "Porn Again." *Campaign* 213 (December):46–50.

Hussey, M. 1995. "Book Review: Defending Pornography." *On the Issues: The Progressive Women's Quarterly* VI:48.

"Ken." 1995. Personal interview. New York.

Kendall, C. 1993. "Real Dominant, Real Fun?: Gay Male Pornography and the Pursuit of Masculinity." *Saskatchewan Law Review* 57:21–58.

———. 1997. "Gay Male Pornography After Little Sisters Book and

Art Emporium: A Call for Gay Male Cooperation in the Struggle for Sex Equality." *Wisconsin Women's Law Review* 12(1):21–82.

Kleinberg, S. 1987. "The New Masculinity of Gay Men." In M. Kaufman (ed.), *Beyond Patriarchy: Essays by Men on Pleasure, Power and Change*. Toronto: Oxford University Press.

Koppelman, A. 1988. "The Miscegenation Analogy: Sodomy Law as Sex Discrimination." *Yale Law Journal* 98:145.

Lerner, G. 1986. *The Creation of Patriarchy*. NY: Oxford University Press.

MacKinnon, C. 1987. *Feminism Unmodified*. Cambridge: Harvard University Press.

———. 1989. *Towards a Feminist Theory of the State*. Cambridge: Harvard University Press.

Mercer, K. 1988. "Race, Sexual Politics and Black Masculinity: A Dossier." In R. Chapman. (ed.), *Male Order: Unwrapping Masculinity*. London: Lawrence and Wisehart.

Patton, C. 1991. "Safe Sex and The Pornographic Vernacular." In Bad Object Choices (eds.), *How Do I Look? Queer Film and Video*. Seattle: Bay Press.

Pharr, S. 1988. *Homophobia: A Weapon of Sexism*. Little Rock, AR: Chardon.

Reti, I. (ed.). 1993. *Unleashing Feminism: Critiquing Lesbian Sadomasochism in the Gay Nineties*. Santa Cruz: HerBooks.

Rich, A. 1980. "Compulsory Heterosexuality and Lesbian Existence." *Signs: Journal of Women in Culture and Society* 5(4):63–79.

Ross, B. 1995. *The House That Jill Built: A Lesbian Nation in Formation*. Toronto: University of Toronto Press.

Russel, D. 1995. "Nadine Strossen: the Pornography Industry's Wet Dream." *On The Issues: The Progressive Women's Quarterly*. VI:32.

Sherman, J. 1995. "Love Speech: The Social Utility of Pornography." *Stanford Law Review* 47:661–710.

Simpson, M. 1994. *Male Impersonators: Men Performing Masculinity*. NY: Routledge.

Stoltenberg, J. 1990a. *Refusing to Be a Man: Essays on Sex and Justice*. NY: Penguin.

———. 1990b. "You Can't Fight Homophobia and Protect the Pornographers at the Same Time—an Analysis of What Went Wrong With Hardwick." In D. Leidholt and J. Raymond (eds.),

The Sexual Liberals and The Attack on Feminism. NY: Pergamon.

Strossen, N. 1995. *Defending Pornography: Free Speech, Sex, and the Fight for Women's Rights.* NY: Scribner.

Stychin, C. 1992. "Exploring the Limits: Feminism and The Legal Regulation of Pornography." *Vermont Law Review* 16:857–910.

———. 1995. "I'm Ready For My Cum Shot Mr De Mille: Gay Porn is Hot, Dirty and Sometimes Sad." *Outrage* 147 (August):12–15.

"Thomas." 1995. Testimony presented at the First Australian Conference on Violence Against Lesbians and Gay Men. Sydney, NSW.

Torres, F. 1993. "Lights, Camera, Actionable Negligence: Transmission of the AIDS Virus During Adult Motion Picture Production." *Hastings Comm/Ent. Law Journal* 13:89–107.

CHAPTER 10

Alcoff, L., and E. Potter. 1993. "When Feminisms Intersect Epistemology." In L. Alcoff and E. Potter (eds.), *Feminist Epistemologies.* NY: Routledge.

Berstein, R. 1983. *Beyond Objectivism and Relativism: Science, Hermeneutics, and Praxis.* Philadelphia: University of Pennsylvania Press.

Brittan, A. 1989. *Masculinity and Power.* Oxford: Blackwell.

Brod, H. (ed.). 1987. *The Making of Masculinities.* Boston: Allen and Unwin.

Bunch, C. 1975. "Not For Lesbians Only." *Quest* 11(2):17–32.

Clatterbaugh, K. 1990. *Contemporary Perspectives on Masculinity.* Boulder, CO: Westview.

Connell, R. 1983. *Which Way is Up?* North Sydney: George Allen and Unwin.

———. 1987. *Gender and Power.* Stanford, CA: Stanford University Press.

———. 1989a. "Cool Guys, Swots and Wimps: The Interplay of Masculinity and Education." *Oxford Review of Education* 15(3): 291–303.

———. 1989b. "An Iron Man: The Body and Some Contradictions of

Hegemonic Masculinity." In M. Messner and D. Sabo (eds.), *Critical Perspectives on Sport, Patriarchy and Men*. Champaign, IL: Human Kinetics.

Frank, B. 1987. "Hegemonic Heterosexual Masculinity." *Studies in Political Economy* 24:159–70.

———. 1990. "Reflections on Men's Lives: Taking Responsibility." *Our Schools/Ourselves* 2(3):69–77.

———. 1991. "Everyday/Everynight Masculinities: The Social Construction of Masculinity Among Young Men." *The Canadian Sex Research Forum Journal of the Sex Information and Education Council of Canada* 6(1):27–37.

———. 1992. "Hegemonic Heterosexual Masculinity: Sports, Looks and a Woman, That's What Every Guy Needs to be Masculine." *The Institute of Social and Economic Research Papers* No.3 (Spring):271–303.

———. 1993. "Straight/Strait Jackets for Masculinity: Educating for 'Real Men.' " *Atlantis* 18 (1 and 2):45–59.

———. 1995. "Masculinity and Schooling: Educating for 'Real Men.' " *The South Australian Educational Leader* 6(2):1–11.

Haraway, D. 1988. "Situated Knowledges: The Science Question in Feminism and the Privilege of Partial Perspective." *Feminist Studies* 14(3):575–99.

Harding, S. 1990. "Feminism, Science, and the Anti-Enlightenment Critiques." In L. Nicholson (ed.), *Feminism/Postmodernism*. NY: Routledge.

———. 1993 "Rethinking Standpoint Epistemology: 'What is Strong Objectivity?' In L. Alcoff and E. Potter (eds.), *Feminist Epistemologies*. NY: Routledge.

hooks, B. 1984. *Feminist Theory: From Margin to Center*. Boston: South End.

———. 1990. *Yearning: Race, Gender and Cultural Politics*. Toronto: Between The Lines.

Kaufman, M. (ed.). 1987. *Beyond Patriarchy: Essays by Men on Pleasure, Power and Change*. Toronto: Oxford University Press.

———. 1993. *Cracking the Armour: Power, Pain, and the Lives of Men*. Toronto: Viking.

Kidd, B. 1987. "Sports and Masculinity." In M. Kaufman (ed.), *Beyond Patriarchy*. Toronto: Oxford University Press.

Kimmel, M. (ed.). 1987. *Changing Men: New Directions in Research on Men and Masculinity*. Newbury Park, CA: Sage.

Kimmel, M., and M. Messner. 1992. *Men's Lives*. NY: MacMillan.

Kinsman, G. 1996. *The Regulation of Desire*. Montreal: Black Rose.

Lather, P. 1991. *Getting Smart: Feminist Research and Pedagogy With/In the Postmodern*. NY: Routledge.

————. 1992. "Critical Frames in Educational Research: Feminist and Post-Structural Perspectives." *Theory Into Practice* 31(2):87–99.

Lyotard, J. 1984. *The Postmodern Condition: A Report on Knowledge*. Minneapolis: University of Minnesota Press.

Messner, M., 1987. "The Meaning of Success: The Athletic Experience and the Development of Male Identity." In H. Brod (ed.), *The Making of Masculinities*. Boston: Allen and Unwin.

————. 1989. "Masculinities and Athletic Careers." *Gender and Society* 3:138–40.

————. 1990. "When Bodies are Weapons." *Changing Men* 21:36–8.

Messner, M. and D. Sabo. 1990. *Sport, Men, and the Gender Order*. Champaign, IL: Human Kinetics.

Nicholson, L., and M. Fraser. 1990. "Social Criticism Without Philosophy: An Encounter Between Feminism and Postmodernism." In L. Nicholson (ed.), *Feminism/Postmodernism*. NY: Routledge.

Polanyi, M. 1958. *Personal Knowledge*. London: Routledge and Kegan Paul.

Pronger, B. 1990. *The Arena of Masculinity: Sports, Homosexuality and the Meaning of Sex*. NY: St. Martin's.

Sabo, D. 1986. "Pigskin, Patriarchy and Pain." *Changing Men* 16:24–6.

Sands, R., and K. Nuccio. 1992. "Postmodern Feminist Theory and Social Work." *Social Work* 37(6):489–94.

Smith, D. 1987. *The Everyday World as Problematic: A Feminist Sociology*. Toronto: University of Toronto Press.

Steedman, M. 1987. "Who's on Top? Heterosexual Practices and Male Dominance During the Sex Act." In B. Young (ed.), *Who's On Top? The Politics of Heterosexuality*. Toronto: Garamond.

Stoltenberg, J. 1977. "Toward Gender Justice." In J. Snodgrass (ed.), *A Book of Readings for Men Against Sexism*. Albion, CA: Times Change.

Yeatman, A. 1993. "A Feminist Theory of Social Differentiation." In L. Nicholson (ed.), *Feminism/Postmodernism*. NY: Routledge.

Contributors

BLYE FRANK is a faculty member in the Department of Education at Mount Saint Vincent University in Halifax. He teaches courses in social theory and masculinity, gender and education, and research literacy. In addition, he is a registered counselor and has a practice working with men in the areas of gender and sexualities. His research area is masculinity and schooling.

WALTER ISAAC is a massage therapist and bodyworker in private practice in Winnipeg. He majored in English and psychology at the University of Manitoba and taught English in high school for twelve years. He became interested in body oriented therapies in the early 1970s and was trained in massage therapy in Toronto in 1975–76. One of Walter's major interests involves cross-cultural approaches to meditation and healing. He is a student of Dakshong Tulku Rinpoche, a Tibetan meditation master, and has studied with Chagdud Tulku Rinpoche, a Tibetan meditation master and physician.

MICHAEL KAUFMAN lives in Toronto. Since the early 1980s he has worked with men throughout North America and overseas to challenge sexism and redefine masculinity. He is a founder of the White Ribbon Campaign. He formerly taught at York University, and now makes his living as a writer, public speaker and workshop leader. His six books include *Beyond Patriarchy: Essays by Men on Pleasure, Power and Change* (Oxford University Press 1987), *Cracking the Armour: Power, Pain and the Lives of Men* (Viking 1993), *Theorizing Masculinities* (co-edited with Harry Brod, Sage 1994) and *Community Power and GrassRoots Democracy* (co-edited with Haroldo Dilla, Zed 1997).

CHRIS KENDALL was raised in Winnipeg, studied at Queen's University and the University of Michigan and now works and enjoys the warm weather in Perth, Western Australia, where he is a law professor at the School of Law, Murdoch University. Chris teaches in the areas of law and sexuality and critical jurisprudence and continues to do research on gay male pornography, its effect on gay male identity and the too frequently ignored links between homophobia and sexism.

MICHAEL KIMMEL is Professor of Sociology at State University of New York at Stony Brook. His books include *Changing Men* (Sage 1987), *Men Confront Pornography* (Crown 1990), *Against the Tide: Profeminist Men in the United States 1776–1990* (Beacon 1992), and most recently *Manhood in America: A Cultural History* (Free Press 1996) and *The Politics of Manhood* (Temple University Press 1995). He edits *Masculinities*, a book series for the University of California Press, and a research annual series for Sage Publications. He is national spokesperson for the National Organization for Men Against Sexism in the U.S. and lectures extensively on campuses in North America and abroad.

JOE KUYPERS is a lecturer in Justice Studies at Edith Cowan University in Perth. Prior to emigrating to Australia, Joe held academic appointments as associate professor at the Faculty of Social Welfare, University of California at Berkeley, and as associate professor at the Faculty of Social Work, University of Manitoba. Joe received his Masters degree in psychology from Roosevelt University, Chicago, Illinois, and his Ph.D. from the Committee on Human Development from the University of Chicago. He received his license as a Clinical Psychologist from the State of California.

Joe's areas of teaching and research have included clinical theory, ethics and social work practice, adulthood and aging, crisis intervention, men's issues and male violence. His recent work has focused on violence, power and masculinity. Among his published works are *From Thirty to Seventy* (with Henry Maas, Jossey Bass 1974) and *Man's Will to Hurt* (Fernwood 1992).

JOHN STOLTENBERG is the author of *Refusing To Be a Man: Essays on Sex and Justice* (Penguin/Meridian 1990), a radical examination of male sexual identity that has been adopted in hundreds of courses—in gender studies, philosophy, religion, psychology, sociology, law and political science. John's next nonfiction work, *The End of Manhood: A Book for Men of Conscience* (Penguin/Plume 1994), is a practical guide to everyday relationships—how to live as a man of conscience in love, in sex, in families, among friends. His most recent book, *What Makes Pornography "Sexy"?* (Milkweed Editions 1994), is about an experiential workshop in which men assume poses from pornography and then talk about how it felt. He is presently at work on a book about sexual orientation.

John is co-founder of Men Against Pornography and a frequent speaker and workshop leader at colleges and conferences. He holds a master of divinity degree from Union Theological Seminary in New York City and a master of fine arts in theater from Columbia University School of the Arts.

He lives with the writer Andrea Dworkin in Brooklyn, New York.

LAURENCE THOMAS teaches in the philosophy and political science departments at Syracuse University, where he is also a member of the Judaic Studies Program. The author of two books, *Living Morally: A Psychology of Moral Character* (Temple University Press 1989) and *Vessels of Evil: American Slavery and the Holocaust* (Temple University Press 1993), and numerous articles. Laurence has lectured in the U.S., England and Israel.

CLARK WOLF is an assistant professor of philosophy at the University of Georgia in Athens, Georgia. His interest in feminist issues was piqued when he was a student at Oberlin College in Ohio. Clark's research focuses on issues in political philosophy, and he is currently writing a book on justice between generations. Since the birth of his daughter Rachael, Clark has been especially interested in problems of justice and gender, and justice in the family. Clark dedicates his chapter to his daughter.

BERT YOUNG has for many years been involved in pro-feminist/anti-sexist work and has offered numerous workshops on these subjects in Canada, the United States and Central America. Recently Bert coordinated a revision of the sexual harassment policy at John Abbott College in Montreal. Bert teaches courses on sexuality, gender relations, work and the family.